Serving God
Serving Time

By

PS Chilson

authorHOUSE™

1663 LIBERTY DRIVE, SUITE 200
BLOOMINGTON, INDIANA 47403
(800) 839-8640
WWW.AUTHORHOUSE.COM

First published by AuthorHouse 08/17/05

ISBN: 1-4208-5721-5 (sc)

Library of Congress Control Number: 2005904869

Printed in the United States of America
Bloomington, Indiana

This book is printed on acid-free paper.

Acknowledgments

To my husband, Doug, for all your encouragement.
Without your support my writing would not be possible.

To Steve Catalano for the pencil
drawing on the book cover.

IN LOVING MEMORY

August William Bernstein
October 8, 1918 - October 3, 1985

*When I made mistakes as a teen
I found out you were a little tough.
The many lessons that you taught me,
I now understand why you were so rough.
I remember your hardy laughter
And your pleasant smiles I recall.
Memories of you that I have,
The number indeed is not small.
Sometimes you disappointed me,
You weren't the perfect dad,
But, you were mine,
The only one that I had.*

*Your daughter,
PS Chilson*

Mary Grace (Whitethorn) Bernstein
January 2, 1918-March 29, 1989

*You were so special in my life.
Not only my mother,
But my best friend
Like no other.
As I go about my daily work,
So many tasks to do,
I want so much to pick up the phone,
Dial your number and talk to you.
Then, I realize that I can't.
You aren't there anymore.
You are with God
Behind Heaven's door.*

*Your daughter,
PS Chilson*

Some of the people involved wish to remain anonymous. Names followed by (*) are fictitious names and are in no way related to anyone specific, only through pure coincidence.

Ames, Cindy *	Sharon's friend
Brady, Shawna *	R.N. at Reed Clinic
Berman, Dr. Alan	Suicidologist
Best, Ilene *	Cleaned the manse
Boutelle, Rev.	Bill's friend
Brogan, Vince *	Funeral Director
Burns, Dr. Howard	Toxicologist
Colby, Joan *	Guthries' elderly friend
Conner, Myra *	Bill's lover
Cruse, Ann	Statz pharmacist
Dubrook, Mamie *	Elder at church
Fenski, Susan	R.N. in emergency room
Gerhard, Sally *	State's Attorney secretary
Guthrie, William	Defendant aka Bill & Dr. Bill
Guthrie, Danielle	Guthries' youngest daughter
Hensley, Dr. Rick *	Associate with Reed Clinic
Hewitt, Derrik	Suzanne's son
Hewitt, Les	Suzanne's husband
Hewitt, Suzanne	Guthries' oldest daughter
Hilton, Jon	K-Mart pharmacist
Hoff, Bonnie	Sharon's sister
Hoff, Vic	Sharon's brother-in-law

Hofmann, Steve	Beadle County Deputy
Holst, Nancy	First responder
Hutchins, Darrel	State computer specialist
Kelly, Tracy	Deputy State's Attorney
Lindberg, Jerry	DCI investigator
Mansgrove, C. *	First responder
Martin, Eugene	Presiding trial judge
Mathison, Roger	State chemist
McGrath, Dr.	Psychologist
Minor, Patricia *	P.A. at Reed Clinic
Moore, Michael	State's Attorney
Neilson, Eddy *	Bill's friend in WY.
Neilson, Karen *	Bill's friend in WY.
Orton, Cindy	Fingerprint specialist
Perry, Don *	Executive Presbyter
Polo, Janice *	Cleaned the manse
Provance, Larry	Sharon's brother
Provance, Thelma	Sharon's sister-in-law
Randall, Dr. Brad	Forensic pathologist
Reed, Dr. Richard	Sharon's employer
Robbins, Judd	Forensics specialist
Rogers, Dr. Lola *	ER doctor
Rivers, Lexi *	Guthries' middle daughter
Rivers, Mitch *	Lexi's husband
Sands, Kate *	Cleaned the manse
Scott, Lisa *	Reed Clinic receptionist
Sheridan, Jim	Chief Deputy Sheriff
Traverse, Keith *	Associate with Wilson
Waldner, Michael	Computer specialist
Wilson, Gregory *	Defense attorney

May 14, 1999

Wolsey, South Dakota
Population 450

The Rolling Wheel Cafe is buzzing with regular customers early on a Friday morning. The grill, one half filled with bacon and sausage, sizzles as the cook cracks open eggs to fill the other half. A group of men discuss items of interest regarding their small rural community, as they gulp down cups of black coffee while waiting for their breakfast. The waitress approaches the table with another pot of coffee. Carter Mansgrove, carpenter by trade and life-long resident, rises from his chair.

"Whatcha doing, Carter, leaving already?" the waitress asks.

"Yup. I have a lot to do today and drinking coffee all morning is not on the top of my list." Pulling loose change from his pocket, he tosses several coins on the table.

"Don't forget the tip," Monica says chuckling.

Carter smiles. "Wouldn't think of it." Again, he reaches into his pocket, retrieves more coins and lays them in her extended hand. "See you tomorrow." He bids everyone good-by and heads for the door.

Nancy Holst, seated at a table by the large picture window, greets Carter as he walks by, then focuses her attention out the window. In no time at all she becomes mesmerized admiring the beautiful sunny day and doesn't hear Monica approach her table.

"What can I get for you today, Nancy?"

"Oh, my!" Nancy shrieks as her hand goes over her chest. "A heart pump would be nice."

"Cute, real cute," Monica replies. "Sorry, I didn't mean to startle you."

Nancy takes a deep breath to regain her composure. Chuckling she says, "No harm done. I'm just a few years older now. A couple of pancakes sound good, Monica, and a strong cup of coffee would be great."

Monica grabs a cup off the table, rights it and fills it with coffee, then asks lightheartedly, "Should I ring a bell before I approach with your pancakes?"

Nancy smiles. "No, but, I'll be sure to watch for you."

Nancy strikes up a conversation with a customer at a nearby table while waiting for her food. A few minutes pass and Monica is back with a plate of pancakes. "More coffee?"

"Not right now, thanks," Nancy replies. "Maybe a little later."

Carter arrives home and parks his '92 Dodge pickup in the driveway. A pager attached to his belt sounds off. Though he is retired from the Wolsey Volunteer Fire Department, he helps out when they are short-handed. He quickly rushes into the house, dials in to get the message, then rushes back to his pickup. Needing someone trained in CPR, Carter drives back to the Rolling Wheel Cafe to get Nancy Holst. Having reached the parking lot, he steers his pickup as close as possible to the large cafe window where she is sitting. With both hands he presses hard on the horn on the steering wheel to get her attention. Looking up from her food, Nancy sees Carter motioning to her, drops the fork in her hand, and quickly rushes out to his pickup.

"Get in. I need you to go with me," Carter shouts. "There has been a drowning reported at Pastor Guthries' house." Hearing Nancy's door slam, he steps firmly down on the gas pedal and speeds out of the parking lot.

The manse, located next to the Presbyterian Church, is only a short distance from the cafe, so they arrive there quickly.

Carter and Nancy enter the house. Hearing someone yelling, they proceed into the hallway and find Pastor Guthrie in the bathroom. Dressed in a baggy jogging suit, he is kneeling by the bathtub sobbing, while his wife Sharon lies naked and motionless in the empty bathtub. "I came home from the church and found her." Dr. Bill wails as he moves away from the tub. "I drained the water."

Carter pushes past Dr. Bill and immediately feels Sharon's neck for a pulse. "Nancy, she's still warm," he yells. "We have to do something quick!"

"Help me get her out of the tub!" Nancy shouts to Carter.

"I tried to get her out," Dr. Bill sobs, "but she's too heavy." Sharon, only five-foot four inches tall, is a fairly plump woman.

They carefully remove her slippery body from the bathtub and lay her on the bathroom floor. "There's not enough room in here to do CPR," Nancy states.

Dr. Bill quickly declares, "I … I … tried to give her CPR."

Carter and Nancy grasp Sharon again and pull her out of the bathroom. As she lies immobile on the carpeted hallway floor, Nancy begins administering mouth-to-mouth resuscitation. As she begins chest compression, water squirts out of Sharon's mouth. They roll her over. Nancy pushes on Sharon's back to remove the water from her body and again they roll her onto her back. "Carter, I need help. Call and see if Peggy is home," Nancy says, then proceeds with the chest compression.

Carter rushes into the kitchen and phones Peggy Stevens, a nurse who lives across town. She picks up on the second ring. Carter quickly explains the circumstances and tells her that she is needed at the Guthrie residence.

Dr. Bill, stationed at Sharon's feet, keeps asking if his wife is okay. Nancy hears him, but doesn't answer. In no time at all Peggy enters the manse and immediately rushes into the hallway to assist Nancy. After a moment, she notices that Sharon is not responding and her lips are grayish blue. "We need to put in an airway, NOW!" She's handed a tube and quickly inserts it into Sharon's throat. After the insertion is complete she leans over Sharon. "No air --- continue with the CPR. Did anyone call for an ambulance?"

"I ... ah ... I ... ah ... I called 911," Dr. Bill stammers.

Within moments a siren screams. Two EMT's enter the house and relieve Nancy and Peggy. They continue administering CPR, as they hook Sharon to a monitor and observe her vitals. "Go get the stretcher! We need to transport her now!" one EMT yells.

Sirens blaring in a small town quickly bring out spectators. Several people have gathered across the street from the manse. "Do you know what happened?" A bystander asks.

"No, but it must be serious."

"Is it Dr. Bill again?" Another asks. "It wasn't that long ago that the ambulance was here when he was almost electrocuted."

The EMT's place the unconscious Sharon on the stretcher and quickly carry her outside. Everyone inside the manse follows closely behind and watches as she is loaded into the back of the ambulance. The doors slam shut and with red lights flashing they are off to the hospital located in Huron, approximately thirteen miles southeast of Wolsey.

"It's not Dr. Bill; he's standing right over there," a bystander points out.

Dr. Bill states that he needs a ride to the hospital. Peggy says that she can give him a ride, but must first stop at home to get her purse. She looks down at his bare feet, informs him that he needs to put shoes on, and then follows him into the manse to retrieve his shoes.

1964

Scottsbluff, Nebraska

The excitement is building at Platte Valley Bible College. Bill Guthrie and Sharon Provance, along with their fellow classmates, file out of the school to enter the waiting bus that will take them to a weekend rally retreat. Sharon settles into a seat next to her friend, Cindy Ames. The driver pulls the door shut as the last students are seated. He quickly wheels the large vehicle out of the parking lot, turning it south towards the Wildcat Hills, a little chip of Wyoming stuck in the panhandle of Nebraska.

Chatter is constant during the short ride, but the second the bus enters a parking area the students become quiet and patiently wait for the driver to bring the bus to a stop. They grab their sparse belongings, hastily exit the bus, and walk quickly to a picnic area located by a rock shelter.

The students stand motionless for a time as the wonderful smells of pine trees and flowers are delivered to their noses by a light flowing breeze. Off to their left, in an open pasture area, numerous buffalo graze lazily on abundant green grass, as baby calves frolic playfully.

They are anxious to explore the beautiful area where God's hand has touched, so the students separate into small groups and scatter. The delightful afternoon passes quickly. When dusk approaches, they again assemble in the picnic area and watch the beautiful peach-colored sunset. Several students collected scraps of wood and twigs while exploring, so they begin building a campfire while others venture off to gather long, thin sticks for roasting hot dogs and marshmallows.

After all the hot dogs are consumed, the group gathers around the campfire to listen to the beautiful violin music being played by the guest lecturer and his son, a professor at the college. The stars seem to march across the sky as if keeping time to the sweet melodies flowing from the violins.

After completing several lively tunes, the two musicians invite Sharon to fetch her violin and join in with them. Her voice sticks in her throat as she humbly accepts their invitation. She thoroughly admires these gentlemen and is ecstatic to be asked to play along with them. The threesome strum a few more tunes before retiring their instruments, then join in with the students who are sitting around the campfire roasting marshmallows over the crackling flames.

Sharon sits down on the ground between Cindy and Bill. After consuming a few marshmallows, Bill nudges Sharon lightly and motions her to follow him. Cindy watches as they quietly slip away from the campfire and climb up onto the roof of the rock shelter

Sharon and Bill huddle together with their hands locked, their legs dangling over the edge of the shelter. The look of love can be seen reflected in their eyes as they stare aimlessly into the light of the campfire below them.

Sharon's dream of being the wife of a minister, a man of God, comes true on June 20, 1965. She faithfully pampers her new husband and treats him like a king. She is especially proud of Bill when he earns his Ph.D.

In 1966, Sharon and Bill welcome their firstborn, Suzanne; then in 1968, another daughter, Lexi. Several years pass. In 1979, to make their family complete, they adopt a baby girl, Danielle, born out of wedlock to a young girl in Casper, Wyoming.

Dr. Bill follows in his grandfather's footsteps. Throughout several years he serves parishes in Wyoming, Oklahoma, and Nebraska as a minister in the Christian church.

Sharon earned a Christian Education degree while in college, so she assists her husband in several duties at the various churches. On Sundays, using her amazing talent with puppets, she manipulates the puppets to promote messages to the children during the children's sermons.

Dr. Bill makes a choice to change religions in 1993. Prior to taking five ordination exams required to become a minister in the Presbyterian faith, he is hired at a church in Orleans, Nebraska. A short time later he successfully completes the exams and becomes ordained in the Presbyterian faith.

June 1996

Wolsey, South Dakota

The meeting of the session is called to order. Eight members of the governing board are discussing the employment of a full-time minister to oversee their small Presbyterian churches in Wolsey and Bonilla. It has been over a year since they have had a full-time minister, and it is always a difficult task to find one willing to come to their tiny towns.

Mamie Dubrook, who does the paperwork for the churches and takes minutes during the session meetings, produces résumés from several candidates. The board studies all of the résumés, and then after considerable discussion they agree that Dr. William Guthrie's résumé is very impressive. He writes:

The ministry has been my first love for over thirty years. Ministry entails more than just an hour or two on Sunday morning.

Ministry means sitting in a hospital with a family waiting for surgery to be completed and Counseling the family when the outcome is unfavorable. Sitting with a widow/widower after a spouse dies. An example listed was in 1995. Dick's wife was suffering from terminal cancer and I went to visit their home each week to pray and see what I could do. When she went into the hospital, I visited her daily. When the call came that she had passed away I hurried back to the hospital and sat with him, comforted him, cried with him, and waited for the family to arrive. The next day I went to his home to see what I could do. For two weeks after the funeral I met with him for prayer and moments of tears. When Dick came to the next session meeting he said, "You don't know how much our pastor means to me. He is my pastor, but even more he's my friend."

Ministry means going to a disgruntled member and guiding him/her through personal problems and speaking with teens who are crosswise with their parents and resolving family problems.

Ministry means presenting a Sunday sermon in such a way that the congregation understands it and is benefited by it. The message should make the congregation feel they have been fed, challenged, comforted, and loved.

Ministry is also having fun. At a county fair in 1992, there was an event called "pig wrestling." The next Sunday I announced that if church attendance would reach one hundred twenty-five four times during the year and one hundred fifty one Sunday during the year I would head a pig wrestling team the next summer. The congregation rose to the challenge and met it, so we got muddy, slimy, greasy, sticky, and dirty, but it all came down to having some clean Christian fun. The greatest advertisement for the church was that the preacher wasn't afraid to get dirty and have fun.

Ministry means helping teachers and training them to do their jobs better. After teaching several training courses, on one occasion, a woman took me aside and said, "I have always needed ideas on how to present a lesson more effectively to my class and you have provided me with some great new tools." A new convert once asked me to teach her how to teach Sunday School so I took her some books on teaching and sat with her for an hour a week for ten weeks. She now teaches each week and is very capable.

Ministry means sitting with first and second graders and teaching them how Jesus healed the leper ... or adults ... why God punished his people with wandering for forty years in the wilderness.

Ministry means keeping in shape and maintaining good health. I walk two miles a day, read a good book every week, and do my best to read through the Bible three times a year. I enjoy hiking, archery, hunting, fishing, camping, and dog training.

Teaching and example are the style of leadership I feel most comfortable with. Christ set the example with a perfect life and punctuated it by teaching twelve disciples a way they could change the world. The world can be changed by example and teaching.

I once met a man who confessed his addiction problem to me and told me he was going to leave his family to get himself straightened out. We prayed together and talked. After Counseling with him, he accepted Christ and with his family's help, he broke his addiction and became very active in the church.

At the center of my faith is my reliance to God. God is the center of my life; all that I am and ever hope to be depends on the strength that comes through the Father, Son, and the Holy Spirit. Through Christ's living presence in my life I am empowered to respond to God's claim on me, both in word and deed. I commit my life to God's authority in the world and to the church.

On the major issues of the world today the minister must be wise as a serpent and harmless as a dove. Where sin is involved ministry must deal with it in a scriptural manner so as not to get caught up in axe grinding. I don't get caught up in political parties nor do I stand in condemnation or praise of either. I deal with how I feel Christ would deal with the issue and go from there. I have never been quick to make any snap judgments, but try to weigh the issue by the Word of God, or the Book of Order.

Preaching is my greatest joy. The skills I possess are strong in the areas of preaching, Counseling, and evangelism. I find a real joy in preparing and delivering a sermon and feel my speaking skills are above average. I use several styles of preaching. At times I present a series of sermons on a particular subject or book of the Bible. One Sunday after church a nearly blind woman came up to me and said, "Your sermon really touched me this morning as I have been having some real problems with my family." She asked me to come to her home that afternoon to talk. We talked and prayed and cried together and resolve came to her life.

Counseling is a constant testing ground. We have raised three daughters, each one presenting her own challenges to us. I have also had clinical training. When we came to Orleans, there was a very disruptive ten-year old boy that started fights with his brother or any boy that crossed him. One day I took him fishing and discovered a very nice young man under the tough exterior. I continued to give him all the attention I could, but discovered he needed much more attention that I could give. In the community was a farmer that had recently lost his wife and needed companionship. I turned the young boy over to this man and they became very good friends and spent a lot of time together. The boy's attitude changed and he no longer felt like he needed to fight at every drop of the hat.

Evangelism is solving problems in the church that make it more appealing to the whole. We had a young family in our congregation that had small children who were disruptive to our services. This was causing problems with the older members who were having difficulty hearing the worship service. This could have been handled in a way that we would have lost one side or the other, but a win-win process was arrived at. We held a Junior Church in the basement during only the sermon portion of the services, so the children still learned about being a part of the regular services, but had more of a message at their level.

June 1996

Orleans, Nebraska

Bill enters the kitchen. "Sharon, has the mail come yet?"

"Yes, I put it on the dining room table."

He rushes into the dining room, snatches the mail from the table, and quickly whips through a stack of letters. Spotting a letter from the Wolsey Presbyterian Church, he briskly tears open the envelope and quickly scans the contents. "Sharon!" he yells out. "I have a new church!"

Sharon enters the dining room. "What did you say?"

"I've been accepted at a church in South Dakota. Actually, it's two small churches. One is located in Wolsey and the other in Bonilla, a small neighboring town."

Sharon smiles. "That's wonderful, Bill. When do they want you to start?"

"As soon as we can get packed and moved. The manse in Wolsey will be ready for us when we get there."

"How about your mother?" asks Sharon.

"You handle it, I have too much to do," he answers.

Nanette Guthrie, also referred to as Nannie, lives in a nursing home in Alma, Nebraska, and is their only living parent. Bill always leaves it up to Sharon to be his mother's main caregiver. Even though Nannie often makes Sharon feel that she isn't good enough for her son, Sharon never allows that to alter her responsibilities towards her mother-in-law.

Whenever Nannie is in need of something, she always makes sure that she receives it. A few phone calls later arrangements are made to move her to a nursing home in Huron, thirteen miles from Wolsey.

Nannie grew up on a pecan plantation deep in the South. Her father was a pulpit supply pastor to the surrounding towns that needed a preacher and also sold remedies and a line of health needs for those who would invest their belief and money in his products.

Her passion was taking care of sick people, so she became a nurse. In September of 1940, she married her husband William. When she was told the devastating news that she would not be able to have children, she accepted it, but to her surprise four years later Bill was born.

Very sadly, Nannie could not conceive again, but later she and her husband adopted a baby girl. A patient at the clinic that she worked for became pregnant and wanted to leave her baby to someone with a good home.

William died after forty years of marriage. Throughout the years Nannie suffered from depression, an illness that affected several of her family members. Depression was not addressed in her day and medications were not available to combat her illness.

Her most important legacy was that of a Christian upbringing. God was very important to her. She found solace in reading the Bible and speaking of her relationship with the Lord. She was always a willing participant in prayer and welcomed any time to be in prayer.

Her strongest wish was trying to keep the family intact and her greatest hurt was not always being able to maintain that wish.

May 14, 1999

Huron, South Dakota

Suzanne grabs a towel, wraps it around her body, and quietly tiptoes into the bedroom, so as not to wake her husband who works nights. Hearing the phone ring, she quickly throws on a bathrobe and rushes out of the bedroom to answer the phone before it rings again and wakes Les. Recognizing her son's fourteen-year old friend's voice, she says, "I'll get Derrik."

"Wait, Mrs. Hewitt, wait!" the caller yells abruptly. "I want to talk to you. I have been listening to our scanner and there has been an accident at the manse. They said a female has drowned. I thought they might be talking about your mom and that you would want to know." Shock sets in; a gray area develops in front of Suzanne's eyes.

"Mrs. Hewitt, are you there? Did you hear what I said?"

Suzanne shakes her head to clear the fog floating around her head. "Yes, thank you for calling --- I have to go," she utters and lays the phone back in the cradle. Standing motionless, her legs weaken and her head starts spinning, so she leans against the wall to steady herself. A loud slamming of a door brings her back to reality. The children have left for school. Struggling for strength, she heads into the bedroom.

"Les, you need to get up, now!" she cries out loudly, throwing off her bathrobe and reaching for a pair of jeans.

Les sits up in the bed. "What's ... the matter?"

"Hurry --- get dressed. They've taken Mom to the hospital."

Chadron, Nebraska

Larry Provance is hard at work at his lumberyard when his son approaches. "Dad, you need to sit down. I have some bad news. Suzanne just called and said that Aunt Sharon has had a bad accident and is at the hospital in Huron."

His face drops. "Did she leave a phone number?"

"Yes, it's on your desk."

Larry rushes into his office. Hands shaking, he dials the hospital and informs Suzanne that they will be there as soon as they can. He adds that he will contact Bonnie and Vic. Bonnie is his and Sharon's sister who live in Scottsbluff, Nebraska.

Huron hospital

Suzanne and Les are in the waiting room next to ER when her dad and Peggy enter. "Have you seen your mother?" Bill abruptly asks.

"No, they won't let us in. They're trying to get a heartbeat and get her breathing on her own." Without hesitation, Suzanne immediately asks her dad what happened.

"I hid the Benadryl from her...."

"Dad, what happened?" Again, she asks with more urgency.

"I woke your mom up, then I got up and went over to the church to do my morning prayers. When I came back to the house I could hear water running, so I went into the bathroom and found her in the bathtub. I grabbed her, pulled her out of the tub, and then I called 911."

8:02 a.m., Dr. Lola Rogers enters the emergency room. "What do we have here?" she asks.

"A drowning," replies the ER nurse. " She doesn't have any pulse, she's extremely cold, and her skin is very white, except from her chest up."

Dr. Rogers orders an IV started, then gives Sharon four cc's of epinephrine to stimulate her heart. Three minutes pass and still no pulse. She administers another four cc's of epinephrine and then checks the rhythm strip. It shows anginal electrical stimulus, but still no pulse. They use electrical shock to get the pulse going. Nothing --- still no pulse.

"Susan, we need to put her on artificial respiration. Call anesthesia to come and put a tube in." Dr. Rogers gives Sharon another dose of bicarb to raise her pH. Her blood pressure is still high, but she begins to show a nice rhythm. A blood gas, blood test, and urine test are ordered.

Dr. Rogers orders Susan to put in a nasal gastric tube and suck out the contents of Sharon's stomach to avoid choking and vomiting.

Susan carefully inserts the tube into the back of Sharon's nose and down into her stomach, then hooks the tube to a wall suction unit. After 500 cc's of stomach contents are collected, she reports to Dr. Rogers that there is nothing floating around and everything looks pretty normal.

"Have the other tests come back yet?" Dr. Rogers asks.

Susan grabs a clipboard with the test results. "Yes, Doctor, her blood gas is dangerously low even after the bicarb we gave her earlier."

Dr. Rogers pauses for a moment. "How about the urine test?"

Susan looks again at the clipboard. "The benzodiazepines came up positive ... over 300 nanograms per mill."

"Get her ready for transport," Dr. Rogers orders. "We must get her to Sioux Falls."

Danielle Guthrie enters the waiting room. After Suzanne called her youngest sister in Brookings where she goes to college, she drove the seventy-five miles to Huron in record time. Dr. Reed, Sharon's employer, enters a few seconds later. Danielle quickly asks him how her mom is doing.

"I wish I could give you all better news. I'm so very sorry, and I hate to say it, but it doesn't look very good. We're getting ready to transport her to Sioux Valley Hospital."

Danielle wipes away the tears trickling down her cheeks. "May we see her?"

"Yes, but only for a few minutes," Dr. Reed states. "We need to get her to Sioux Falls immediately."

The family members gather around Sharon's bed. The tears they have held back begin to flow and any feelings of hope vanish quickly. As they view her poor condition, a sense of helplessness sets in. After several minutes they leave and make plans for the 120-mile drive to Sioux Falls.

Scottsbluff, Nebraska

Before leaving home Larry and Thelma receive a call stating that Sharon's condition has deteriorated and she is being transferred from the Huron hospital to Sioux Valley Hospital in Sioux Falls. They call Bonnie and Vic to relay the news.

During the first part of the drive they remain speechless until Larry, worry clearly etched on his face, breaks the silence. "What now? How can Sharon be so accident-prone? First that accident with the string, then that electrical thing, the overdose, and now this."

"I don't know, Larry, but let's not second guess anything. We have to leave it in God's hands that she'll be okay."

Sioux Valley Hospital
Sioux Falls, South Dakota

Larry and Thelma enter the waiting room. "Larry, I'm so sorry - oh, I'm so sorry," Bill cries out and throws his arms around his brother-in-law.

Breaking the embrace, Larry immediately asks, "What happened, Bill?"

At first Bill can't seem to talk, but suddenly the tears stop flowing and he becomes composed. He motions Larry and Thelma to follow him. They enter a small room where his grandchildren are sitting. The children get up and leave the room. Bill proceeds to tell them what happened to Sharon. "Sharon drowned in the bathtub. I had gone over to the church like I normally do, and when I came back, I saw the water, and went into the bathroom…"

Larry enters ICU and advances toward the bed. He stops when he is about three feet from the bed, shakes his head, and looks again. That person lying in the bed doesn't look like his sister. The patient's eyes are swollen shut, the face is puffy, and there are tubes going everywhere, hooked up to various machines. He turns back toward the door. " I must be in the wrong room," he whispers to a nurse who has entered ICU. "Where is Sharon Guthrie?"

Seeing the pain in his eyes, she replies compassionately. "I'm sorry, sir, but you are in the right room."

Larry, extremely shocked, watches the nurse check each of the machines before she leaves. He advances slowly to the left side of the bed and grasps one of Sharon's icy cold hands. A tremor runs through his body as tears begin trickling down his cheeks. *"Oh, baby sister, what happened to you?"* he says quietly and begins to pray. *"Lord; please take care of my beloved little sister. She is good, she is kind, she is one of your faithful followers. Amen."*

Lexi, the Guthries' middle daughter who lives in Oklahoma with her fiancé Mitch, arrives at the hospital and enters the waiting room. "What happened, Dad?" she asks without hesitation.

Again, Bill tells his story of going to the church to do his morning prayers and coming home to find Sharon in the bathtub.

May 15, 1999

Larry and Thelma are at the motel. They rise from a restless night's sleep, get dressed, and leave for the hospital. Bill has a migraine and chooses to stay at the motel.

The second they enter the waiting room, Larry gets a phone call from Bonnie and Vic. They have arrived in Sioux Falls, but have gotten lost, so he leaves to meet up with them to show them the way to the hospital.

Bonnie enters the waiting room. "How's Sharon this morning?" she asks immediately.

"The doctor hasn't been in yet to give us a report," Suzanne tells her aunt. The words are hardly out of her mouth when the doctor enters the room. Everyone becomes silent. With care, he tells the family that Sharon didn't show any improvement during the night, then adds that there isn't any more that they can do for her at this point.

"Doctor, there has to be something!" Suzanne blurts out.

"I'm so sorry. Sharon is not showing any brain activity, and without that she will not have any quality of life."

"What are you trying to tell us?" a family member asks, knowing deep down what the doctor is saying.

The doctor speaks the words that every doctor hates to tell loved ones, "Without brain activity you may want to consider taking her off life support."

"No, we can't!" Suzanne screams out.

"Are you sure this is the only recourse?" Larry asks.

"I'm so sorry," The doctor utters. "We have done all we can do for her. I'll leave you now, so you can discuss it as a family. Let me know what you decide. My prayers are with you."

The family is stunned - shattered - heartbroken. How could this be? No one knows what to say. After a few minutes of silence, Larry asks them to all hold hands. *"Lord, we ask that you give us guidance in making this difficult decision. We trust in you Lord that you will take care of our Sharon and that you have prepared a place for her. Amen."*

Even though the doctor told the family that Sharon would never have quality of life without brain activity, this devastating news doesn't make their decision any easier. They rely on their faith, knowing that the Lord will take care of her. They inform the doctor of their decision to remove Sharon from life support.

They all enter ICU one last time. Each family member, one at a time, walks to Sharon's bedside, and then quietly leaves the room. Sharon's daughters are the last ones to leave. Feeling as if someone is ripping their hearts from their bodies, they say good-by to their mother.

The family gathers in the waiting room attempting to understand what has taken place. They must now go back home and make preparations for Sharon's funeral. No one has eaten much, so they decide to meet at a restaurant in Sioux Falls before making the three-hour drive home.

Bill chooses to ride back to Wolsey with Larry. As they are driving down Dakota Avenue in Huron, he gives Larry directions to the Brogan Funeral Home. Vince Brogan greets Bill with a handshake. "Lose another parishioner, Bill?" he asks, assuming that is why Bill is here.

"Well, sort of ... it's my wife."

Vince is taken off guard. "I'm so sorry, Bill. You have my utmost sympathy."

"Thank you," Bill replies and then asks to look at the caskets.

Vince shows them to a large room where rows of caskets are on display. "I'll leave you now, but if you have any questions, please let me know."

Bill begins walking up and down in between the rows with Larry following behind. He stops at a wooden casket with white silk lining, pauses for a second as he runs his fingers over the silk, then proceeds to another, then another, then another. After a time, he chooses one and informs Vince of his choice.

"Are we looking at Tuesday or Wednesday for the funeral, Bill?" Vince asks.

"Monday if that works for you?"

A bit stunned, Vince replies, "That doesn't leave us a lot of time."

"The family is all here, so there's really no reason to wait," answers Bill.

"I'm sure we can work it out," Vince replies. "I will need information for the newspaper and the memorial folders as soon as possible."

"No problem," Bills answers. "I'll have someone call you in a little while with what you need."

Suzanne and family arrive home. She immediately heads for the phone to call her mom's friend who's been waiting for an update. Suzanne knows that Cindy wouldn't want her to beat around the bush, so she immediately tells her that Sharon has died.

Feeling as if someone just took a two by four and whacked her behind the knees, Cindy quickly grabs a chair and sits down. "Oh, Suz, how terrible!"

Suzanne explains that her mother wasn't showing any brain activity, so the decision was made to remove her from life support.

"Oh, Suzanne, what can I do for you?"

"I'll need you at the funeral, Cindy."

"Of course, I'll be there. Just let me know when you decide on the day."

"The funeral is Monday in Wolsey."

"Ohhhh ... you know that already?" Cindy utters in surprise.

"Dad feels there's no reason to put it off since all of the family is here."

"I can understand that," Cindy replies.

"I have to go now. I need to make some more calls."

Cindy's voices breaks up. "My prayers - go - with you." She pushes the off button on the phone and lays the receiver in her lap. The tears that she has been holding back flow from her eyes and down her cheeks. Grabbing a tissue, she wipes them away as more continue pouring out. *"Not Sharon! Not my sweet Sharon!"* she yells out angrily. They had planned to have lunch together next week, which they had often done.

Now there won't be anymore lunches with her good friend and no more gab sessions. She just can't believe this.

Cindy sits like a puppet with broken strings as memories of Sharon run rampant through her mind. Their meeting at youth rallies prior to college, attending Bible College together, and becoming very good friends the last few years, since they both had moved to South Dakota.

. Sharon was in the choir at college and served as class representative. She was upbeat and very positive and always had a good word for everyone. If anyone were ever down and out, Sharon would always bring smiles to their faces. She was a very kind person.

A black cloud forms in Cindy's mind as she begins thinking about Bill. He has always seemed strange to her and at times, very sullen. She knows that his dad had been verbally and physically abusive to him. Even so, she can't excuse the catty way he would act at times. He would make snide remarks that he thought were funny, but they weren't.

Cindy always felt that Sharon could have done better than to marry Bill, but she could never tell Sharon that. Sharon was forever Bill's enthusiastic cheerleader supporting him through anything and everything, never putting him down, as he did to her when they were out in the public. Sharon was so very proud of Bill when he earned his Ph.D. Tossing the negative thoughts aside, Cindy folds her hands and bows her head. *"Sharon ... my good friend, the Lord has prepared a place for you. May you rest in peace. Amen."*

Kate Sands, a member of the Wolsey Presbyterian Church, receives a phone call at her home informing her that Sharon has died. She phones Janice Polo and Ilene Best, two other ladies of the church, and requests their help to clean the manse before the family returns.

Word of Sharon's death travels fast. Parishioners and friends begin bringing food to the manse the moment they hear the news. Several church ladies arrive at the manse to prepare the evening meal for the family. Cakes, cookies, hot dishes, hams, and cans of coffee line the countertops in the kitchen.

Bill receives numerous phone calls throughout the afternoon and evening, and spends a lot of time explaining to each caller what happened to Sharon. Larry, sitting close enough to overhear his conversations, begins to wonder why Bill's story keeps changing ever so slightly as he speaks to each caller.

May 17, 1999

Monday, two days after Sharon was removed from life support, the family and her co-workers meet at the manse to walk together to the church for the funeral. Patricia Minor, a physician's assistant from Reed Clinic where Sharon was employed, enters the manse. Bill approaches her immediately and gets right in her face, forcing her to take a step backwards. "Patricia, I didn't know anything about the second prescription that was filled. Sharon apparently filled that prescription for Temazepam and must have been taking it without my knowledge."

"I didn't know two prescriptions had been filled," answers Patricia, a perplexed look on her face. She is very sensitive to the fact that he is talking about this now. "Bill, as far as I know only one prescription was filled. Sharon told me that you had lost the written prescription and asked me if I would mind calling a second one in for you."

"I didn't know anything about that."

Sharon's brother, Larry, close enough to hear Bill and Patricia Minor talking, becomes extremely puzzled as to this discussion regarding pills. Bill hasn't said anything to him about any pills, but now seems quite insistent that Sharon had gotten into medications prescribed for him. Everyone has been anxiously waiting for the results of the autopsy ordered by law enforcement, but no mention of pills has been brought up. Larry approaches the twosome. Patricia takes advantage of the moment to gracefully move away. "Bill, are you insinuating that Sharon was suicidal?" Larry quickly asks.

"Everybody knows that."

Extremely upset now, Larry explodes. "Bill, tell me who knows that. I want names, so I can talk to them."

Les approaches, cutting the conversation short. "Bill, we need to go over to the church. Suzanne is already over there."

"Yes, I guess it's time." Bill turns away from Larry and walks to the front door.

Suzanne sees Cindy enter the church, walks away from her mother's casket, and throws herself into the arms of her mom's good friend. "Sorry, I wasn't at the house, but I needed to be here with Mom for awhile."

"I understand, Suz," Cindy whispers.

Suzanne releases Cindy. "We have reserved a place of honor at the front of the church for you and the rest of the people from work."

Cindy's heart skips a beat. "How nice that you think of us at a time like this."

"Mom would have wanted it this way."

Cindy watches Suzanne walk away. She takes a deep breath and slowly advances towards Sharon's casket. Her feet feel like she is wearing cement shoes. Viewing her wonderful friend lying in state is much more than she feels she can handle, but realizes it's time to bid Sharon farewell and turn her over to the Lord. She stops briefly for a second and takes another deep breath.

"Cindy, are you okay?" asks a concerned co-worker standing behind her.

"Yes, just give me a second. Go ahead of me. I'll be along shortly." Cindy wipes away a large tear and bows her head. *Help me, Lord. Please give me the strength I need at this moment. Amen.*

Her feet instantly become lighter and she finds herself next to Sharon's casket. Not able to will herself to look at Sharon's face, Cindy brings her head up just high enough to see that Sharon is wearing a lovely peach-colored outfit. She places one of her hands over Sharon's folded hands and with the other hand holding a tissue she dabs at the river of tears flowing out of her eyes. *"Oh, my beautiful friend, I will miss you terribly. I will never forget you,"* she whispers. Sharon's hands begin warming under Cindy's hand.

Cindy lifts her head a little higher and looks at Sharon's face. She suppresses a sudden impulse to poke her and say, *"Wake up sleepy head."* Carefully she leans over the edge of the casket and plants a kiss on Sharon's forehead. A large tear leaves Cindy's eye and drops onto Sharon's cheek.

As Cindy prepares to leave the side of the casket, a bright light suddenly hits her in the eye. A shiny brass cross that is placed in the middle of the casket cover above Sharon's head is glowing. A warm feeling passes through Cindy's body. Accepting this as a sign from God that Sharon will be safe in His hands, she bids her friend good-by. Raising a tissue to her eyes, she dabs at her tears and walks away to the front of the church.

Cindy seats herself next to a co-worker, reaches over, and pats her hand. "See that beautiful bouquet on the left," she softly whispers.

"They are all so beautiful, which one?"

"That one to the left of the stand holding Sharon's violin. It has Smarties attached to sticks mixed in amongst the flowers."

"Yes, I see it. It's very beautiful."

A smile appears on Cindy's face, the first smile since she heard about Sharon's accident. "Sharon would give Smarties to the children when she was done with her children's sermon," Cindy whispers to her co-worker, then becomes silent. She opens up the memorial folder scrunched in her hand, and begins reading silently.

In Loving Memory of
Sharon A. Guthrie
November 25, 1944 - May 15, 1999
First Presbyterian Church,
Wolsey, S.D.
Burial - Wolsey Cemetery
Sharon Provance is survived by her husband,
William Guthrie, three daughters,
Suzanne Hewitt (Les), Lexi Rivers (Mitch),
Danielle Guthrie, four grandchildren,
one brother, Larry Provance (Thelma),
and one sister, Bonnie Hoff (Vic).
She was preceded in death by her parents...

Cindy can't read anymore. She shuts her eyes, attempting to delay the tears that are building. Insane thoughts again invade her mind. *"I still can't believe this ... this just can't be true."* Her instincts tell her that there is something wrong here - she can feel it.

"We are here today to celebrate the joining of Sharon with the Lord to reside in His House forever," says Reverend Boutelle. "I will begin today by reading from Psalms 9, verses 13 through 16."

She was employed at various places ... Cindy wipes away tears as she again attempts to read the memorial folder ... *more recently being the Reed Clinic.*

"Dr. Guthrie, Sharon's husband, will be doing the eulogy today," announces Rev. Boutelle.

Cindy's head pops up sharply. She watches Bill rise from his seat and walk to the lectern. Her mind is going wild. *"I can't believe that he's doing this."*

"I would like to talk about Sharon," Bill begins, "and tell you what a wonderful wife and mother she was. My darling Sharon was a great help to me in the church. My darling Sharon gave the best children's sermons."

Cindy is appalled. This is the phoniest thing that she has ever heard in her life. *"He looks as if he's acting --- he appears much too happy to have just lost his wife."* She closes her eyes and guilt feelings begin to rush in. *"What's wrong with me? These people were my good friends. This is the second time I'm thinking that this is screwy, that something is wrong here. Why am I thinking like this?"*

"Lunch will be served here at the church after the service at the cemetery," Rev. Boutelle states. "The Guthrie family invite you all to join them."

Sharon's casket is wheeled down the center aisle of the church while the organist plays one of Sharon's favorite hymns. Tearfully, the mourners watch as the family and friends follow behind the casket.

At the cemetery, family and close friends gather under a tent with Sharon's casket directly in front of them. Others move in as close to the tent as possible. Rev. Boutelle opens a marked place in his Bible and begins reading, "The Lord is my Shepherd, I shall not want. He makes me lie down in green pastures." The families, feeling as if someone is taking a knife and slashing out their hearts, hold tight to each other as the minister finishes the 23rd Psalm.

Family members, one at a time, place a long-stemmed rose on Sharon's casket. Rev. Boutelle then asks everyone to bow their heads. After a short prayer, he shakes hands with each family member extending his condolences. Others who have made the trip to the cemetery approach the family and extend their sympathies.

Cindy, being one of the last ones in line, steps up to Bill. "I'm so sorry," she begins. "There just aren't words...." Before she can finish, Bill leans over and grabs her. "Give us a kiss," he says; then kisses Cindy directly on the mouth. Horror written all over her face and extremely shocked, Cindy quickly pulls away from him. Normally, she is never without words, but this action has rendered her speechless! She turns on her heels and walks briskly away from him.

"Girls!" Bill calls out to his daughters as they walk back to the cars. "I would very much appreciate it if you would remove all of your mother's things from the house as soon as possible. You can keep her clothes or give them away ... whatever you want. I also want her cow collection removed. I may remarry someday and I don't want them in the house." Having reached his vehicle, he opens the car door and gets in, leaving his daughters looking stunned and speechless.

May 18, 1999

The day after their mother's funeral, the three sisters face another sorrowful day. They arrive at the manse in Wolsey to grant their father's request to remove their mother's belongings from the house. They unload various sizes of empty cardboard boxes from the back of a van and enter the front door. Anxious to end this stressful task, but hesitant to start, they stand motionless and silent in the living room. Feelings of emptiness and sadness pass through their bodies. Even though this is their father's home, they feel as if they are intruding.

Suzanne quickly breaks the silence suggesting that they start in the bedroom. Shivers travel up and down their spines as they each carry an empty box into their parents' bedroom. They open the closet door where their mother's clothes are hanging neatly and remove one article of clothing at a time, making the difficult decision to keep it for themselves or place it in a box for the Salvation Army.

"I feel that Mom would want Cindy to have this," Suzanne states when she pulls out a red Nebraska Cornhuskers sweatshirt. A subdued tear slowly slips from one of her eyes as she remembers how her mother loved this sweatshirt. "Cindy was raised in Nebraska and I'm sure that she would be thrilled if we gave this to her. How do you guys feel about it?" Lexi and Danielle agree that it is fine with them, so Suzanne lays it on the bed. "I will deliver it to Cindy later."

Tears suddenly burst out of Lexi's eyes as she pulls a light blue dress from the closet. "I remember when Mom wore this. She always looked so nice in it."

As the good memories are shared, tears flow among the sisters. They finish the clothing, then concentrate on their mother's shoes lined up on the floor of the closet. The chest of drawers is emptied, and then they come to Sharon's jewelry box. The three sisters sit on the bed and as each piece of jewelry is removed, they make the decision to keep it or give it away.

"Well, that should be everything in here," Suzanne states. They grab the filled boxes and move them into the living room. "I guess we should pack up her cow collection next."

"Suz, would your girls like some of Mom's cows?" Lexi asks. "After all they are the ones who got her interested in collecting them."

"Thanks for thinking of them --- they will be thrilled," Suzanne replies. She carefully finishes wrapping a cow statue in newspaper and places it in a box.

"Suzanne, why don't you just take them all home, let the girls go through them and pick out what they want to keep," Danielle suggests.

"Thank you, they would love that."

They finish with the cow collection and proceed to the living room to pack Sharon's collection of plates, dolls, and miscellaneous items.

Within a few days, Lexi and Mitch travel back to Oklahoma while Danielle returns to college in Brookings. Suzanne attempts to get her home life back in order and take over the care of her grandmother, Nannie, in the nursing home.

A few days after the funeral Dr. Bill packs some clothes and leaves Wolsey to visit with his good friends, Karen and Eddy Neilson in Wyoming. After staying with them for several days, he drives to Oklahoma to officiate at Lexi and Mitch's wedding; then returns home to continue his ministry.

August 27, 1999

Beadle County State's Attorney Michael Moore is in his office with Deputy State's Attorney Tracy Kelly.

"Deputy Sheridan has received a copy of the warrant and has left for Wolsey to arrest Bill Guthrie, so he should be behind bars soon," Moore states.

The phone rings. "Excuse me a moment, Tracy. Hello. Yes, that's okay ... sounds good. Talk to you later. Sorry, that was Candice," he replies. "She needed my input on a wedding matter."

"How are the wedding plans coming along?" Tracy asks.

"Great! Candice is doing a great job and has almost all the preparations done. The honeymoon is my contribution, but until I know when the motions hearings will start, I'm not sure how many days we can be gone, and that worries me a little."

"How are the nerves holding up?" Tracy asks.

"Are you talking about the wedding coming up in five weeks or the trial?"

"Both, I guess." Tracy replies.

"Well, to be truthful, right now, I'm a little more nervous about the trial. I have never prosecuted a murder case in the seven years I've been a lawyer and with only circumstantial evidence looking at us, this is going to be a tough one."

Tracy chuckles lightly. "Hey, Mike, remember, this is also your first wedding."

"I know, but at least I know where I stand there. With no large insurance policy looking at us as motive, this business regarding Guthrie's affair still going on with that woman in Nebraska should help us. Adults just don't drown in a bathtub, so it looks like we're going to have to prove that Guthrie put sleeping pills into his wife's chocolate milk."

"Hey, everything will work out," Tracy encourages.

"Thanks for the vote of confidence. I'll need a lot of help and I know I can count on you." He opens up the Guthrie folder lying on his desk and begins sorting through it.

Deputy Jim Sheridan and Deputy Steve Hofmann arrive at the manse. Dr. Bill is not home, so they drive around town looking for his car. After a thorough search of Wolsey, they don't spot his car anywhere, so decide to take another pass by the manse. They see him drive into the alley behind the manse, so they follow and park behind him.

"What can I do for you?" Bill asks, very little emotion showing on his face as he exits his car.

"Bill, I have a warrant to arrest you for the murder of Sharon," Deputy Sheridan states. "You have the right to remain silent and stop questions at any time. Anything that you say can be used as evidence against you. You have the continuing right to consult with and have the presence of an attorney. If you cannot afford an attorney, an attorney will be appointed for you. Do you understand these rights?"

"Yes," Bill answers softly.

"Do you wish to waive these rights and talk to us at this time?" Deputy Sheridan asks.

"No."

Deputy Hofmann places the handcuffs on Bill and escorts him to the patrol car. He is transported to Huron

Huron Daily Plainsman

The family of Bill and Sharon Guthrie would like everyone to remember that people are innocent until proven guilty. Please remember that our family has lost a wife, a sister, a mother, and a grandmother. We stand as a family and with God and ask the Christian community to be with us in prayer through this whole time. Thank you.

Bill's arrest is also upsetting to the Committee of Ministry in the Presbytery. They grant him a leave of absence with full salary and benefits and place a temporary supply pastor at the Wolsey and Bonilla churches. They state that Dr. Bill Guthrie is a minister in good standing and firmly believe in the premise of being innocent until proven otherwise. The interim executive of the Presbytery states that they intend to proceed pastorally and to be supportive to Guthrie, his family, and the churches. The members of Wolsey and Bonilla Presbyterian Churches voice strong support for their minister.

August 30, 1999

The day of his arraignment, Bill Guthrie, dressed in his jail attire, a blue jumpsuit, sits quietly on a cot reading passages from his well-worn Bible

Deputy Sheridan approaches. "Well, Bill, are you ready for your big day?" he asks, as he places a key into the lock.

"Do I have a choice?" Bill chuckles nervously as he rises from the cot and walks toward the cell door.

"You can leave that here. We have one in the courtroom."

A puzzled look appears on Bill's face. Then he realizes that he is still holding his Bible. "Sorry, didn't know I was still holding it. Nerves, I guess." Bill walks over to the cot, lays the Bible down, then returns. Sheridan places the cuffs around Bill's wrists and they proceed out of the cell area to the east exit door of the jail.

The Beadle County Courthouse is located only a few steps away from the jail. Deputy Sheridan and Bill walk through the parking lot, enter the south door of the courthouse, take a left, and enter the elevator. Bill's knees weaken, as the elevator door closes. The old elevator whines as they travel the short two-floor climb to the courtroom.

They exit the elevator and are immediately greeted by Gregory Wilson, Bill's attorney. He shakes Bill's hand and directs him into the courtroom. Wilson lays his briefcase on the table in front of them, opens it, and begins to pull out a stack of papers before sitting down.

"How long do you think this will take?" Bill inquires.

"I would guess approximately fifteen to twenty minutes."

"What do I have to do?"

"When the judge addresses you, just answer, 'Yes, Your Honor, or no, Your Honor.' "

Judge Eugene Martin enters the courtroom. "For the record it's now 2:21 p.m., August 30, 1999. The matter before this court is the State of South Dakota versus William Boyd Guthrie. Mr. Guthrie is present in court and is represented by his legal counsel, Gregory Wilson. Michael Moore and Tracy Kelly, representing the State, are present. Mr. Wilson, have you received a copy of the indictment?"

"Yes, Your Honor."

"Mr. Guthrie, do you understand that you are being charged with the murder of Sharon Guthrie?"

"Yes, Your Honor."

"I further advise you that this is a Class A felony in the State of South Dakota and the penalty is death or life in prison in the State Penitentiary. A lesser sentence than death, or life in prison, may not be given for a Class A felony. Do you understand this, Mr. Guthrie?"

"Yes, Your Honor."

"If you are unable to obtain counsel, I will appoint an attorney to represent you. The county will pay for it, and any monies paid out on behalf of the court-appointed attorney will result in a lien against yourself and your property. You have the right to confront and cross-examine all of the witnesses that appear against you. You have the right to have subpoenas issued on your behalf to secure the presence of witnesses that you may wish to come and testify. You have the right against self-incrimination, which means that you do not have to give any testimony on this matter. You have a right to a speedy public trial with an impartial jury here in Beadle County, if you so desire. If you enter a plea of not guilty, the presumption of innocence, which you now enjoy, will continue with you throughout the trial. The burden is on the State to prove all of the elements of the charge beyond a reasonable doubt. The jury must reach a unanimous verdict, and if the jury finds a verdict of guilty, and if the Court accepts it, it would amount to a conviction and subject you to punishment. If you enter a plea of guilty or a plea of nolo contendere, that means that you do not argue with or dispute any of the facts set out in the indictment. If you enter a plea of guilty, you will have waived your right to trial by jury here in Beadle County, waived your right to confront and cross-examine the witnesses against you, and waived your right against self-incrimination. Do you understand this, sir?"

"Yes, Your Honor."

"Do you have any questions regarding what you have been charged with?"

"No, Your Honor."

"Do you have any questions regarding any of the legal rights that I have set forth?"

"No, Your Honor."

"Do you have any questions regarding the penalty involved?"

"No, Your Honor."

"Mr. Guthrie, are you prepared at this time to enter a plea to this charge?"

"Yes, Your Honor."

"What is your plea, Mr. Guthrie?"

"Not guilty."

"A plea of not guilty will be taken, entered, and filed. Mr. Guthrie, do you wish to have a jury trial?"

Guthrie remains silent. Gregory Wilson answers for his client. "Yes, Your Honor."

"Mr. Wilson, are there any motions that you want to bring to the Court's attention at this time?"

"Yes, Your Honor. I'm filing a motion for release of the grand jury transcript and a discovery motion. I would ask that the Court address the issue of the transcript at this time. With fairness to the State, since Mr. Moore has not had a chance to review the discovery motion, I will simply file it. I will trust that he will provide discovery on the issues that he doesn't have any objection to, and we can address the objected matters at a later date."

"Is there any resistance from the State to the motion for the release of the Grand Jury transcripts?"

"No, Your Honor," answers Moore.

"Your Honor, I have one other matter that I would like to address. On the way over here today I heard a news report on the radio concerning the charges against my client. Quotes were attributed to Mr. Moore purportedly describing various statements made by Mr. Guthrie and offering the State's theory of how certain elements of the offense were committed. I believe, Your Honor, that it extends beyond the rules of professional conduct, and I would like to ask that the Court instruct the State to refrain from such further comment."

"I will take this under advisement. Anything else, Mr. Wilson?"

"Yes, Your Honor. I do not believe that bond has been set for my client."

"Are there any comments from the State, Mr. Moore?"

"Yes, Your Honor. The State would ask for a significant bond to be set in this matter. Even though Mr. Guthrie has lived here for three years, it has come to my attention that he has been suspended from his church as their minister, so he has really no reason to stay here since he is not originally from this area."

"Mr. Wilson?"

"Obviously, the charges are very serious, Your Honor. Nonetheless, I would ask the Court to consider that law enforcement has had a number of contacts with my client since May 14th, the date of the alleged offense, and have taken no action in the ensuing three months. Apparently, they did not perceive him a flight risk at the time, nor perceive him as a threat to the community, so I would ask the Court to set a reasonable bond in this matter, such that he would have some hope of posting."

"The fact that Mr. Guthrie is charged with an offense punishable by death, such a release will not reasonably assure his appearance, so he will be held without bond," Judge Martin states.

Judge Martin, Michael Moore, and Gregory Wilson meet to review three hundred questionnaires of prospective jurors that have been returned. Each person summoned has been informed that knowingly failing to comply with the summons is a crime punishable by a fine, jail term, or both.

One hundred prospective jurors are immediately removed from the list mainly because they have already formed an opinion. Of the remaining two hundred people, one hundred are contacted to be questioned the first day in four groups of twenty-five. The following day, the remaining one hundred people will be also be questioned in four groups of twenty-five.

Approximately seventy people are then selected and their names are placed on a list. Mr. Moore and Mr. Wilson then conduct what is called a *strike down*. They pass the list of names back and forth and each take a turn removing a name from the list. Fourteen names are needed to make up a jury of twelve with two alternates, so once this process is completed, the fourteen jurors are contacted by mail and informed of the date and time to report to the courtroom for the first day of the trial.

January 12, 2000

Trial Day One

After several months of motion hearings, the first day of the murder trial begins. Deputy Sheridan escorts the defendant into the courtroom. During his trial Guthrie is allowed to wear street clothes instead of jail attire.

Eight women and six men are escorted into the courtroom by the bailiff. Twelve are seated in the jury box and the other two, just to the right of the jury box. All fourteen will hear the evidence. At the completion of the trial, Judge Martin will announce the names of two alternates and they will be excused, and the remaining twelve will determine a verdict.

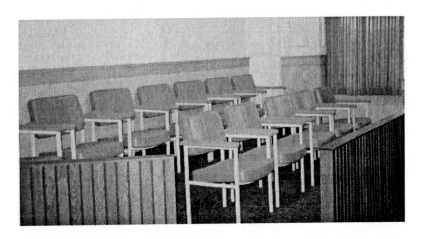

The courtroom is not a large room, so several chairs have been added along the two sides of the room to accommodate more seating space, and a speaker system has been installed. Family members, court personnel, press, and numerous residents and church members of Wolsey and Bonilla fill the available seats. As many as twenty-five spectators are turned away due to lack of seating. Most have never sat in a courtroom before and definitely not for a murder trial. Other than the shuffling of papers by the attorneys, the courtroom is deathly silent.

Judge Martin enters. Everyone stands until Martin is seated. "The record may reflect that all members of the jury are present, counsel are present, as well as the defendant. Mr. Moore, you may read the indictment."

"The State of South Dakota versus William Boyd Guthrie, Indictment for Homicide, Murder in the First Degree. The Beadle County Grand Jury charges on or about the fourteenth day of May, 1999, in the county of Beadle, State of South Dakota, William Boyd Guthrie did commit the public offense of Homicide, Murder in the First Degree. In that, he did cause the death of Sharon Guthrie without authority of law and with a premeditated design to effect the death of Sharon Guthrie. Dated the twenty-seventh day of August, a true bill, by the grand jury foreperson. To that charge the defendant has pled not guilty."

Judge Martin speaks. "Before the attorneys begin, I wish to make a few comments to the people in the general audience. You are certainly welcome here, but, if I detect, see, or hear, anything that is of an emotional outburst, or I feel that one of you is attempting to do something to influence the jury, you will be ushered out immediately. Also, when the trial is in recess for the lunch hour, you must leave the courthouse. There are seats reserved for court personnel and the press, which leaves the other seats on a first come, first serve basis.

"Now, ladies and gentlemen of the jury, at this time, the attorneys will make their opening statements. The State will tell you what they feel they are going to show and prove and also, what the evidence is in this case. When the State is done, the defense will have the opportunity to make their opening statements."

State's Attorney Michael Moore proceeds to the front of the courtroom and faces the jury. "There are four ways people die. They can die of a natural death --- it can be an accident --- it can be suicide --- it can be homicide. In this case the State will tell you that Sharon Guthries' death was not of natural causes, that she didn't die of an accident, and that she didn't commit suicide. That leaves us only one. The evidence will show you that Sharon's death was a homicide, and that the defendant, William Guthrie, killed her.

"Sharon Guthrie died in a bathtub on May 14, 1999. A pathologist will testify she drowned in that bathtub because of a large amount of a drug called Temazepam that was found in her system. She did not have a prescription for Temazepam, but William Guthrie did. So, how did she get this Temazepam in her system? In order to answer that question you are going to have to listen to the evidence. You will hear about an affair that the defendant has been having since 1993, and also, you will hear about several incidents that happened to Sharon in the months prior to her death. A computer expert will inform you of the results that he found when he researched the defendant's computer. During the course of this trial you will hear testimony from many witnesses, including Sharon's family. Thank you."

"Ladies and gentlemen of the jury," Gregory Wilson for the defense begins. "I am going to begin by telling you a very important story. It's the last day of school before Christmas and the kids are bringing gifts to their teacher. Jimmy, whose dad owns a bakery, comes up first. He gets halfway to the teacher's desk and the teacher says, *'I can smell it from here. It's fresh bread from your dad's bakery, isn't it Jimmy?'* He replies, *'yes.'* The next one up is Janey, whose dad owns a grocery store. It is obvious that the way the gift is wrapped that it's a fruit basket and the teacher again guesses correctly. Johnny, who is next, comes walking up to the desk carrying his gift. The bottom of the gift is kind of wet. It's a small town and the teacher knows that Johnny's dad owns a liquor store. She says, *'Johnny, I wonder what this is?'* Johnny quickly says, *'It's a puppy!'* Now, I would surmise that you were all thinking it was liquor from Johnny's dad's liquor store, but you got ahead of yourselves. Remember --- facts are stubborn things. Think about the facts first in this case and reach conclusions later. That is what this story is all about --- reaching conclusions before you know the facts.

"Much of what the State says will be true, but when you hear about the affair for the tenth time ask yourselves, *'Why am I hearing about this affair for the tenth time?'*

"You are going to hear Bill's credibility called into question, but don't get so tripped up in trying to catch him in a lie that you miss when he tells the truth. When in doubt, look to what other people say happened. Look to what Sharon says happened. You need to remember that the evidence comes from the witnesses. Listen to the evidence when it comes in --- the difference being in the details. Bill gave an extensive statement to law enforcement. You will see some inconsistencies, but don't be so intent to look for the inconsistencies that you miss what is consistent with what other witnesses say.

"The drug Temazepam that was in Sharon's system was from Bill's prescription, but there were also two other drugs in her system. Whose prescriptions were they from?

"You will hear from a psychologist who calls himself a suicidologist. He will give you his opinion, but again --- do not miss the facts. The evidence is going to come at you in bits and pieces.

Focus on catching the details as they come in and catch all of them.

"What is required of you as a juror is not to decide the case until you have heard all of the evidence. Hopefully, the story that I just told you demonstrates how easy it is to jump to conclusions. Don't get caught in that trap. Wait and hear the whole story from each witness, make notes and watch for the details. When all of this is done, both the State and I will be back to make our closing arguments, and I am confident that at that time you will return a verdict of not guilty."

Witness for the State - Deputy Jim Sheridan
Questioned by Moore

"Deputy Sheridan, please explain the photographs I have here."

"I took these inside the Guthrie home in Wolsey on May 14, 1999. Photo A is the bathroom showing a stand with a plant on it and an extension cord under it located next to the bathtub.

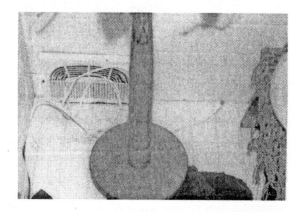

B is an overall picture of the bathroom. It's not discernible, but the floor is wet and the dark materials on the floor are wet towels.

C is the bathtub and I assume that the articles in the tub are nightclothes and a bathmat."

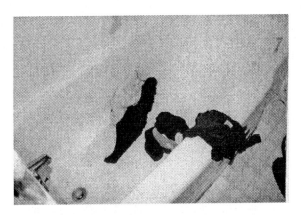

"What did the defendant tell you when you spoke with him at the hospital?"

"Mr. Guthrie said that he and Sharon had gotten up about 7:00 a.m., that his normal routine was to go over to the church to do prayers and devotions, so he left the house. When he got home, he walked down the hallway and saw that the carpet was wet, so he opened up the bathroom door, and found his wife in the bathtub. He pulled the plug to drain the water and wrestled with her, trying to get her out of the tub, but was unable to do so because she was too heavy."

"What did you do next?"

"We interviewed people in the Wolsey area, members of the church and people that had responded to the incident. Background investigations were done on both the victim and any potential suspects. I then contacted Agent Jerry Lindberg, who works for the South Dakota Division of Criminal Investigation, to assist me. After we were informed that Mrs. Guthrie had a large amount of prescription drugs in her system, an autopsy was ordered."

"Deputy Sheridan, please explain the medications that I have here."

"On May 17th, I asked Les Hewitt to gather up all the medications that were in the house, then I picked them up at 1:30 that same day. We had checked on the prescriptions and found that a prescription for Temazepam had been written by Patricia Minor for William Guthrie, was filled, and picked up at K-Mart on April 29th of '99. Then that same day Patricia Minor also phoned in a prescription for Temazepam to Statz Drug for William Guthrie, and that prescription was also filled and picked up."

"Deputy Sheridan, please open the bag and take out the prescription marked State's 3a. What does it say on the bottle and how many pills are left in that bottle?"

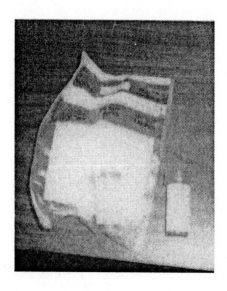

"This is a script bottle of fifteen, 30-milligram Temazepam, prescribed for William Guthrie and filled at Statz Drug on May 12, 1999. There are six capsules in the bottle."

"When you interviewed the defendant on June 9th, what did he tell you about Sharon's sleepwalking?"

"Mr. Guthrie indicated that she had been sleepwalking since '75 - '76 when they lived in Wyoming, said that it has been a problem several years. He told us about a time prior to the move to South Dakota when they had gotten out of bed and found a pair of his muddy boots sitting in front of a chair in their home. Sharon asked him why he had worn the muddy boots into the house, and he claimed that he hadn't. He told her that someone must have broken into the house, so he checked the exterior of the house, but found no forcible entry. He indicated he was sure that she had been sleepwalking, had put his boots on, and had come back into the house with the mud on them."

"What did he tell you regarding Sharon's more recent sleepwalking incidents?"

"He said Sharon had a liking for chocolate milk, would go to the refrigerator during the night, and wander around the house. He said most of the time he would sleep through these incidents, *'Slept like a log,'* I think is how he put it."

"What did the defendant tell you regarding the incident when Sharon quit breathing?"

"He indicated that he was sleeping pretty soundly when apparently something woke him. He noticed that Sharon wasn't breathing, hollered at her loudly several times, and then she woke up or started breathing again. He said he suspected that she was suffering from sleep apnea. I think that he mentioned there was a time frame where he took her to the doctor's office."

"What was Mr. Guthrie's response when you asked him if he was trained in CPR?"

"He said that he wasn't."

"What did he tell you regarding the incident when Sharon was taken to the doctor because she was groggy?"

"He said Sharon had been up and he thought that she had gotten into some Benadryl because there were empty bottles of Benadryl sitting on her nightstand. She was having heart palpitations is how he referred to it, that her heart was racing and when he held on to her she was shaky, so the next day they made an appointment and he took her into Dr. Reed's office around 2:00 p.m."

"When did you find out that the defendant was having an affair with Myra Conner?"

"May 20, 1999."

"What did he say when you asked him about the affair?"

"He denied having an affair with anyone, said that it was a counseling session. When she would come to his office he would leave the door open, so nobody would think that there was anything going on, and then he left it at that. We proceeded to explain to him that we had some pretty solid information that there was something going on between him and Ms. Conner. After further prodding, he finally admitted they had had an ongoing affair."

"Did he tell you when he had told Sharon about the affair?"

"He said that he told her in January of '99, which supposedly was the last contact that he had with Ms. Conner."

"Did he also tell you that Sharon was upset about him having this affair?"

"Yes."

"What did the defendant tell you about Sharon's suicidal tendencies?"

"He stated that she had threatened suicide two years ago when he was gone on a camping trip. Sharon told him if he didn't come home right away she was going to do something to herself, so he returned home."

"Did he talk about red Solo cups?"

"Yes, he asked me if I saw the red Solo cups and I told him that I saw just one."

"Deputy Sheridan, did you do any additional follow-up investigation to confirm or deny some of the other things that he told you during the interview?"

"Yes."

"Please explain this photo that was taken on July 27th, the day of the search."

"This shows the relationship of the church with the office attached to the church and the front door of the house."

"I also have a photo of the inside of the church office taken that day. Deputy, when you seized the Corsair computer from the office, was the computer on or off when you arrived there?"

"It was off. We turned it on to see if we could find e-mails or evidence that might be germane to the case, but after about an hour of trying we were unable to get by the password. We then turned it off and delivered it to the evidence room at the Beadle County Sheriff's Office."

"When was the computer taken to the DCI lab in Pierre to be analyzed and then brought back to the evidence room?"

"I checked it into their evidence room on July 30th, and I brought it back to our evidence room on November 29th."

"Deputy Sheridan, what did you do with the computer when you brought it back from Pierre?"

"You asked me to have the hard drives removed, so on December 1st, I had an employee at Office Supplies come to the evidence room and remove the two hard drives from the computer. I left Huron on December 5th and traveled to Lake Tahoe, Nevada. On December 6th, I delivered the hard drives to Presentation Dynamics, Inc. at Incline Village at 9:00 a.m. That same day, at 3:00 p.m., I picked up both hard drives and brought them back to Huron."

"Please explain the care that these hard drives have received to prevent them from becoming damaged?"

"The hard drives were wrapped in an anti-static bag to prevent any static electricity, and the mailing-type envelopes with little air bubbles were used to prevent any damage."

"Deputy Sheridan, I'm showing you a bottle of medication that was found on the headboard of the bed at the Guthrie residence. Please read what it says on the bottle."

"This is a script bottle for fifteen, 30-milligram Temazepam from K-Mart pharmacy in Huron. It was filled on May 13th of '99 for William Guthrie. The physician's name is Patricia Minor."

"How many pills are left in this bottle of Temazepam?"

"There is one capsule."

"I have a picture here showing another pill bottle. Where did you find this bottle?

"I found that one on the headboard of the bed in the master bedroom, which is located on the northeast corner of the house."

"I have no further questions, Thank you."

Cross-examine by the Defense

"Deputy Sheridan, what was the first thing you did to preserve evidence at the Guthrie house?"

"We photographed it, identified it, and bagged it."

"When was that done?"

"The day of the search on July 27th of '99."

"A little over two months after Sharon's death. Is that correct?"

"Yes."

"What did you do to preserve evidence at the Guthrie house on May 14th?

"Nothing."

"How about on May 15th?"

"Nothing."

"So, Deputy Sheridan, May 15th was the first day that you learned that there was a drug overdose, and two days later you retrieved some prescriptions from the house. Are those prescription bottles from both Sharon Guthrie and Bill Guthrie?"

"Yes."

"When you recovered these pills, did you know that you were dealing with a prescription drug overdose?"

"Yes."

"Were you were looking for the source of the drugs?"

"Yes."

"How would you have handled these pill bottles if you were concerned about fingerprints?"

"Most likely differently."

"Was any effort made to determine if there were any fingerprints on them, or preserve them if there were?"

"No."

"Was there any effort made to preserve Sharon Guthrie's fingerprints?"

"No."

"Deputy, am I correct in understanding that you tried to activate the computer while it was still in the church office, but you were unable to get by the password?"

"Yes, that's correct."

"During the time that the computer was at the DCI lab in Pierre, is it correct that Mr. Hutchins did, in fact, access records on the computer while it was in his possession?"

"Yes, he did."

"And then in December, for some apparent reason, wasn't a different computer expert from Nevada utilized?"

"Yes."

"Through your investigation, were you able to determine that the Temazepam prescription of Bill Guthrie's was filled four times, and that at least one of those times, it was picked up by Sharon Guthrie?"

"Yes."

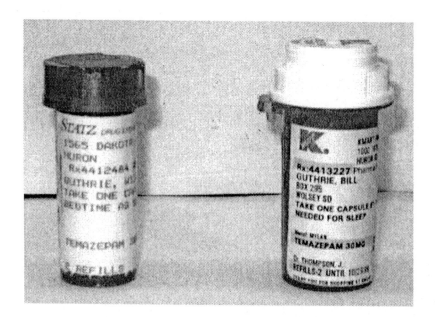

"Do I understand correctly, Deputy Sheridan, that you actually have one bottle from Statz Drug and one bottle from K-Mart, but that you never attempted to take fingerprint information off the bottles to determine whether Sharon had handled them, and haven't done that to this day?"

"That's correct."

"Are you generally familiar with the fingerprint process and what needs to be done to preserve an item for possible fingerprint analysis?"

"Yes."

"With the handling of these bottles as it's been, and your understanding of fingerprint techniques, Deputy Sheridan, could they now be successfully fingerprinted?"

"Well, … for yours and mine probably, but not something that was there six months ago."

"I have no further questions."

Witness for the State - Darrel Hutchins
DCI Computer Support Specialist, Pierre, S.D.
Questioned by Moore

"Mr. Hutchins, what effect does Norton Utilities have on a computer when you are working on it?"

"Norton Utilities is a program that allows you to look at the data on a computer. It also allows you to look at hidden and deleted files and files that are left on the hard drive. Norton will not change the actual files, but will update the date of the last access on the computer files. By using the *read only* mode, you can tell when someone has looked at a file on a particular date."

"How many days do you think that it took you to examine the computer?"

"Approximately four days --- if I remember correctly."

"Did you ever turn the computer on while it was in your possession?"

"Yes, one time I made a mistake. I accidentally plugged it in, allowing it to boot under it's own operating system. After it was fully running, I safely shut it down."

"What does that action do to a computer when you start it up?"

"It would be the same as if you turned a computer on and off normally each day when the normal operating system can modify files as part of its normal startup sequence."

"When you were looking at this computer and using Norton Utilities, did you find anything that you felt was relevant to the investigation?"

"I was asked to look for certain information. When I found some that I felt was relevant, I printed it out. I printed out the contents from the hard drives regarding the e-mail folders, which included the deleted e-mails, and I also found information regarding drugs."

"Did we ask you to do further investigation on the computer?"

"Yes, but my supervisor needed me for other projects, so I was unable to do so."

"When you were done with the computer, what did you do with it?"

"It was secured back in the forensics lab evidence room by the evidence personnel."

"I have no more questions. Thank you."

Cross-examine by the Defense

"Mr. Hutchins, are you specially trained in computer forensics?"

"No, I am not a forensic examiner, but I do assist the investigators."

"Are you aware that there is software available which allows a forensic computer specialist to access computer data without changing the files and will not change the last access date?"

"Yes, I am aware of that, but we did not have that software or equipment at the time I was asked to do this examination."

"Aren't we talking about a thousand bucks worth of software and hardware combined, Mr. Hutchins?"

"The last one that was purchased for the Sioux Falls Police Department was twenty-six thousand dollars worth of equipment and software."

"You stated that you actually allowed the computer to boot on its own. Wouldn't allowing the computer to boot in that fashion have the net effect of destroying some of the information that was stored on the hard drive?"

"Booting the computer on its own is the same as booting on any normal day on its own and would have the same effect. It can modify files as part of the operating system's normal operation."

"When you say modify files, does that mean it can cause information stored on the hard drive to be posted?"

"Yes, under some circumstances, if the operating system has the procedure for doing that."

"Mr. Hutchins, were you ever instructed to look for a suicide note?"

"No, I was not."

"Thank you. No further questions."

Judge Martin questions Mr. Hutchins. "Is it correct to say that booting the computer can have the effect of the loss of some information?"

"The accidental booting using normal operating system as part of the normal operating system startup will sometimes clear its working areas, so that it can do its normal operations."

"Okay, but does that mean that you may lose something, but it doesn't change the information that's stored in there?"

"The information that's stored in the areas where the process needs to modify is not changed."

"Thank you. Anything else, Mr. Wilson?"

"Yes, Your Honor. Mr. Hutchins, I'm a little bit confused. I'm not a computer expert, but I have had a little bit of this explained to me. Is it correct that booting up a computer can, in essence, push some information off the hard drive to make room for more information?"

"The areas are available for other information to write over them, but on computers when it's done that way, it is taken out of the directory and the information is left on the hard drive, but it can be overwritten by a later action on the computer."

"So, Mr. Hutchins, the act of booting up the computer may, in fact, overwrite something or cancel out something that was already there. Correct?"

"If it does, it will leave information on the computer that it has done so."

"Thank you, no more questions."

Witness for the State – Judd Robbins
Computer Forensic expert from Nevada
Questioned by Moore

"Mr. Robbins, when someone asks you to do forensic work on a computer, in basic terms what you do?"

"Basically I play detective. The computer is an electronic equivalent to paper in a person's house. A detective will look through a house to find pieces of paper, scraps of evidence that might apply to a case. I look through the hard drives and occasionally a diskette. Sometimes additional technology like zip drives also have electronic information, so I look through bit by bit, byte by byte, word by word, instruction by instruction. With input from the lawyers, as to what the case might be about, I search for things that are relevant.

"In this case, the lawyers told me that there was something regarding drugs. I looked through the entire hard drive for anything that had the word *drug* in it, which might be a note, a memo, an e-mail or a reference to a website on the Internet. I didn't know what I was looking for at that point, other than exploring. The real neat thing about computer forensics is that with pieces of paper, where every piece of paper you look at has something on it, you can read through it line by line and say that's relevant, but with a computer you can hide things. Hiding in some cases is sometimes purposeful and sometimes it's not purposeful at all; it's just the way the computer works.

"When you look at computer-defined evidence there are four general classifications of cases and things that you can find. One is something that's just sitting there in plain sight. For example, the file on a computer could be twenty to thirty pages and could have a label which says, '*Sent to Mike 12/14.*' That is its label and it tells me immediately what it is --- just some copies of what I found that might be relevant to this case. It's a file and it's now in my notebook. I can find it, I can identify it by name, and it's easy to understand what it is.

"Another piece of paper might represent a different file. This is a piece of paper that at the end of today is going to be garbage. So I might delete this, crush it up, and throw it into a trash basket. If you come to my folder tomorrow, you wouldn't find that piece of paper because I threw it away; but if you knew where to look, you could find it in the deleted area of my computer. I have just undeleted this, retrieved it completely, read it, and the data was there. Whatever it was is completely useful to me and completely meaningful. It was nominally deleted, but it doesn't get truly deleted and disappear forever in a computer when you just say delete. So that's a second class of information that computers can present in a case like this. It can simply be deleted because the computer needs the space. I have a friend who called me up two days ago and said, *Judd, my computer only has fifty megabytes left on it, what can I do?'* I told him it was time to delete some files to make space. You can delete things to make space, but at least for awhile they are retrievable. I like this one because there is a time period during which you can delete files and they still are retrievable. I advise every lawyer who calls me regarding cases like this, that the sooner you can hold the computer in abeyance the more likely, if there is any evidence there, I or someone like me can find it again for them.

"The third area called unallocated space, which is when the computer has things that are no longer needed, it will free up space for the programs to reuse. It's like having a stack of paper with writing on one side and I want to use the backs of the paper to do other work. I could pull off one sheet that I had made notes on that were important and place it in my briefcase for reference later. Depending on my mood, I might take a sheet from the pile from either end or the middle of the stack. I may make some notes, fold it up, and put it in my jacket pocket. The point is that all of this unallocated space in the computer contains potential places for evidence. People don't think about that when they delete the file or when the file becomes available. Allocate means set apart. I pulled that piece off one end, I pulled a couple pieces off the middle, and then pieces from the other end, so what is left is called trace evidence in a computer forensic sense.

"The fourth one called slack space is kind of neat. In school, when blackboards were used extensively, teachers would write all over the blackboards filling them. Then they might start erasing from the left and write in the newly erased space, but the stuff that they wrote at the beginning of the class was still on the right. Some teachers would leave the information on the board and when the next class came in, a different teacher would have to decide what to erase without messing up the teacher who was there prior and might need it tomorrow. Generally, you don't have a choice when you start erasing. You start from the left usually because that's how we write. You begin to erase from the left and fill in new things for your class. For instance, there are four blackboards and you only erase and write on three of them, leaving what has been written on the fourth blackboard on the right. Residual data is still on the fourth blackboard because it's still there from the first class, but the other three boards have been written over. The writing on the first three boards is never retrievable again because it's been erased and overwritten. On the fourth board there would be evidence that might be useful regarding what went on in the previous class.

"In computer terms, in classic cases like this, the slack space sits at the end of the file. If you start writing over from the beginning of the file, the last pieces of data might be something interesting, important, or relevant. Also, a file might say it's a picture of someone's front lawn, but I would look there because at the end of the picture, there may be some hidden text in it.

"Even though the file says it's an e-mail that is one paragraph long, the back end of that file that was reused could be a word processing document with some other text of importance. It also could be a piece of an Internet website that was looked at, and the computer did not need all the extra space at the beginning.

"Those are the general areas a computer expert looks at to see what, if any, evidence exists anywhere on a hard drive. What I did regarding this case was look through the whole hard drive at all of the possible areas that still had names that were never erased. I looked at areas that had been deleted, but not overwritten, and were completely retrievable. I looked at areas that had been deleted, unallocated, made available, and not used again, and in part, sometimes reused, but still with data remaining that was of use. I looked at areas that had been reused completely and where there was some slack at the end of the data that turned out to be germane."

"Mr. Robbins, what did you do with the hard drives when you received them from Deputy Sheridan?"

"I copied each hard drive to a large lab computer. I have a number of software that I use, but the major one I used, in this case, is called Encase and is used by many law enforcement officers and personnel around the country. I made exact digital copies of the hard drives that I could keep in my lab to analyze, so that Mr. Sheridan could take the original hard drives home with him at 3:00 p.m. that same afternoon.

"I consolidated the two digital copies into a larger file on the computer or set of files, which the software can be assigned to search. I can instruct the software to look at every bit on the computer overnight while I am sleeping. The first night I asked to look for the words *drug* and *Temazepam*, which were some key words in the case. When I came in the next morning, the computer told me all the times and all the places, exactly where they were, where it had found the word *drug* and several other words that I had directed it to find. I looked at all the places that the software had identified where it had discovered the word *drug* in the middle of other information. There weren't any references to the specific word *Temazepam,* but there were five references to something called Temazepam, that was related to the word *drug.*

"Other drug names were found on the same page under drugs, namely Methcathinone, Ativan, and Lorazepam. I decided I needed to do some subsequent searches, so the next evening I directed the software to do additional searches for those drugs to see if they would lead me into anything that was related and meaningful.

"Each day that week, Monday through Thursday, I directed the computer to look for something more, and then I looked at all the results of the searches. I spoke with the prosecutor about what I had found. As a result, the searches and those discussions would lead me to further analysis. In each case, the word might be a part of e-mail, might be part of a website, or part of an entire set of pictures that came off a website. By the end of Thursday, I had found everything that I thought I could find that related to the facts, the evidence, and the discussions, so I printed out copies of my original evidence and sent it to you, Mr. Moore. I told you to take a look at it over the weekend and on Monday we discussed which of them seemed to have some meaning. I looked at those particular ones in more depth, because when you find the word *drug* in the middle of a bunch of computer code, you don't necessarily know exactly what it's going to look like when you print it out. An Internet website looks good, easy to read, highlighted text and bold text, but the codes that make that happen are sometimes difficult to read and look like three or four languages. If someone translates it for you, that's easy, but the original French and German might not be so easy to read. The computer language looks that way.

"Even if the word *drug* might be in the middle of it, to translate it into what it might really appear to be on a website is an extra chore. I did that chore for each of the websites and the text files that had apparent meaning. We then looked at those the following week and many of those particular pieces of evidence you will see here today."

"Mr. Robbins, what is this paper I have here?"

"This is an e-mail from William Guthrie to his daughter Lexi, dated April 16, 1999, which was on a Friday. I found this e-mail in what's called the draft folder of the Netscape program. Netscape enables you to either produce the Internet or send and receive e-mail. Most people when they write an e-mail they send it. This particular indication says it's a draft and it was never sent. It was stored in what's called the temporary or drafts folder."

> Hi well your mother continues to keep me on my toes even in the middle of the night. Wednesday night tuesday evening she got up turned on all the lights walked into the kitchen was there about 15 min. and returned to bed, with a glass of chocolate milk. I asked her what she did she said nothing this was about 2:00 a.m. then about 3:00 she did the same thing. then about 4:30 she did it again this time after about ten min. I got up to check on her she passed me in the hall without acknowledging I was there. At 7:00 a.m. I woke her up for work and she wobbled into the bathroom and a few min. later she was asleep in the tub with water running all over the floor. I woke her up got her out of bed ant then started my investigation. She during the night at some point had ingested something like 15 to 20 benidril and God knows what else. She has been sleep walking now I figure for about 3 months and just now I'm realizing what she has been doing talk about

feeling stupid. Well I got her to the Dr. and he did some tests and he feels she has some sleep disorder her brother has. Well I put up all the meds last night where she can't find them and we got some sleep last night. She got up twice in the night and I knew then what she is doing. Well so much for that now I will keep you posted on the continuing saga of How the Guthries' churn...
I love you Dad...

"Mr. Robbins, please tell us about the website, Worst Pills Best Pills that was visited on the defendants computer."

"I didn't find any date associated with this website; just the fact that it was clearly accessed and displayed on the computer screen. I copied two pages on a website identified as a Consumer's Guide to Avoiding Drug Induced Death or Illness."

"Please read the highlighted portions."

"It says consumer's guide to avoiding drug-induced death or illness and includes top selling drugs that are among the one hundred and sixty *do not use* drugs discussed. It includes at least a dozen drugs here, and Ativan and Temazepam are among those drugs."

"Will you please tell us what I have here marked State's Exhibit 10?"

"This is the result of a Web search for information, the display that appears, when someone goes to a website to a search engine. It compares to someone going to the information desk at the library and asking to point them in the direction of books or magazines that can help them on the subject matter that they are researching. A search engine on the Web does the same thing except it lists things for you. You can then click on an item that interests you. With a search engine, you just simply type in a phrase or a word and the result on the screen will list pages that contain information. For example, with the word *ephedrine*, it will list ten pages that contain information about *ephedrine* and say that two thousand twenty-one matches were found."

"Mr. Robbins, please explain why you have a date and a time written at the top of this one."

"This search was done on April 27, 1999, at 10:29 p.m. In some cases, as in the preceding one, you can't identify it when something was displayed on the screen because it's just facts. In other cases, you can identify when it was displayed on the screen because there may be an attached date and time information behind the scenes. For instance, when there are advertisements that appear on the Web, they often contain a date stamp as to when they are advertising. You can read that the advertisement was printed out on the screen at the same time as the web page, then conclude that the web page was displayed at that date and time. An example would be when an advertisement for the Vitamin Shoppe is at the top of the screen, often there is information at the bottom of the page as well. In many cases with this evidence, I was able to accurately identify the date and time of display."

"What do I have here marked as State's Exhibit 11?"

"This is the result of another search using a search engine called Lycros. It shows two websites that were found containing information about the drug Lorazepam. I couldn't get a date stamp on this one. This is one of those examples where I found this in unallocated clusters and any of the date sampling that existed had been stepped on and overwritten."

"Will you please read the highlighted portions?"

"Ativan - Lorazepam - Oral. This medication is used for anxiety. It is used to produce drowsiness and reduce anxiety prior to surgical or medical procedures. It may also be used in the treatment of seizure disorders."

"Please explain what I have here marked State's Exhibit 12."

"This is a copy of the actual website that was displayed and viewed on the screen for the information about Ativan, Lorazepam with oral uses, side effects, precautions and dosage information about storage of the drug and precautions."

"Mr. Robbins, is it common that you would get more detailed information on a search result, than what you are looking for?"

"Yes. The search result is a series of what are called links, which are easy ways to retrieve the pages that could be located anywhere in the world on the Internet. If you click on that link, you can get the full details of the page that is being displayed on your screen."

"Just for clarification. The one where you never found a web page in the computer that corresponded to the top. Does that mean that it wasn't accessed because you didn't find it?"

"Not at all. The fact that you might not be able to find it in what's left of my file here doesn't mean that I didn't have it an some earlier point."

"I have here State's Exhibits 13 and 13a. What are these?"

"Number 13 is a nine-page document, and 13a is a five-page document, which represent fourteen pages of the Ambien website that's put on the Web by a drug company called Searle. The middle pages are missing. I found these in one of the unallocated places on the disk where the beginning part and the end part were visible, but the middle parts had been stepped on, removed or deleted somehow."

"Mr. Robbins, please read the highlighted portion in Exhibit 13."

"Ambien, zolpidem tartrate, is a non-benzodiazepine hypnotic in the imidazopyridine class and is available in five milligram and ten milligram strength tablets for oral admission."

"Would you please read 13a for the jury?"

"Ambien, five-milligram tablets, are capsule-shaped, pink, film coated, identified with markings of AMB 5 on one side and 5401 on the other side. Then it indicates a little table of bottles, cartons, and dosages. It also says that Ambien ten-milligram tablets are capsule-shaped, white, film-coated, and identified with markings of AMB 10 on one side and 5421 on the other side. They are supplied as a bottle of a hundred and also available in cartons."

"Please explain State's Exhibit 14."

"I found this in unallocated space on the hard drive. It is the first eight pages of a website that was displayed and brought into the computer from the Internet. In the middle of the eighth page, the trace evidence was stepped on, and that's all I could retrieve. It is information regarding what's called TCA or tricyclic anti-depressants. It says TCA's are among the leading causes of morbidity from drug overdoses in children and adults."

"Why is there a date at the bottom of all of these exhibits?"

"That is simply my request to my printing program to put the date there when I printed this out and while looking at the evidence. It indicates the file number, where I have stored the evidence on my computer for rapid retrieval if it is needed for subsequent discussions with the attorney."

"Were you able to determine a date that it was viewed on the computer?"

"No, I was not."

"I have State's Exhibit 15. Please explain what this is."

"This is a search that was initiated on May 4, 1999, for websites containing information about Temazepam. It contains the two pages, which is the website itself, and then other several pages, which are the actual behind-the-scenes computer code that generates the display of the website."

"Mr. Robbins, how many results on the first page show a search for the drug Temazepam?"

"On the first ten websites that were found there are a total of four hundred twenty-five that the search engine has. You can look at the first ten; and if they are not what you want, you can click and go on to the next ten and so forth. If you find what you want, you can click that you are done."

"Please explain the back part of this exhibit, the *behind the scenes* as you called it --- *the French or German* that we can't read."

"The last five pages are the actual code on the Internet called HTML meaning Hyper Text Markup Language. The browser is placed in this simple easily understood two-page website. The back of this *behind the scenes* includes the data and the time of day in which these things happened. This particular one that has *behind the scenes* text says that it was presented on May 4, 1999, at 7:07 p.m. and twenty-one seconds after that."

"What is this search marked State's Exhibit 16?"

"This was done on April 3, 1999, for anything that could be found on the subject of bathtub accidents. This is actually the third page that was displayed with *behind the scenes* information. It indicates that two previous pages of information had already been looked at."

"Mr. Robbins, you indicate the date stamps you looked at on the second page. Please explain."

"This is part of the *behind the scenes* indicating date information. On page one of this website, it says business news on April 3rd, and sports news on April 3rd. That might suggest superficially that this happened on April 3rd, but it wouldn't necessarily be enough for me to be sure. I looked behind the scenes at additional information that showed weather in Sioux Falls and Watertown for that weekend; more specifically, it showed horoscopes. On the second page there are three links you can click on. One that indicates that you can get today's horoscope, which was dated behind the scenes, April 3rd, and two other buttons that say you can get yesterday's and tomorrow's horoscopes for April 2nd, or April 4th. Put it all together and it tells me that it was done on April 3rd."

"This search where you indicated that this was at the top, it said *back* and *next*, and so, this person had already looked at one through twenty. Was this actually displaying twenty through thirty, Mr. Robbins?"

"In *behind the scenes* text, the two buttons *back* and *next* would enable this person to go *backwards* or *forwards* in the search. Going backwards would show choices eleven through twenty. We have already looked at some evidence that showed the top ten searches or first ten searches. In this example, the HTML code, behind the scenes, indicated that you could go back to the second group of ten because you have already seen the second group of ten. It only goes forward. In the first group of ten search results, you have to click on some sort of button that says *next* to get to the next group. If you have done this twice you are in the third group and the code to display the third group would have indicated that you had already looked at ten, twenty, or fifty. So, this code was remaining enough to tell me that the person looking at this had already seen two groups of ten, and that these buttons at the top would get him the next group, the fourth group of ten, that he or she wanted."

"Please explain State's Exhibit 17?"

"This is another search engine for something called bathtub accidents. The *behind the scenes* code indicated that twenty-five choices had already been viewed regarding bathtub accidents and that the next group that would be displayed would start at choice number twenty-six. This was found in the unallocated space on the disk."

"I have State's Exhibit 18. Please explain."

"This is another search done on a search engine called Excite. The search was for bathtub accidents and was seemingly begun on April 21, 1999, at 10:20 p.m."

"Please explain number 18a."

"This is the Internet language that produced the web page in exhibit number 18. It indicates two dates: the searching date, which was initiated on searching, and at the end of the code that says the search began on April 21st, at 10:20 p.m. There is an advertisement displayed at the beginning of this code that says it was put on approximately twenty minutes after midnight on April 22nd. This suggests to me that we have a web page that was being displayed. There was some movement to one group or another during that two-hour window where the same page was being displayed or additional choices were being displayed that the advertisement is just the only thing that's being updated for time. Since the search indication was that it was being initiated a couple hours earlier, we have a window in this case where we know some activity was going on for two hours here with this particular search."

"How many possible matches does it show?"

"It says these are the top ten matches out of eighty-seven thousand, nine hundred forty-nine possible hits. This engine could show you all of these choices, if you wanted to sit and look at them; but most people would never look at that many."

"What is this marked State's Exhibit 19?"

"This is another web search using the Excite search engine which was done on April 22, 1999, at 12:19 a.m. It shows the top ten matches out of two hundred thirty-five thousand possible sites that contain information about household accidents."

"Mr. Robbins, you stated that the bathtub accidents search on the Internet ended at 12:19 a.m. Is it correct to say that this search was done on the computer about that same time?"

"We have a window time during which searches were happening and initiated because advertisements were being displayed on the screen. So within that window, I have results of things that were dates and times. I can't be sure what might have exactly come first or second, but based on the fact that these were fragments, I can say that these searches happened roughly during this two hour window of time."

"Please explain State's Exhibit 20."

"This is another search for bathtub accidents controlled by Netscape. It shows a series of websites that can be clicked on that might have information. The interesting thing about this one is that you have some things that relate to bathtubs and some things that just relate to accidents. One thing you need to realize is, that when you look for things on the Internet, and when you ask for bathtub accidents; you will get a large number of websites. That is why you get these ridiculously large numbers of eighty-seven thousand or two hundred thirty-five thousand. Some of those websites are just about bathtubs and some of those might be about accidents. The most likely ones are the ones that they show you first, the ones that have information about both bathtubs and accidents. This would explain why, when you do an Internet web search and put together a couple of words, you don't always get exactly what you are looking for so you have to go clicking around."

"Mr. Robbins, were you able to determine a date that this search was done?"

"No."

"Please explain State's Exhibit 21."

"This is another Internet search for bathtub accidents that produced two websites containing information from the Indiana Prevention Resource Center regarding Methcathinone. I thought this might be relevant to a drug-related case, so I printed it out. The search was specifically for bathtub accidents, but produced information about Methcathinone. I did not get a date for this search."

"I have State's Exhibit 22 and 22a. Mr. Robbins, please explain what these are."

"This is a list of all the files on both hard drives. It lists every file on the hard drive, the file name, where I found it, and dates of when the file was created, when it was last written on or modified, and when it was last touched, accessed, or looked at by anybody. This is sort of the key information for everything I looked at. The listing includes not only the files with names that are still visible, but also indications of where and in what part of the unallocated space or slack space I might find things."

"Mr. Robbins, from looking at and analyzing these files, are you able to tell when this computer was used, the particular dates and times that it was used, or when a file was changed and created?"

"Yes, sir."

"Please explain to the jury why it has a lot of dates that say date of last access, August 4th, August 5th, or August 6th.

"I asked you about that when I first started looking at the evidence. Apparently, the State had seized the computer on or about July 27th and turned on the computer on that date, which accounts for a number of last written times on the computer. Mr. Hutchins also accidentally allowed the computer to be turned on August 4th, which accounts for a number of dates of last access occurring on August 4th. I told you right away that you probably lost evidence that you might otherwise have found because of his carelessness. Computers should not be turned on because when normal processing occurs on a Windows machine like this one boots up, things get stepped on. The operating system juggles space on the disk to enable it to start up and do various kinds of checks. In some cases, like on this computer, there are times that things happen that are automatically set up to happen. When Windows was opened, the swap file dated August 4th, meant that Windows started and it did its little swapping or juggling act at 6:57 p.m. on August 4th. Evidence like that Serle Ambien website, if that would have been found in the Windows swap file, then that would directly and immediately explain while the middle of it got stepped on because the Windows itself did some juggling. So we lost part of that, or who knows completely what was lost? When you do things like that, you lose evidence you never knew you had. I continued looking and found other evidence, but this indicates to me that the carelessness of turning the computer on allowed things to happen.

"This computer was also set up to do something called Microsoft Office. There is a program called *fast find* and it does an index just like in a library. In writing the index, it accesses a whole series of files on the drive, so that it can quickly find those files later if somebody asks it to find data on the hard drive. When they do that, it influences the last access date. In fact, all but one of the dates is August, of which August 4th appeared in the last accessed column. This simply means that somebody either looked at the data or accessed it for the purpose of creating an index. Regarding this computer, that is the explanation for the access date of which the Microsoft program actively started under automatic control when the power was turned on. The other last written single entry of August 4th, happened when Windows started up and did its juggling. If you just shut it down, which is what Mr. Hutchins told me that he did, it would concur that only that one date changed in the last written column and nothing else happened that would influence any of the contents of the files."

"Mr. Robbins, do I understand correctly that what Mr. Hutchins stated about using Norton Utilities would possibly change the last access file?"

"Anything that pulls up a file for reading on the screen or pulls a file off the hard drive to see information about it would change the last access date. So, yes, the Norton Utilities program would change the last access date. By changing the last access date, you lose potential evidence, but you don't change the contents of the evidence if you can still find it."

"Referring to these exhibits, was the computer used during the two weeks before May 14th?"

"Yes, sir. The computer was clearly being used from May 12th, May 11th, May 10th on a regular basis, and many files have been influenced, in the week before May 14th."

"After May 14th, was the computer still being used on a similar basis?"

"Yes. Starting on the 15th, 16th, 17th, 18th, --- pretty regular. Actually, even more activity during the week after the 14th."

"Thank you. I have no further questions."

Cross examine by the Defense

"You noted, Mr. Robbins, that the computer did continue to be used after May 14th, and all the way up to July 27th, until the State took it into its possession."

"Yes."

"Not that anything that remained was changed, but isn't it a fact that when the computer was started up by law enforcement officials on July 27th, the likelihood is that some information was lost?"

"Yes."

"Mr. Robbins, if a person typed a document, then printed it without saving it under a specific document name, could that possibly be found in the computer?"

"It is possible, yes."

"You indicated that you used Encase, a software designed not to affect what is stored on the hard drive. Do you know if that is a particularly expensive software?"

"I think the basic version costs a few hundred dollars and the professional version would cost over a thousand dollars."

"So --- for approximately a thousand dollars we can have professional software that doesn't change the data stored on the hard drive, and actually for even less money, one could get software that does the same thing, just doesn't have all the bells and whistles. Correct?"

"Essentially, yes."

"Were you ever asked to search for a suicide note?"

"No, sir, I was not."

"And in fact, you didn't, did you?"

"Not explicitly, no."

"What are your fees for your services in this case?"

"I charge three hundred and fifty dollars an hour plus expenses."

"Mr. Robbins, please refer to the exhibits that were introduced in the course of your testimony. Would you please tell the jury what exhibit numbers where you did not find any indication of when they were accessed?"

"Numbers 9, 11, 12, 13, 13a, 14, 20 and 21."

"Would it be fair to state, that with the exception of the unsent e-mail or the draft of the e-mail, that there is no indication as to who would have accessed these documents other than someone using this computer?"

"What do you mean by accessed?"

"I am asking if there is any indication of who conducted the searches, or who accessed the Internet sites?"

"The suggestion from where I found many of these things was that Mr. Guthrie accessed the Internet sites. That was based primarily on the fact that the Netscape browser is set up with sub directories and the primary one in use was Dr. Bill or labeled Dr. Bill."

"What were the other directories labeled?"

"Temporary Internet files was the primary one, but most of the indications of caching or storing information referred to Dr. Bill's cache."

"So, is it correct, Mr. Robbins, that somebody accessed this Internet site and then stored the information on the computer?"

"Site or sites. To access all of these sites somebody certainly had to log in to the Internet, initiate searches for things, and go to the different websites that were displayed. Those are the facts."

"Did that operator cause the information to be stored on the computer?"

"That's not known by the operator. Most of these things were all stored automatically by the browser, which is part of its mechanism for accessing, storing, and displaying, all in a temporary fashion, so that the space can be reused for efficiency purpose. The person controlling the browser has the option to make copies of these things and save them on their hard drive if they like, but most people don't do that. They look at the information and then go away. You can print it out or you can save it. In all of these cases, it was automatically saved and it was in temporary holding places that would be automatically overwritten by Netscape whenever it needed the space again."

"That's what I am getting at, Mr. Robbins. Is it correct then, that all the information was saved on the computer without any action by the operator?"

"Yes, that's correct."

"For that matter, is it correct that the operator of the computer would not have any knowledge that the information was being saved?"

"That's usually correct."

"As I understand, Mr. Robbins, you stated that the basic rule of maintaining computer evidence is to unplug the computer and get it to someone who knows what they are doing. Apparently, this did not happen in this case, did it?"

"Apparently not, sir."

"I have no further questions."

Redirect by the State

"Mr. Robbins, you testified that you didn't search specifically on the computer for the word *suicide*. What key words and what searches did you do?"

"Day one I searched for anything that had the following key words in it: Temazepam, Temazepam, Ambien, Myra, Connor, drug store.com, Lexi, bathtub, water, and drug. The next day, I searched for Methcathinone, Ativan, Lorazepam, Benadryl, Tylenol, codeine, Allegra, Claritin, Zolpidem, and Sharon. By the second day, I had figured out from the e-mails that Mr. Guthrie's wife's name was Sharon, so I searched for anything that might have been from her, to her, or related to her. The third day, I searched for the word *sleep*; and subsequent searches in that four-day window were for *Searle.PDF*", which is the name of a type of presentation file that I saw reference to. I also searched for the name Myra."

"Mr. Robbins, is it correct that all of those searches either resulted in a hit or they didn't?"

"That's correct."

"Did you look at them when the result was a hit?"

"Yes, I looked at every single one."

"I have no other questions. Thank you."

Redirect by the Defense

"Mr. Robbins, did you try looking for terms or words such as *good-by, sorry, Mom, love, or love you*?"

"No, I did not."

"Thank you, no more questions."

Tracy Kelly for the State questions Nancy Holst. Ms. Holst was the EMT who responded to the Guthrie home the day of the drowning. She testifies that she was a member of the governing board when the defendant was the minister at her church. She states that Dr. Bill made a special request of the session to see a counselor once a month in Nebraska, saying that it was private and that he didn't want to get into it, but that it wouldn't interfere with his duties.

Cross-examine by the Defense

"Ms. Holst, when you arrived at the Guthrie house, was Sharon undressed, as though she had been bathing?"

"Yes."

"Was the water drained from the tub?"

"Yes, but she was still very hot from the bath water."

"Was Sharon somewhat of a large woman?"

"Yes."

"Was Bill sobbing when you were at the house?"

"Yes."

"Do you have any knowledge of any medications that Sharon was taking?"

"She told me that she wanted to lose weight for the wedding and was willing to try anything, but other than Phen-fen, I don't know of any other medication that she took."

"Did you know that Sharon had been on a Holter monitor?"

"Yes, I did."

"Do you have any knowledge of what Bill's prayer habits were?"

"No, but I would see them almost every morning about 7:45 at the Rolling Wheel Cafe having their breakfast."

"Ms. Holst, are you familiar with the benefits that Bill received as the minister of your church?"

"I am familiar with them, but I don't remember them. There is a list stating the minister's salary, insurance, retirement, and pension. It really didn't mean anything to me --- we were just glad to have a minister."

Witness for the State – Peggy Stevens
Questioned by Moore

Ms. Stevens testifies that she got wet from the bottom of her legs up to her knees while assisting with the CPR on Sharon. When asked if she noticed if Mr. Guthrie was wet when she helped him put his shoes on, she replied that he wasn't wet. At the hospital she heard him say that he had hidden the Benadryl from Sharon.

"Ms. Stevens, tell us about a previous time that you responded to the Guthrie house."

"It was around April 23, 1999, sometime between 10:30 or 10:45 p.m. I was told that Dr. Bill was helping Sharon wash her hair in the bathtub and was shocked by a lamp. When I arrived at the house, he was lying on the bed moaning. It took a few minutes for him to respond and every time I would touch him, his hand would recoil. The ambulance arrived and they transported him to the hospital."

"Were you able to make any observations of his body for burn marks?"

"Yes. When I arrived, he only had underwear on, so I checked him to see if there was any burn entrance or exit. The skin wasn't burned or broken. I couldn't see or find anything."

"Thank you. I have no further questions."

Cross-examine by the Defense

"Ms. Stevens, is it fair to say that Bill was genuinely concerned about Sharon's condition the day of the drowning?"

"Yes."

"When Bill told you that he had hid the Benadryl from Sharon, was that a concern that you understood him to be expressing, that she might be on some drugs?"

"I guess it was my understanding that she was using it for sleep."

"I have no further questions."

Susan Fenske, the nurse who assisted Dr. Rogers in the ER at the Huron hospital is asked to demonstrate the suction type tube that she used on Sharon. She testifies that after the stomach fluid was collected, the fluid was determined to be very typical, kind of watery with a yellow color, and that no pill fragments were visible in the fluid.

Witness for the State – Dr. Lola Rogers
Questioned by Moore

"Dr. Rogers, do you have any idea how long Sharon had gone without having a heartbeat?"

"No, but CPR is very important. Number one, to get the oxygen in, and number two, to stimulate the heart so that the oxygen circulates to the brain, but to the rest of body as well. Sharon was never breathing on her own."

"What tests did you order prior to moving Sharon to ICU?"

"We ordered a normal routine drug panel of the blood and urine. Urine would show earlier drugs that had already been cleared by the body, and the blood would show what was there. We can also check for Tylenol level and aspirin level, and if it is an intentional overdose of Tylenol, it would be in the blood. We tested for eight different drug families. The benzodiazepines, which are central nervous system depressants, showed positive --- it was over three hundred nanograms per mill."

"Is that a high amount or a normal amount?"

"It's a normal screening cutoff."

"Is Temazepam or Temazepam considered a benzodiazepine?"

"Yes."

"Is it correct that the other tests done on the blood and the gastric contents were not done at your hospital, but were sent out to be tested?"

"Yes, that's right."

"I have no further questions, Your Honor."

Cross-examine by the Defense

"Dr. Rogers, is it correct that Lorazepam and Ativan are also benzodiazepines?"

"Yes."

"When was the urine sample drawn?"

"I believe that it was drawn at one o'clock."

"Thank you. No further questions."

Judge Martin adjourns for the day. He cautions the jury that it is their duty neither to converse among themselves or with anyone else on any subject connected with this trial, nor to form or express any opinion thereon until the case is finally submitted to them. He further cautions that they not listen to the television or radio or read any newspapers regarding this matter.

January 13, 2000

Trial Day Two

Witness for the State – Dr. Brad Randall
Pathologist at the Laboratory of Clinical Medicine
Questioned by Moore

Dr. Randall performed the autopsy on Sharon Guthrie in Sioux Falls. He explains that an autopsy is a careful examination of a deceased person. The skin, organs in the abdomen, the chest, neck, and the brain, are examined for evidence of injury or disease. Occasionally, an autopsy is used for identification, but its prime purpose is to discover why the person has died. If it is already known why a death occurred, an autopsy can also uncover other illnesses or injuries a deceased person might have had. An autopsy also has the purpose of recovering evidence and documenting injuries that can be presented in a court of law or any other legal hearing.

"Dr. Randall, what were your findings on your visual examination of Mrs. Guthrie?"

"The pertinent findings were those of height and a rough estimation of weight. On the outer surface of her body she had some bruising in the right shoulder that appeared to be related to medical therapy. There was some bruising on her left shoulder of uncertain origin. There was a small bruise and scrape on her left elbow, some bruising on the inside of her left arm that appeared to be of a medical origin, and a small scrape on the back of her right fourth finger. On the corner of her mouth, there was a little scrape, which also appeared to be medically related. There was a large area of bruising over her anterior chest, which is the type that is commonly seen in people that have been aggressively resuscitated with CPR, usually done by EMT's and others out in the field."

"What were your findings after you completed the internal exam on Mrs. Guthrie?"

"I documented that there was some bruising in the muscles on the left side of her windpipe. Also, there was a large area of bruising in her chest underneath what was seen on the skin surface, and some fractured ribs, which is commonly seen with aggressive resuscitation. There were signs of early pneumonia in her lungs, again consistent with someone surviving a period of time in a brain dead situation in ICU. Her liver was enlarged and showed considerable fatty change. The subsequent examination of her brain showed areas of cell death in the brain, which is consistent with the brain being deprived of oxygen for a period of time prior to death."

"Dr. Randall, what was the connection regarding the bruising on her neck?"

"The origin of that bruising was unclear. It was certainly possible that it could have been inflicted when the effort was made to insert the tube into her airway during the resuscitation. It could also have been caused by pressure to her neck from other causes. The extent of this bruising did not appear to be life threatening."

"Based on your external and internal exam of the deceased, were you at the point to determine what caused her death?"

"Not based on the autopsy examination alone. As a part of any death investigation, I had to pull together the information from the autopsy and the circumstances in which the decedent came to be deceased. I usually talk to witnesses at the scene to determine what the circumstances were when the body was found. After compiling that information with the autopsy report, I was then able to determine the cause of her death as drowning."

"What was significant to you regarding the toxicology report?"

"I did a chemical analysis on her stomach fluid, which had been removed shortly after she arrived at the hospital in Huron. The results were reported only as positive or negative, so there weren't any numbers involved. The results showed positive for Oxazepam in small amounts, Lorazepam in moderate amounts, and Temazepam in large amounts."

"What were the results of Sharon's blood tests when she was in the Huron hospital?"

"The results showed the presence of Lorazepam at twenty-four nanograms per milliliter, Oxazepam at fifty-seven nanograms per milliliter, and Temazepam at one thousand eight hundred forty nanograms per milliliter."

"Please explain the words *therapeutic, subtherapeutic,* and *overdose* that you have noted on your report."

"The first two are noted as subtherapeutic, and the Temazepam is referred to the summary for discussion of the interpretation of that amount. This means when you consume the drug there will obviously be a period of time as you wait for it to absorb. Then the level will come up to what we call a therapeutic level, where it delivers the response that it's supposed to; then it will tail off into a subtherapeutic range. This means that Sharon had taken the drug and was either in the very early phase of absorbing it or was in the phase where it had reached its peak and had no longer become effective, but was still present in her body."

"Do you consider the Temazepam amount to be an overdose amount?"

"Yes, sir."

"What effect would it have on Sharon with these other two drugs in her gastric contents and her blood?"

"The Lorazepam and Oxazepam, probably by themselves had no particular effect, but the Temazepam amount most likely was significantly intoxicating. In my opinion, the Temazepam would eventually render her unconscious."

"Based on these levels, in your opinion Dr. Randall, how many Temazepam pills, at thirty milligrams each, would Sharon have had to ingest to get to that level?"

"We use a standard formula, so that would be about five tablets or capsules."

"Is that how many you believe she took?'

"No, sir."

"Please explain."

"We know there were pills still in Sharon's stomach because the gastric contents that were analyzed at the hospital show large amounts of the drug still in her stomach. Other factors that can affect this would be the speed in which the material is flowing to the intestines and the stomach. For example, an individual that might be stressed, their digestion will slow down, and then the absorption rate will slow down. It has been my experience that when we get up into the high concentration that this equation, which you can find in many of the common toxicology textbooks, simply doesn't work. It grossly underestimates the amount of capsules that actually have to be consumed to come up with a particular concentration."

"Doctor, you stated that stress slows down absorption, so would a person almost drowning, or drowning, put the body under stress?"

"Certainly."

"Would that slow down the absorption rate?"

"There is no way to know whether it actually would, but certainly it would be one of those conditions that you could expect."

"Dr. Randall, in your opinion, based on the levels and your experience in the field, how many pills would you say that Sharon consumed?"

"Somewhere in the vicinity of about twenty pills."

"In your opinion, can someone take twenty pills accidentally?"

"No."

"Based on all of this, and the fact that she drowned in the bathtub, what significance does this drug have to determine the cause of Sharon's death?"

"It is quite significant in the cause of her death, but primarily in the determination of the manner of death."

"Based on that, Doctor, what is the reason that she drowned in the bathtub?"

"In my opinion, she was incapacitated from the Temazepam and would not have drowned in the bathtub if it were not for the drugs in her system."

"Why did you prepare a death certificate and then later prepare a corrected death certificate?"

"The families and various other institutions like to have a death certificate filed as soon as possible after a death. Often we don't have everything we need to know to accurately complete the death certificate at the time, so we will often say something to the fact that we are waiting for further information. Then, when that information comes in, we amend the death certificate to reflect what we believe is the actual cause and manner of death."

"Was drowning an autopsy finding for you?"

"No."

"Will you explain why you couldn't find that?"

"The finding of water in the lungs is not a particularly good marker of drowning; it only indicates that someone has been in the water. In a drowning the brain is deprived of oxygen, which doesn't leave any particular marker in the body. In a case like this, where the individual is removed from the water, whatever water might have been in the lungs is drained out or absorbed rapidly by the body. It really doesn't leave any external or internal marks of an individual having drowned. The only evidence we see is that the brain was without oxygen for a period of time. So the determination of drowning as a cause of death really depends upon the circumstances in which a body is found. A body that has been recovered from beneath water, either in a bathtub or body of water, with no other reason to be dead, we consider that they have drowned."

"Why have you marked *could not be determined* on the death certificate in the box under manner of death?"

"Pending, natural, accident, suicide, homicide, and could not be determined are the six different choices. It requires that you pick one of them. In this case the death was not natural and, in my opinion, not accidental. With the information available to me, I could not decide whether the manner of death was suicide or homicide; so, therefore, I checked *could not be determined*."

"I have no further questions."

Cross-examine by the Defense

"Dr. Randall, we know that Sharon ingested at least five of the thirty milligram capsules of Temazepam, but beyond that, aren't you speculating as to how many she actually ingested?"

"Sir, I am basing that opinion on my experience, which I believe is a little beyond speculation."

"You also stated that you observed some bruising at the base of the neck around the windpipe. Can you describe Sharon physically, such as her height and weight?"

"She was five foot four inches tall and weighed somewhere between one hundred eighty to one hundred ninety pounds."

"Doctor, are there any particular deviations to the general procedures that are utilized when a person is heavy set and perhaps has a short thick neck?"

"Yes, sir, there are."

"The toxicology screen showed three drugs in Sharon's stomach contents. Isn't it a fact that the Oxazepam and the Lorazepam were prescribed to her?"

"Yes, that's my understanding."

"Is it consistent with your experience that the taking of multiple prescribed drugs is consistent with an intentional overdose that is self-administered?"

"Yes."

"In other words, suicide?"

"Yes."

"Dr. Randall, I believe that you indicated in the toxicology screen that Oxazepam and Lorazepam were in significantly lower levels, actually in subtherapeutic levels, which would indicate that either she had just taken them or had taken them combined some time earlier. Is that correct?"

"That's correct."

"Do you know whether Oxazepam and Lorazepam are available in capsules or tablets?"

"I believe they can be found in either formulation, but I am not sure exactly what was used in this case."

"Would those drugs commonly be prescribed to be taken in combination?"

"I can't comment on that, I'm not a psychiatrist."

"You are a doctor, correct?"

"Yes, but those drugs would commonly be prescribed by a psychiatrist or a general or family practitioner and are prescribed for psychiatric purposes."

"Isn't it a fact, Dr. Randall, that if Sharon had consumed a large quantity of capsules of Temazepam, that they would have clumped together?"

"That is one of the things that happens when a large number of capsules are ingested. That is true."

"Doctor, isn't it correct that gel capsules are designed to dissolve and will generally dissolve within an hour?"

"Yes, sir."

"You performed the autopsy on Sharon some twenty-four hours plus after she was first found in the bathtub. Wouldn't it certainly not be a surprise that no gel caps were found in the autopsy?"

"That's correct."

"You also noted that there weren't any gel caps found in the stomach contents that were drawn while Sharon was hospitalized. Did you view the stomach contents yourself?"

"No, I did not."

"In your opinion, Dr. Randall, are we are talking about twenty gel caps clumped together?"

"That's a possibility --- yes."

"A clump approximately the size of a tennis ball?"

"I think that would be a little large."

"Okay --- how about the size of a golf ball?"

"Perhaps."

"I have here what is called a gastric lavage tube. Would a clump of capsules the size of a golf ball pass through this tube?"

"No."

"Wouldn't this be the type of tube that was used by the ER nurse to extract the stomach contents of Sharon?"

"It certainly could have been, but I am unaware of what particular tube was used."

"Did you review Sharon's medical records for her hospitalization prior to her death?"

"No, I did not."

"Doctor, let's say a person takes a substantial number of Temazepam pills, whether it be five, ten, or twenty, would the number of pills taken, assuming it's five or more, affect how quickly they are absorbed into the system?"

"Yes."

"In what way?"

"The greater number of capsules or tablets taken, the more inefficient the absorption will be, and you wouldn't get a steady state of absorption at higher concentrations."

"So, Dr. Randall, if a person took a number of gel caps of Temazepam, whether it be five or ten, wouldn't the person start feeling the effects within as little as fifteen minutes?"

"That depends on the circumstances, but that's certainly possible."

"Would the effects of the Temazepam then be amplified by the Oxazepam and Lorazepam if they were already present in Sharon's system?"

"To some degree --- yes, sir."

"What length of time would it take for Sharon to go from a nontherapeutic dose of Oxazepam and Lorazepam to an overdose of Temazepam?"

"I don't think there is any way to objectively determine that. Potentially within fifteen to thirty minutes, but I can't give you an exact answer."

"Doctor, how long would it take for the peak levels of the drug Temazepam to be reached after ingestion?"

"There is no way to calculate that. If you use the single small dose levels, you have about an hour and a half, but with large doses, the peak levels can be delayed for a considerable time afterwards."

"As an example, Dr. Randall, let's take five pills consumed at one point in time. When would you expect those pills to peak?"

"I honestly don't know. When you deal with something other than the peak levels that have been calculated at low doses, you are really conducting an experiment at that point. You would have to either perform the experiment yourself, do the research and see if someone else has done the experiment."

"The one thousand eight hundred and forty nanograms per milliliter of Temazepam that was found in Sharon's system is not a commonly known fatal amount. Isn't that correct, Dr. Randall?"

"That is correct."

"From your examination, isn't it indicated that Sharon was submerged in the water for no more than a few minutes?"

"That is correct."

"Will you please tell us your autopsy findings regarding Sharon's liver?"

"She had fatty change in the liver, where the liver is actually replaced by fat, and her liver was enlarged."

"As a doctor, can you explain the potential causes for the condition in which you found her liver?"

"The most common cause is chronic alcohol abuse. The next most common cause being nutritional, which can be seen in individuals that are starving, either truly starving, or physiologically starving with diabetes. It can also be seen in a variety of toxic drug exposures."

"Would a one-time toxic drug exposure cause this enlargement or fatty accumulation?"

"It could, but it would be very unusual."

"Dr. Randall, wouldn't it be more likely a prolonged exposure to drugs over time?"

"Yes."

"Do you know what type of drugs in particular?"

"The most common ones are the hydrocarbon drugs --- not drugs, but toxins. For example, carbon tetrachloride, pesticides, and herbicides --- that sort of thing. All of the alcohols are capable of producing this; and, of course, ethyl alcohol is most commonly associated with it."

"Doctor, would pharmaceutical drugs designed for human consumption produce enlargement of the liver?"

"As a rule, no."

"Under what circumstances would they?"

"One example would be methotrexate, which is used in cancer therapy. Most of the antibiotics and psychoactive drugs, such as tranquilizers, are not associated with this sort of change in the liver."

"To reiterate, Dr. Randall, would the finding of multiple drugs in Sharon's system, particularly the two that were prescribed to her, be consistent with a self-administered intentional overdose?"

"Yes, it would."

"Thank you. No more questions."

Redirect by the State

"Dr. Randall, when a person takes a gel cap pill, how does it get from his stomach into his system?"

"That is a very complex question. The drug companies spend a great deal of time working with drugs. Some capsules or tablets they want to absorb in the stomach or the small intestine as quickly as possible, and some they want to absorb more slowly. When you open up a capsule you will see a powder, which is usually not a pure drug. It contains the drug, along with some sort of matrix, such as starch or sugar. The drug companies spend a lot of time designing these matrixes to decide how fast or how slow a drug will be absorbed.

"If I took a pure drug, placed it in a capsule, and had you swallow it, that could be an entirely different absorption than what you might get from the druggist or pharmacist. Once the drug is released in the stomach and the small intestine, some drugs simply go through the lining and get absorbed by the bloodstream and then are carried into the body. Other drugs have to be physically carried across by transport chemicals in the lining of the stomach or intestine. Those drugs can be absorbed quickly, or slowed up, if there are other things competing for the carriage of that drug.

"What it all boils down to is a very imperfect science that often is far different than what you would get from just reading a toxicology journal and seeing what the half-life of a particular drug is. It may be much different in real life."

"Dr. Randall, you were asked by Mr. Wilson that if twenty capsules were consumed, would they possibly clump together. Can you explain what clump together means?"

"The gelatin capsule is nothing different than Jell-O. If you put Jell-O in water it will dissolve slowly. The amount and the speed in which a capsule dissolves depends on how much water is around it, whether it's bumping up against something else, whether the whole capsule is available to be dissolved, or just part of the capsule is available. If all of the drugs are taken together, the gel can get kind of sticky, and they will clump together. So, instead of having a lot of capsules, you have one great big capsule. Much of the service of these individual capsules is actually bound to other capsules, so the only thing that is going to dissolve is on the outside. In that situation, the absorption can slow down quite a bit."

"What is the other possibility?"

"If someone would want to maximize the absorption, speed it up and make it go as fast as possible, the capsules could be opened up and the raw drug inside the capsules could be mixed in some liquid and then ingested."

"What happens to these capsules as they dissolve in the stomach?"

"Once the capsule is gone, it depends on what is on the inside of the stomach. Again, if it's bonded together with something that isn't designed to absorb real quickly, there may be lots of residue left. On the other hand, basically if it's in with sugar or something like that, once the capsule itself is dissolved, there is nothing left."

"Is it common to find capsules or remnants of capsules in the stomach if the stomach is pumped right after ingesting these pills?"

"If the stomach is pumped immediately after or within several minutes after, it would be common to find residue of the pills."

"Is it correct, Dr. Randall, that these capsules break apart, get smaller, and eventually dissolve?"

"That's correct."

"Is that done by the acid in the stomach?"

"In part. If you just took the capsules and put them in a beaker of water, they will eventually dissolve."

"Doctor, is it correct to say that all of these different factors affect how they are absorbed into the body?"

"Yes, that's correct."

"Is this why you have a problem with the formula that says that everybody that takes this many pills is going to be at this level, no matter what, because you don't see that in practice?"

"That's correct."

"In your opinion, do you feel that Mrs. Guthrie ingested at least twenty pills?"

"In that neighborhood, but it's an incalculable amount. In my experience, that is the ballpark figure that I have seen with people that have taken overdoses of this category of drug."

"Dr. Randall, in your experience, is this mathematical formula very accurate as to what is actually taken?"

"Not in high concentrations, but it works well in low concentrations."

Redirect by the Defense

"Dr. Randall, when you speak of your experience in estimating the number of capsules ingested by Sharon, are you talking about your experience in autopsies of suicides?"

"Yes."

"Did you state that it's common to find remnants of gel caps if the person's stomach is pumped within minutes of ingestion?"

"Yes."

"How about within an hour of ingestion or more?"

"I would find it very unpredictable."

"Isn't it a fact, Doctor, since no gel caps were found in Sharon's stomach contents that it does not have any particular meaning?"

"It's a negative finding, that's correct --- it has no particular meaning. The presence would have meant something --- the absence doesn't."

"The presence would have meant that the gel capsules had been consumed intact, but the absence doesn't mean that they weren't consumed intact. Correct, Dr. Randall?"

"That's correct."

"I have no further questions."

Janice Polo, a member of the church, assisted two other ladies in the cleaning of the Guthrie home before the family returned home from Sioux Falls. She testifies, when questioned by Tracy Kelly for the State, that when cleaning the bathroom, she found a wet towel in the bathtub and some in the sink. When she cleaned the bedroom, she found a change of clothing lying on Sharon's side and took them home to wash. On the nightstand, located on the right side of the bed, she saw a half drunk Diet Coke and on the headboard of the bed there was an empty red Solo cup.

Cross-examine by the Defense

"Ms. Polo, when you arrived at the Guthrie house at approximately one-thirty, did you notice whether the hall carpeting was wet?"

"Yes, there was a fan running on it to dry it."

"Did you notice if the bathroom floor was wet?"

"There wasn't any water on the bathroom floor, but along the tub there were some damp areas where the linoleum had come up a little."

"Did you see a red Solo cup on the nightstand?

"I think it was on the nightstand when I picked it up."

"Ms. Polo, looking at this photograph, isn't the Solo cup on the headboard?"

"Yes."

"The nightstand that you referred to, is that on the right side of the bed --- Sharon's side of the bed?"

"Yes."

"In this photograph of the bedroom the red Solo cup is in the middle of the headboard. Do you have any way of knowing whether that Solo cup was there when you were at the house?"

"No."

"Isn't it correct to say that one Solo cup pretty much looks like another?"

"Yes."

"I have no further questions."

Redirect by the State

"Ms. Polo, you claimed Sharon's side of the bed was on the right side. Is that correct?"

"It would be the right side if I were lying in bed."

"Thank you, nothing further."

Redirect by the Defense

"Now, I've gotten a little confused." Mr. Wilson hands Ms. Polo a photograph. "When you look at this photo, is this the same nightstand that's depicted in this picture with the bottle of Coke on it?"

"Correct."

"Thank you. No further questions."

Ilene Best, questioned by Tracy Kelly for the State, testifies that when she vacuumed the manse she noticed the carpet in the hallway was damp. She observed some women's clothing in the entryway to the master bedroom. It appeared to her that Sharon had just stepped out of them because they were all wadded down in one spot. She stated she did not remove the clothing that she found in the master bedroom. Also, she did not see any wet clothes in the home.

Witness for the State – Kate Sands
Questioned by Moore

Ms. Sands cleaned the kitchen at the manse. There were some red plastic cups on the table and the counter, which she threw away because they were dirty. She couldn't remember if there was anything in them. She wiped up some flour that was scattered on the countertop to the left of the sink.

"Humor me, Ms. Sands, what does flour look like?"

"White powder."

"Was it just dusting across the countertop?"

"Yes."

"When you were in my office I took apart a Temazepam capsule and spread it out on the table. What did the inside of that pill look like to you?"

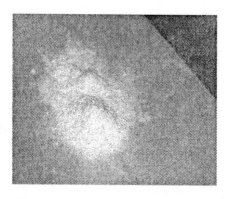

"It looked like scattered flour."

"Were you surprised as to how much powder was in that one capsule?"

"Yes, I was very surprised."

"When was the last time that you saw Mrs. Guthrie alive?"

"I saw her at Frosty's two days before she drowned in the tub. She and Bill always stopped there to eat before they went to church in Bonilla."

"Did you notice if she was upset about anything?"

"No --- she was just excited about her daughter's wedding."

"I have no further questions, thank you."

Cross-examine by the Defense

"Ms. Sands, prior to her death, did Sharon talk with you about going on a cruise with Bill?"

"Yes."

"Since Sharon was trying to lose weight, did she talk to you about taking diet pills?"

"No."

"You stated that this white powdery substance on the countertop in the kitchen looked like flour to you. Is there any reason to think that it was anything but flour?"

"It was in the kitchen, so I just assumed it was flour."

"Fair enough. Thank you, no further questions."

Witness for the State – Myra Conner
Questioned by Moore

Ms. Conner works as a sales representative for a gift line in the areas of the northern half of Kansas and the southern half of Nebraska. She had become a friend to Bill Guthrie in May of 1992, then a few months later their friendship turned into an affair. She has three children and was divorced in July of 1995.

"Ms. Conner, how did you meet the defendant?'

"I was an active elder on the session at our church. Our church in Orleans was interested in hiring Dr. Guthrie. I was not on the pastoral committee, but I was asked to go to Beaver City and hear him preach at a Good Friday service."

"The defendant was a minister at the Christian Church. What affiliation were you?"

"Presbyterian."

"When was he hired as a minister at your church?"

"About six weeks after I heard him preach."

"When did your relationship with the defendant grow into more than just friends?"

"In December of 1993 --- just before Christmas, he kissed me in his office at the church."

"What happened after this kiss?"

"We stayed away from each other quite a bit. He had an accident and was in the hospital for awhile, so it was probably two months before anything else happened."

"Ms. Conner, what happened in February of 1994?"

"The company I worked for had a market in Omaha, so I went there to set up our product. Bill came there and stayed with me one night."

"Did the two of you become intimate then?"

"Yes."

"How often would you see each other in Orleans?"

"A couple of times a week."

"Where would you meet up with each other?"

"Down at the river or out in the country, wherever we could be together."

"Ms. Conner, were you and the defendant intimate during those times that you were together, as you say --- those couple of times a week?"

"Yes, we were."

"What is the population of Orleans?"

"About four hundred and ninety people."

"How long after this affair started did you first realize that people were starting to talk about you and Bill?"

"Probably nine months to a year."

"Ms. Conner, did anybody specifically from the church question you about the affair?"

"No."

"What did you say to the defendant about these rumors?"

"I told him that it was getting too dangerous for us to be seen together and I didn't like it."

"Why was he afraid of being caught?"

"I think it was more because of his job than anything. The Presbyterian church had just put in a new law that was established for gays, but it also included heterosexuals. It stated that if they were caught in any kind of immoral doings they could be dismissed from their jobs."

"What did you decide to do about these rumors?"

"I just denied them."

"Did the defendant ever deny these rumors to the congregation?"

"Yes, he did."

"When was that, Ms. Conner?"

"It was around Thanksgiving of '94 or '95 during Sunday morning services."

"Were you aware that he was going to deny these rumors?"

"Yes."

"Did he ever tell you about the incident that happened to him in Lincoln, Nebraska, in September of '93?"

"Yes. He told me the following July --- about six months after the relationship started."

"What did he tell you?"

"He said that he was in a motel in Lincoln when a male and female truck drivers pushed him into a room, raped him, beat him, and sodomized him."

"Ms. Conner, did the defendant ever have any physical problems being intimate with you?"

"No."

"Did the rumors stop after he denied the rumors to the church?"

"No."

"Was he ever asked to leave the church?"

"I don't know that he was ever asked to leave our church, but suggestions were made that maybe it would be better for him to move on."

"Did you talk to him about his moving away?"

"Yes, I did."

"What did these conversations entail?"

"We talked about how close he could be, so that we could still see each other occasionally."

"Did the two of you talk about his relationship with Sharon before moving to South Dakota?"

"Some."

"In your understanding, Ms. Conner, did the defendant and Sharon have a good relationship?'

"I thought it was pretty typical. There were arguments and fighting over little things, and they were not communicating very well."

"Did he tell you anything about his sex life with his wife?'

"He said that there wasn't any."

"Did you and the defendant talk about the possibility of his leaving Sharon and what would happen after that?"

"We talked in general terms about him being single at some point, so that we could be together."

"Did he ever tell you that he was going to divorce Sharon?"

"He mentioned the fact that he would at some point."

"Ms. Conner, during your relationship, did he ever tell you that he had filed divorce papers?"

"Yes. He said that he had started papers a couple times."

"Were you pressuring the defendant to leave Sharon?"

"No."

"Did you talk to him about your frustration in having to sneak around?"

"Yes, but he would always say that eventually we would be together."

"Did this relationship continue when the defendant moved to Wolsey?"

"Yes. We talked on the phone at least once a day; and if he could get away, he would meet me at the location where I was working."

"Who would call whom?"

"I had an 800 number, so he could call me anytime that he wanted."

"Did you call him at the house?"

"Yes."

"Did you call him at the church?"

"Yes."

"What time of day or night would you usually call him?"

"Usually first thing in the morning before I went to work and sometimes in the afternoon if I was home."

"Did you accumulate some very large phone bills, Ms. Conner?"

"Yes, I did."

"How often would you physically see the defendant after he moved to Wolsey?"

"We tried to see each other once a month, but sometimes it would be two months before we could be together."

"Where would you meet?"

"Usually during the week he would come to wherever I was working. Hayes, Kansas, is probably where we met the most since I would stay in the same motel quite a few nights when I worked out of Hayes. The ones that I can remember are St. Paul --- sometimes in O'Neill."

"What did you do during these meetings?"

"If we were in Nebraska, we would stay in the room and I would go out after food and get a movie to watch. Sometimes, when I was in Kansas, he would travel with me."

"Were you still being intimate with him?"

"Yes."

"What were the excuses that the defendant gave his wife when he was supposedly going to Nebraska?"

"He was supposed to be meeting a counselor and one time he attended a pastoral school in Hastings. He found something to tell her when he came to Hayes, but I don't remember what it was."

"To your knowledge, did Mrs. Guthrie know about the affair?"

"I always assumed that she did."

"Did she ever confront you with her suspicions?"

"No."

"Ms. Conner, when this relationship ended in January of 1999, who broke it off?"

"I did."

"Where were you when you told him you didn't want this affair to continue anymore?"

"I can't remember for sure, but I think I met him in Grand Island or Hastings. I didn't tell him that night --- I couldn't. I waited until I got home; then I phoned him."

"What was the reason that you broke off this affair?"

"I told him I was tired of sneaking around."

"What was his reaction?"

"I don't remember exactly, but he wasn't very happy."

"After you told the defendant that it was over, did you talk to him again?"

"Yes, we still talked on the phone. Then in February I met him in St. Paul, Nebraska. I don't know why, but I guess it was to finalize it more."

"Were you intimate with him during this time?"

"Yes."

"Ms. Conner, after you broke it off with the defendant, how often would you say that you talked to him on the phone?"

"It wasn't as much; but when we did talk he would get angry with me, and then we wouldn't talk for a couple of weeks."

"When you told him that it was over, did you leave the window open for him if he ever left Sharon?"

"I told him that I wasn't married to anyone and that I was going to date and do the normal things that single people do."

"Did you kind of leave the impression that you might be interested in getting back together if he ever left Sharon?"

"I don't think I said I would be there --- just that we could date and see how it went."

"What happened when the defendant became aware that you were involved in another relationship?"

"Bill became sort of angry when I told him that I thought it would just finish it off if I told him I was seeing someone else."

"Why did you continue to talk on the phone with the defendant after you told him that you were seeing someone else?"

"I wanted to continue to be his friend."

"In those months when you were with him and talking to him on the phone, did you ever talk about Mrs. Guthrie's health?"

"I think it was in March when he told me that she was walking in her sleep and taking Benadryl tablets."

"How did you learn about her death?"

"I have an answering machine that I can call to pick up my messages. I was in Milwaukee at my daughter's bridal shower; and when I arrived at the airport to fly home, I called to get my messages. Bill had left a message that Sharon had an accident and that her funeral was on Monday. That was all he said, so I immediately called his house. The youngest daughter answered the phone and said that he wasn't home.

The airport was very noisy and I couldn't hear very well; so I waited awhile, and then I called back."

"When you spoke with the defendant, what did he tell you regarding his wife's death?"

"He told me that she had drowned in the bathtub, and he had tried to get her out, but couldn't."

"What day did you receive this message on your answering machine?"

"I believe it was on Sunday evening, May 16th. I talked to Bill several times to see how he was and how the family was doing."

"Did he ask you to meet with him the week after Sharon's death?"

"Yes, he did."

"What did you tell him?"

"Initially I told him no, that I wasn't going to betray the relationship that I was involved in."

"What was his reaction?"

"Bill said that it hadn't taken me very long to betray him, so I hung up on him."

"Did you ever talk with him again?"

"I talked to him a few times, but we didn't talk much after that."

"Did he ask you to meet with him again any time later?"

"No."

"When you spent overnights with the defendant, did he ever do prayers or devotions in the morning after rising?"

"No."

"Thank you. I have no further questions."

Witness for the State – Lisa Scott
Questioned by Kelly

Ms. Scott, not only a member of the Wolsey Presbyterian church, she also worked with Sharon at the Reed Clinic. Sharon was the account manager and did collections and insurance claims. Sharon started work at eight-thirty in the morning and was never late for work and never missed work. She states that Sharon was always cheerful and she couldn't recall that Sharon ever appeared sleepy or lethargic at work.

"Ms. Scott, I want to turn your attention to the week prior to Sharon's death when you, your husband, the defendant, and Sharon were at lunch. What did you observe that day regarding the interaction between Sharon and the defendant?"

"Everything started out real well. We were laughing and joking like always, then Bill started getting a little rude with Sharon. When she would say something he would kind of just --- just cut her off. Then, all of a sudden, he sat back and wouldn't talk to any of us. We didn't know if we had said or done something wrong, so we got up and left."

"When the defendant would come into the office to see Sharon, briefly tell us what you observed regarding their interaction with each other."

"Most of the time it was real good, but I did notice that Bill would talk down to Sharon a lot. At times, when she would say something, he would kind of make fun of her or be rude to her."

"Ms. Scott, please tell us about the incidents that you were aware of in the months prior to Sharon's death?"

"The first one, in late March --- early April, was the string across the basement stairs. When Sharon came to work the next day, she said that someone had broken into their house and put a string on the top of the steps to the basement. She and Bill had gone to a movie and when they arrived home she said Bill asked her to go downstairs and check the washer and the dryer that he had worked on that day. She started down the stairs, tripped on the string, and would have fallen all the way down if Bill hadn't grabbed her.

"Then there was the morning on April 15th, when Sharon was ill. We were still out to lunch when Bill brought her into the clinic. They were in the exam room; and when I finally got to see her, she was completely out of it. Sharon didn't know anything, where she was, or what time of day it was. Bill was very upset because we weren't there when they arrived. He said that Sharon couldn't walk and nobody was there to help him. I asked him how he got her up here and he said that he had to carry her."

"Ms. Scott, did the defendant tell you what had happened to Sharon?"

"When he called earlier in the morning to tell us Sharon wouldn't be in, he said she had a migraine. Other than that, we really didn't discuss it."

"Did that story ever change any other time during that day?"

"Yes. When Bill was standing by my desk. He said, *'I didn't do anything to her, honest --- I didn't do anything to her.'* I told him that I didn't think he did and asked him why he was saying that. He said, *'Well, I just want you to know that I didn't do anything to her.'*"

"Was there anything in your conversation accusing him of anything?"

"No."

"Did Sharon remember anything about this incident when she came back to work the next day?"

"She said the only thing she remembered was having supper."

"When did you learn about the incident involving the lamp that allegedly shocked the defendant?"

"I learned about it when I got to church on the following Sunday morning. One of the ladies in church told me about it."

"When you visited with Sharon at work about the incident, what did she tell you?"

"She said that Bill was going to wash her hair in the bathtub. The light was burned out in the bathroom, so he went and got a lamp and put it on the sink. Then she said she didn't know what happened, other than the dog could have grabbed the cord and knocked the lamp in the tub. She said that they both were about killed."

"What did the defendant say to you the day of the drowning?"

"He said that he hoped she didn't get into his pills again, but was afraid that she did."

"Ms. Scott, in the months prior to Sharon's death, did you ever notice any changes in her, such as being depressed, under a lot of stress, or withdrawn?"

"No. She was just excited about her daughter's upcoming wedding in June and talked about that a lot."

"Thank you, I have no further questions."

Cross-examine by the Defense

"Ms. Scott, you stated that your general observation of the relationship between Bill and Sharon was fairly good. Is that correct?"

"Yes, generally."

"When Sharon told you about the basement stairs incident, did she make it clear to you that if it weren't for Bill's actions, that she would have fallen down the stairs?"

"Yes --- that's what she said."

"Regarding the incident with the lamp, didn't Sharon actually tell you that the dog came into the bathroom and knocked the lamp over?"

"She said that she had no idea, but that was the only thing she could think of that would have caused it to happen."

"Did she ever say anything indicating that Bill was the cause of it?"

"No."

"In fact, Sharon stated that Bill caught the lamp before it hit the water, again saving her from harm. Isn't that correct?"

"That is what she said --- that he caught the lamp."

"So, Bill caught the lamp presumably keeping her from being electrocuted?"

"That is what she said."

"Ms. Scott, did you answer the phone when Bill called in sick for Sharon?"

"I didn't take the first call when he said that she wasn't coming to work. I took the second call when he said that she would not be in to work that morning, but that she may be in that afternoon. I asked him if she had the flu, and he said that she had a migraine."

"You testified that when you got back from lunch that Bill had, in fact, brought Sharon into the clinic, and that he told you that he had carried her in?"

"That's what he said."

"Ms. Scott, there has been some earlier testimony as to Sharon's physical size. You didn't really think Bill carried her in to the clinic, did you?"

"I wasn't there when he brought her in, so I didn't know how he had gotten her there."

"You stated that when you saw Sharon she appeared to be groggy --- somewhat out of it. Did Sharon ever tell you what happened?"

"She said that she couldn't remember anything of the whole day."

"At least not that she told you?"

"Not that she told me."

"In fact, didn't Sharon tell you regarding the string across the stairway that perhaps it was done by someone who she had initiated a collection against?"

"She never said that to me. She just said that someone had broken into their home and tied a string across the stairs. I asked her if the door was broken or a window, and she said no."

"Ms. Scott, according to Sharon, she and Bill had been gone and found this string across the stairs when they returned home, correct?"

"Yes."

"I have no further questions."

Witness for the State – Shawna Brady
Questioned by Moore

Ms. Brady, a registered nurse and manager at Reed Clinic, not only worked with Sharon, but also was her friend. When they went to lunch together, Bill would sometimes join them. The only times Sharon would be late for work would be when she would get behind a semi-truck or a slow car, but would call the office on her cell phone and inform them of the reason. She never witnessed Sharon napping at work or acting lethargic and states that Sharon's attitude was always good.

"Ms. Brady, did it seem like Sharon had any more stress or tension in her life than usual?"

"Other than her daughter's wedding --- no."

"Would you please tell us what Sharon told you regarding the string across the stairway?"

"She said they went to the movies, and when they got home Bill wanted to show her something down in the basement. There had been a string placed across the top step and she almost fell down the stairs, but Bill caught her and prevented her from falling. Sharon said she was concerned that it was her daughter's ex-boyfriend that had placed it there."

"Did they report it to the police?"

"Sharon said they did."

"Would you please tell us what happened the day that Sharon was sick and came into the office in the afternoon to see the doctor?"

"Bill called the office to tell me that Sharon had a headache and would not be coming in that day. Before we left for lunch, I called and spoke to Sharon. She seemed very confused, so I talked to Bill and told him that he needed to bring her in to see the doctor. About two o'clock, when we arrived back at the office from lunch, Sharon was lying on the couch in one of the exam rooms. She was lethargic, her speech was slurred, and she was complaining that the room was spinning. We checked her hand grasps and they were equal. Her vitals were stable, but her speech wasn't right and she was complaining that her head hurt."

"What did the defendant say to you?"

"He came into my office and asked me why we weren't checking her over and doing anything for her. I asked him what he meant by that. He proceeded to tell me that a couple weeks prior she had stopped breathing at home. He said he had to do mouth-to-mouth resuscitation on her to bring her around; then she seemed fine and they went to bed."

"So, he then told you about another incident that happened. Was the ambulance called then?"

"No."

"To your knowledge, Ms. Brady, did Sharon ever report that incident to any of the medical personnel there at the clinic?"

"No."

"Did the defendant tell you what he thought happened to Sharon the day he brought her into the clinic?"

"He told me that he thought Sharon had been sleepwalking and gotten into his pills. I asked him if he had put the pills up where she couldn't reach them so this could not happen again, and he said that he would."

"Ms. Brady, was this the first time that you had ever heard about Sharon sleepwalking and taking pills while she was sleepwalking?"

"To my recollection, yes."

"Were there any other incidents that you were aware of?"

"Yes. Sharon came in one morning and said that Bill had been electrocuted the night before and was in the hospital. She said that the light in the bathroom went out when Bill was washing her hair in the bathtub, so he went to another room to get a lamp so he could see to rinse her hair. The lamp was knocked into the bathtub and when he grabbed the lamp out of the tub, he had been electrocuted. She said that she thought their dog had knocked the lamp over."

"Did Sharon tell you that she saw the dog or heard the dog?"

"No, she did not."

"At the hospital the day of Sharon's drowning accident, what did the defendant say to you?"

"He was concerned that Sharon had gotten into his medications again. I asked him if he had put the pills up where she couldn't get to them, but I don't remember his response."

"I have no further questions. Thank you."

Cross-examine by the Defense

"Ms. Brady, when Sharon told you about the incident that occurred in the stairway, did she make it clear that if Bill had not been there she would have fallen down the stairs?"

"That's correct."

"Did Sharon tell you that she was in the bathtub when the lamp fell into the bathtub?"

"Yes."

"Is it correct that Sharon told you when the lamp was knocked over, that they thought the dog knocked it over?"

"Yes."

"Going back to the incident when Bill brought Sharon into the clinic shortly after lunch, you testified that she seemed confused. Were there any other observations that you made?"

"Her speech was slurred and it was a little hard to understand her."

"Isn't it a fact, Ms. Brady, that when you suggested to Bill that he bring Sharon into the clinic that he did bring her in?"

"Yes."

"When law enforcement interviewed you, didn't you tell them you suspected that Sharon had overdosed on Benadryl?"

"I told them that she had gotten into some medication, but I don't remember specifically mentioning Benadryl."

"Was there anything about the way that Sharon was acting that day that would cause you to think it was Benadryl?"

"Yes --- the slurred speech."

"Did you have any knowledge that Sharon took Benadryl?"

"She took it for her seasonal allergies."

"You stated that when you talked to Sharon the next day she really didn't recall any of the events from the day before. Isn't it true that amnesia is a known side effect of benzodiazepines?"

"I would have to look that up in a *Physician's Desk Reference.*"

"I have no further questions. Thank you."

Witness for the State – Patricia Minor
Questioned by Moore

Ms. Minor, Physician's Assistant from the Reed Clinic, testifies that Sharon was not only her co-worker, but also her patient when she had problems with allergies and sinus infections. She adds that she also treated Bill once in the emergency room at the Huron hospital.

"What was the reason that the defendant came to see you on you April 29th of 1999?"

"Basically, he was having problems with insomnia. He was also having some other problems but asked me not to record them because they were personal, so we just visited about them. I respected that because of the small staff and confidentiality, and I didn't write them down."

"What treatment did you prescribe regarding the insomnia?"

"We discussed sleeping pills to see if we could help get him through a difficult time. I initially suggested Ambien because it's short acting and a person doesn't feel groggy the next day and is able to function. He declined Ambien and also Xanax, saying that he had taken those before and they hadn't worked for him. We settled on Temazepam, which is not my favorite drug. It's not one that I like to prescribe because it stays in the body a long time and causes sleepiness the next day. For some people, it reacts like a hangover."

"Do you remember who brought up using Temazepam?"

"No, I don't."

"Did you give him a written prescription?"

"Yes. I wrote out a prescription for Temazepam, which comes in two strengths --- fifteen milligrams and thirty milligrams. I gave him fifteen pills of thirty milligrams each with the instructions to take one capsule each day at bedtime. This is a two-week supply, which is a reasonable first attempt. I put three refills on the bottle, which would give him enough to get him through two months."

"On that same day, did anyone else talk to you about this prescription?"

"Yes, that afternoon Sharon came into my office. She told me that Bill had lost his written prescription and asked me if I would mind calling in a second prescription for him. It's not uncommon for a person to lose a written prescription, so I told her I would gladly call it in. I asked her if she wanted me to call it into Statz Drug where they normally have their prescriptions filled, and she said yes."

"Do you keep records each time a patient comes to see you?"

"Yes."

"How does the clinic keep records when a person is prescribed a medication?"

"We use what is called a flow sheet as a tool to refer to what medications a person is currently taking. It also helps us to monitor refills and the number of drugs that people are getting."

"Ms. Minor, according to the defendant's medication sheet that goes back to April 1st of 1997, when was the Temazepam prescribed for the defendant?"

"April 29, 1999. The second prescription that I called in is not recorded on the flow sheet because, as far as I knew, the first one was lost. To the best of my knowledge, we refilled it once."

"At my request, I asked you to look through the defendant's medical records that were kept at Reed Clinic and also his medical records from the Holdrege Clinic that go back to 1989 or '90. Were there any notes that he had ever been prescribed Ambien or Xanax before?"

"None that I could see."

"Also, on the records from the Holdrege Clinic, was there any time that the defendant had been in to see a doctor for having insomnia or sleeping problems?"

"No, none that I could see."

"Is it correct that a person can only obtain Ambien and Xanax with a prescription from a doctor?"

"That is correct."

"Ms. Minor, what did the defendant talk to you about the day of Sharon's funeral?"

"Mr. Guthrie invited the entire staff to attend the funeral with the family because we were very close. At the house prior to going to the funeral I had barely gotten inside the door when Mr. Guthrie stated to me that he didn't know anything about the second prescription being filled. He said apparently Sharon had filled the prescription for Temazepam and was taking it without his knowledge. I told him that as far as I knew only one prescription had been filled. Sharon had told me he had lost the written prescription and asked me if I minded calling in a second one for him. He said he didn't know anything about that."

"Did you see the defendant as a patient after Sharon's funeral?"

"Yes, on June 9th. He was suffering from some obvious grief reaction and complaining of insomnia. He said that the Temazepam was not working for him."

"Did you prescribe any medication for him?"

"Yes, I prescribed Ambien."

"Ambien? Wasn't this the drug that he refused before?"

"Yes."

"Did he accept it this time?"

"Yes, he did."

"Is this noted on the medication sheet?"

"Yes."

"Ms. Minor, tell us about Sharon's appointment with you in March of 1999."

"She told me that she had a fullness in her throat and noticed that when she would lie down at night, her heart would race. Aside from her allergies and congestion, she never complained about her health, but seemed quite anxious about the heart racing. She had a history of hypertension and was apparently having some difficulty sleeping, so was concerned that maybe something was wrong with her heart. A thyroid problem can cause pressure at the base of the throat and also cause the heart to race when one is resting, so I did a complete thyroid examination. We recommended a lab machine called a Holter monitor where electrodes are attached to the patient's chest. The patient carries a little box that records each heartbeat, the rhythm, and the rate. The patient also carries a small journal so that every time he or she experiences any symptoms they can be written down and noted each time. It is worn for twenty-four hours and then taken off. During that twenty-four hours Sharon said that she didn't experience anything. She continued to have problems, so we tried an event monitor. It's much the same as the Holter monitor, except that it doesn't record unless you push the button when you are experiencing some symptoms. She pushed the button several times when she felt that her heart was racing, usually when she would go to bed; but each time it was normal. There was nothing that showed abnormal in the event monitor."

"When did you talk to Sharon about the results of her tests?"

"On May 6, 1999, I told her that it was possible that the anxiety of all the planning of the upcoming wedding was causing her to have trouble sleeping, so I suggested a prescription for Lorazepam."

"Did you write her a prescription?"

"Yes, I believe I called it in. I gave her a low dose of one milligram --- half to one tablet at bedtime. The following Monday she came in and told me that she had had the best night's sleep she'd had in months."

"I have here Sharon's medication sheet. Does this medication sheet list all the medications that were prescribed for her?"

"Yes, it does."

"Will you read the different medications and tell us what they are for?"

"Norvasc is for hypertension
Premarin is an estrogen replacement hormone

EES 400 is an antibiotic

Allegra is for sinus and allergies

Relafen, 500 milligrams, is an anti-inflammatory for arthritic pain

Dyazide is for dependent edema

Claritin and Claritan D are for allergies and also congestion

Zithromax pack is for infection

Estratab is for hormone replacement therapy

Lorazepam is for insomnia."

"What did you observe when the defendant brought Sharon into the clinic on April 15th?"

"When I first saw her she was sitting in a wheelchair and just sat there and stared into space."

"Did anyone give you any information regarding what they thought was wrong with her?"

"Shawna Brady, my nurse, said she had taken a lot of Tylenol P.M."

"Did you have a conversation with the defendant that day?"

"Not specifically that I can recall, but Bill was standing at the counter telling Lisa and Shawna how concerned he was about Sharon."

"Ms. Minor, did you have a conversation with the defendant about the incident when Sharon stopped breathing?"

"He told me that Sharon was having so much difficulty sleeping at night that she was sleepwalking. He said that she would get up in the night and drink her milk and take pills. Bill didn't know if she even knew what she was taking. He told me that one night when she was sleeping, she stopped breathing and he was concerned because it was quite a long time. She had a problem with snoring and not breathing, so they suspected maybe there was some sleep apnea there. This time she had stopped breathing for a longer period of time, so Bill felt it necessary to give her some rescue breathing to get her started again."

"Did Sharon ever tell you about this incident?"

"No, she never did."

"Did she ever tell you that she had been sleepwalking?"

"On one occasion, she told me that she had not been sleepwalking during that time. She didn't recall sleepwalking and wasn't aware that she was sleepwalking."

"Ms. Brady, isn't it correct that Sharon did come to you and tell you that she was having problems --- a little anxious at night, but that she never told you any of the things that you had heard from the defendant?"

"Correct."

"I have no further questions."

Cross-examine by the Defense

"Ms. Minor, just so it's clear, you did not testify that Bill asked for Temazepam, did you?"

"I have no recollection that he asked specifically for it. We decided on Temazepam together."

"So, having eliminated your first two suggestions, would Temazepam have been your next logical step?"

"It would have been one that would have been considered."

"Did Sharon report any family history of sleep disorders or sleep apnea?"

"Yes."

"Lorazepam falls into the general class of benzodiazepines. When did you prescribe that drug for her?"

"On May 6, 1999."

"Is it correct that it was in March that she actually started complaining to you regarding her sleeping problems?"

"Yes."

"So, in between the first reports of difficulty in March and the prescription for Lorazepam in early May, you went through a battery of testing procedures trying to eliminate organic problems. Is that correct?"

"Yes. We were checking to make sure that there wasn't a physical problem contributing to all of this."

"Ms. Minor, was it your conclusion that it was not a physical problem in Sharon's case, but a psychological one?"

"I told Sharon that all the tests were normal and wondered whether the difficulty she was having was actually due to the anxiety of the upcoming wedding."

"Sharon reported the family history of sleep apnea or sleep disorder. Did she report any family history of heart disease?"

"Yes, Sharon had hypertension. There is a tendency for cardiovascular disease any time a person has hypertension."

"Did you sometimes give Sharon samples of drugs to try?"

"Yes."

"Would they also be noted on the medical charts?"

"Since I am the one who used the flow sheet, they would be noted if I gave them to her."

"Did Sharon ever express to you that she and Bill struggled financially?"

"Yes, she did."

"Did she ever express concerns to you regarding the financial situation of the clinic?"

"We were, as a clinic, in the turn around process and were working hard to make things financially strong again. She was in charge of the insurance and the billing and that being her department, yes, she would voice concerns about that."

"I want to go back to the prescription for Temazepam that you wrote for Bill. The prescription was for fifteen pills - thirty milligrams each and could be refilled twice. Correct?"

"The prescription could be refilled three times for a total of sixty pills, which should have been enough for two months."

"Is it correct that Sharon was the one that confirmed calling the prescription into Statz the day that she told you that Bill had lost his prescription?"

"Yes."

"Do you know if Sharon had a prescription for Oxazepam?"

"No --- not in the time that I knew her."

"Did Bill have one?"

"It's not one that I had given him, unless he had one in the past."

"I would be talking about a current prescription."

"Not that I am aware of."

"Thank you, no more questions."

Witness for the State – Jon Hilton
Questioned by Kelly

Mr. Hilton explains the procedure that he uses as a pharmacist at K-Mart when a doctor phones a prescription in or a written prescription is presented by the patient. He states that the date and time the pharmacist fills the prescription are logged into the computer, the prescription is checked for accuracy, and then the medications that go into the bottle are labeled and bagged. When the patient arrives to pick up the prescription, he or she signs his or her name on a sheet provided by the store, it is rung up, and then given to the patient. The law mandates that records are to be kept every time a prescription is filled, regardless of whether the prescription is written or called in.

"Mr. Hilton, according to your records, when did you fill the prescription drug Temazepam for the defendant?"

"Temazepam was filled on April 29, 1999, at twelve o'clock noon for fifteen pills; then another one was filled on May 13, 1999, at 4:00 p.m. for fifteen pills."

"According to your signature log, who signed for these prescriptions?"

"Bill Guthrie signed for both of them."

"Would the May 13th prescription have been the refill of the original prescription?"

"This would not necessarily indicate either way. Without looking at the prescription, one would not be able to identify if it was the original."

"What other prescription did the defendant fill at K-Mart that can be used as a sleep aid?"

"Hydroxyz - fifty milligrams was filled on April 2, 1999."

"What is Hydroxyz used for and what are its side effects?"

"It is primarily used for hives, but can also be used for allergic reactions to medication. It causes extreme drowsiness, so it can be used as a sleep aid for some individuals."

"Did the defendant receive a prescription for any sleeping pills after May 13, 1999?"

"On June 9, 1999, he filled a prescription for Ambien - ten milligrams, which is primarily a sleep aid."

"Thank you, I have no further questions."

Cross-examine by the Defense

Mr. Hilton, are the recorded times of the prescriptions the time of day that they are filled or the time of day that they are picked up?"

"That would be the time of day that the pharmacist fills the prescription."

"Do you have any indication as to the time of day that the prescription is picked up?"

"Other than just the day --- no."

"Thank you, nothing further."

Witness for the State – Ann Cruse
Questioned by Moore

Ms. Cruse, a pharmacist at Statz Drug, states that other than filling prescriptions, pharmacists also counsel patients regarding the prescriptions and over-the-counter medications. A pharmacist knows what the medications are, what they will do, and also the side effects.

She explains that when a patient presents a written prescription from a doctor it is given to the cashier and if the person is a new patient the cashier obtains information that is needed by the pharmacist. The information is then entered into the computer, which generates a label. The technician or the pharmacist will pull the drug, count the tablets or capsules, and put them in a bottle. The date and time is then logged into the computer. The computer-generated label is placed on the bottle, the pharmacist checks the prescription for accuracy, then initials it. The prescription is placed in a bag with the receipt stapled to the outside. If the patient is not there, the bag is placed in an alphabetical area to be picked up later. It is required that a patient, or someone designated to pick up the prescription, must sign for it; then the date is recorded. She clarifies that only a pharmacist can take a phone-in prescription from a doctor. She adds that not all pharmacists use forms where it is noted whether it's a phone-in prescription versus a written one, but this is the procedure used at Statz Drug. Medical expense reports are maintained that list all prescriptions received by each patient.

"Ms. Cruse, was a prescription for Temazempam filled for the defendant at your location at 2:30 p.m. on April 29, 1999?"

"Yes."

"Was there another time that a prescription for Temazepam was filled for the defendant?"

"Yes, at 5:30 p.m. on May 12, 1999."

"According to your records, when these prescriptions were picked up, who signed for them?"

"Bill Guthrie signed for the April 29th prescription and Sharon Guthrie signed for the May 12th prescription."

"What can you tell us about the drug Ambien?"

"I referred to a book called *Facts and Comparisons*. Ambien is referred to as a sedative and hypnotic. The book lists the categories, its pharmacology, how it works, how it can be given, its dosage forms, side effects, precautions, and warnings. It tells you the adverse reactions of the drug and the different trial studies that were done of the drug versus a placebo. Placebo is a drug that has nothing in it. It lists what the form of the drug is, the manufacturer, the strength that is available, the dosage forms, and sometimes the color of the tablet for tablet identification."

"What is the dosage form available for Ambien?"

"It only comes in tablet form --- five or ten milligram tablets."

"What form does Xanax come in?"

"It comes in tablet form and also an oral solution."

"What does *Facts and Comparisons* say about the drug Temazepam?"

"Temazepam is listed under the pharmacology of different sedatives and hypnotic drugs. It talks about the dose, its half life, its plasma levels, its protein binding, and how it is excreted through the urine."

"Ms. Cruse, please read the highlighted overdose symptoms regarding Temazepam?"

"Somnolence, which is confusion with reduced or absent reflexes, respiratory depression, apnea, hypertension, impaired coordination, slurred speech, seizures, ultimately coma."

"What is the dosage form for Temazepam?"

"It only is available in capsule form."

"Please tell us the difference between tablets and capsule forms?"

"Tablets are a solid dose, whereas capsules are made out of gelatin that can be pulled apart to expose the powder form of the medication that is inside."

"Thank you, I have no further questions."

Cross-examine by the Defense

"Ms. Cruse, did I understand correctly that Sharon picked up the Temazepam prescription on May 12th?"

"Yes."

"Was Bill Guthrie counseled when he picked up the prescription for Temazepam on April 29th?"

"It is marked on the sheet that he was not counseled."

"Is it correct to say that he was handed the drug, paid for it, and was gone?"

"Correct."

"Referring to Exhibit 40, please read under the title *precautions*, the paragraph regarding indictor for depression."

"Depression: administer with caution in severely depressed patients, or in those of who there is evidence of latent depression, or suicidal tendencies. Hypnotic drugs may intensify signs or symptoms of depression. Protective measures may be required. Intentional overdose is more common in these patients and the least amount of drug that is feasible should be available to the patient at any one time."

Witness for the State – Lexi Rivers
Questioned by Kelly

Ms. Rivers, the Guthries' middle daughter, testifies that she lived with her parents in Hinton, Oklahoma, until the age of twenty-one. When her parents moved to South Dakota, she only saw them about once a year because of the length of the travel, but kept in contact through phone calls and e-mail. Her relationship with her mother had been getting closer because of her upcoming wedding. She typically communicated with her mother on the phone and mainly with her father through e-mail once or twice a week. Her relationship with her father was good.

"Did you ever visit with your father about divorce?"

"No, I didn't."

"Did he ever talk to you about any problems in their marriage?"

"Not really --- he kept it to himself, as well as my mom."

"Were you ever aware that your father was having an affair?"

"Not that he had told us, but I suspected that he was before they moved to South Dakota."

"Did you ever visit with your mother about the prospect of him having an affair?"

"No."

"To your knowledge, did she know about the affair?"

"Not that I know of."

"Did you ever observe your mother and Myra Conner together at any time?"

"No."

"Ms. Rivers, what medical problems of your mother's were you aware of?"

"I knew about her hypertension. We had encouraged her to take hormone pills. She talked a little bit to me about the thyroid problem, but that was about it."

"Did she ever mention to you that she was having trouble sleeping?"

"No."

"In all of the years that you had known your mother, were you ever aware that she had any sleepwalking problems?"

"No."

"Were you familiar with any of your father's medical problems?"

"I was told that whenever he went to the hospital in Orleans it was for his heart."

"Did he ever complain to you about any sleeping problems?"

"No."

"Would your mother drink chocolate milk in the morning and sometimes periodically throughout the day?"

"Yes."

"Will you please tell us about the incidents that you were aware of that occurred in the months prior to her death?"

"Mom told me about the string being on the steps and that Dad grabbed her before she fell. Dad e-mailed me once saying that he had problems waking her up, so he called the clinic. They told him to let her rest; but when he called in again to tell them he couldn't get her to wake up, they said to bring her into the clinic. At that time he told me that Mom was taking diet pills as well as Benadryl, and that the mixture of the two caused her to have problems. Mom called me on the phone after Dad was shocked, said they were having an evening, which is how she put it to me. Dad was washing her hair, and she thought the dog walked in and knocked the lamp over, and when Dad caught the lamp he received a shock."

"Did your mother indicate to you whether she had seen the dog knock over the lamp?"

"No."

"Did you also hear about this same incident from your dad?"

"Yes, he e-mailed me. He told me pretty much the same thing, except he told me that the dog did knock the lamp over."

"After you were notified of your mother's drowning, what did your father tell you when you arrived at the hospital?"

"He told me that he walked in, found her in the bathtub, tried to get her out, but couldn't. He said he was sorry that he couldn't do any more for her."

"Thank you, I have no further questions."

Cross-examine by the Defense

"Ms. Rivers, do you know if your mother ever took her medications with chocolate milk?"

"I think so, yes."

"The day of your mother's death when you arrived at the manse in Wolsey, was there any chocolate milk in the house at that time?"

"Yes, I drank some that was in the refrigerator."

"Did you suffer any ill effects from drinking it?"

"No."

"Can you recall approximately when you and your father started utilizing e-mail as a way of communication?"

"I can't really remember for sure, but it was probably in March of 1999."

"Regarding the day that your father brought your mother to the clinic when she was groggy, did you talk about this with him or with your mother?"

"I talked with both of them."

"What did your mother tell you about that day?"

"She said Dad had trouble waking her up and that she really couldn't remember. She said that she had been taking some diet pills, and they thought maybe the Benadryl caused her not to be able to wake up."

"Did she tell you what kind of diet pills she was taking?"

"She just said they were something herbal that she had gotten from Dr. Reed's wife."

"Do you remember your mother telling you anything about your dad's comments to her after this incident?"

"Yes, he told her to stop taking them."

"Was dieting something that your mother was always struggling with?"

"Yes."

"When your mother talked to you about the incident with the basement stairs, isn't it correct that she made it clear to you that without your father's actions, she would have fallen down the stairs and that he kept her from falling?"

"Yes, that's correct."

"Ms. Rivers, which one of your parents had a tendency to exaggerate or dramatize things?"

"They both did."

"I have no further questions. Thank you."

Witness for the State – Dr. Richard Reed
Questioned by Kelly

"Dr. Reed, on April 23, 1999, you treated the defendant when he thought that he might have been electrocuted. What symptoms do you look for when a person is electrocuted?"

"The person usually will have a burn mark, an entrance wound, or an exit wound, and perhaps some cardiac arrhythmia. There may also be some breakdown of muscle tissue from the energy."

"Did you find any of those symptoms?"

"No, but I admitted Mr. Guthrie overnight to make sure that I wasn't missing something."

"What were the defendant's symptoms?"

"He was very anxious and complaining that he had a lot of pain in various parts of his body, particularly his chest and his arms."

"Dr. Reed, based on those symptoms and your observations, did you come to the conclusion of what his problem might be?"

"I treated him for an anxiety attack, which is probably a diagnosis of exclusion. The patient is extremely anxious, breathing very rapidly, nervous, complaining about a lot of things, but you can't find anything to put your finger on. There are no physical findings other than maybe hyperventilation, rapid breathing, and maybe the heart rate would be up a little bit. Other than that, you can't find anything. Usually there is a precipitating event, such as one feeling like he had been electrocuted or whatever."

"What are some typical causes of anxiety attacks?"

"Anything you are afraid of I suppose. It could be psychological or it could be physical."

"Thank you, I have no further questions."

Cross-examine by the Defense

"In other words, Dr. Reed, could we say that Bill Guthrie received a mild shock and that apparently it scared the hell out of him?"

"Could have, yes."

"Is it correct that a mild shock wouldn't necessarily leave any wounds or anything observable and that he just might have overreacted a little bit to the shock?"

"Yes."

"Could this be what we are basically talking about as far as an anxiety attack and overreaction?"

"In this instance, sure that could happen."

"Thank you. Nothing further."

Witness for the State – Les Hewitt
Questioned by Kelly

"Mr. Hewitt, what took place when you were asked by Deputy Sheridan to retrieve pill bottles from your in-laws' residence?"

"As we collected bottles from the bathroom medicine cabinet and cupboards above the microwave area in the kitchen we wrote down the prescriptions, how many pills were in each bottle, and what they were for. Bill offered all the bottles that he knew of regarding their locations. We put them all in a bag and gave them to Deputy Sheridan."

"Mr. Hewitt, did you ever use the defendant's computer that was in his office at the church?"

"Yes, when Bill had a problem with it, he would call me to help him since I am familiar with computers."

"Was this computer Internet accessible?'

"Yes, it was."

"Did you ever access the Internet on it?"

"Yes, a few times --- probably less than five times."

"Who normally was present when you accessed the Internet?"

"Bill was there one time when we changed his password. I think Mitch was there one time, but mostly Danielle."

"Did you ever do searches for drugs on that computer?"

"No, ma'am."

"Did you ever do searches for bathtub accidents?"

"No, ma'am."

"Prior to Sharon's death, were you aware of the defendant's affair with Myra Conner?"

"No, I was not."

"Were you aware of the trips that he made to Nebraska periodically?"

"Yes, ma'am."

"Do you know the reasons that the defendant gave regarding these trips?'

"There were a number of reasons: counseling because of the sexual assault in Lincoln and also for pastoral reasons."

"Mr. Hewitt, did you ever visit with him about his counseling sessions?"

"No, ma'am, we never spoke about it."

"Did you ever visit with the defendant about his relationship with Sharon?"

"On and off, but not an every day or an every time we went fishing thing. Just here and there, I guess."

"You had a conversation with the defendant in the weeks prior to Sharon's death. Do you recall specifically what the two of you talked about?"

"We were sitting in his truck in the parking lot by Reed Clinic. Bill said that he had something serious he wanted to talk about; then proceeded to tell me that after Lexi's wedding he was going to divorce Sharon."

"What did you find when you went to the manse to look at the stairs after you heard that Sharon almost fell down the stairs to the basement?"

"On the two steps down on one side there is wood and carpeting that come together, forming a ninety degree angle. It looked like somebody had drilled a hole, and there were fresh wood shavings on the carpet. The other side of the wall is concrete and there was a round spot that looked like something had been glued on, then pulled off."

"Mr. Hewitt, when you checked the bathroom lighting the day after the defendant was allegedly electrocuted, what did you find?"

"Sharon asked me to come over and help her replace the light bulbs. The stand in the bathroom normally used for a plant was not there, but an electrical cord was there and plugged into the outlet located underneath the mirror on the medicine cabinet. The fluorescent lights were okay, but the starters weren't working."

"How many lights were in the bathroom?"

"There were three lights in the bathroom, counting the one above the mirror."

"Was that light working?"

"No, ma'am."

"Did you see any problems with Sharon or any changes in her in the months leading up to her death?"

"Other than her being excited about Lexi's wedding in June, no, I did not. Sharon was always bubbly and very upbeat."

"Thank you, no further questions."

Cross-examine by the Defense

"Mr. Hewitt, I have heard a number of people describe Sharon as bubbly and upbeat and others have described her as being very private. Do you agree with the private part?"

"That depends on what you mean by private."

"Was it your experience that Sharon would talk about very personal things with you?"

"No."

"Did she tell you how her relationship with Bill was going?"

"No --- not with me."

"Regarding the light in the bathroom. Do I understand clearly that a bad starter in the fluorescent fixture is one of those devices where you have to take the fluorescent bulb out to replace it with a new starter?"

"Yes, sir."

"When Sharon talked to you regarding the incident on the staircase, did she make it clear to you that Bill kept her from falling down the stairs?"

"Yes, she said that he reached out and grabbed her shoulder."

"Mr. Hewitt, when you looked at the staircase to the basement, is it correct, that except at the very top, the walls on each side of the stair treads were carpet-covered concrete?"

"It was not covered by concrete on the one side underneath."

"So, immediately adjacent to the stair tread on either side there would be a wooden wall. For example, a wooden wall where you could drive a nail or affix something to it?"

"Could be --- could be."

"Did you say there was a hole, I believe, somewhere in the woodwork?"

"Not a hole --- I noticed some wood shavings."

"Was that in relationship to the top, bottom, or middle step?"

"It would have been at the top step."

"Mr. Hewitt, if the string was fastened at the top step and she had sat down after catching her foot on the string, where would she have sat down?"

"She would have sat down at the top of the stairs."

"Over the many years you have known Bill and Sharon, have you had the chance to form an impression of whether Bill or Sharon tend to embellish or exaggerate?"

"Yes, sir, both of them."

"Thank you, nothing further."

Redirect by the State

"Mr. Hewitt, when you saw what appeared to be fresh wood shavings in the stairway, did you investigate to see if there was a hole present?"

"As far as pulling back the carpet --- no. Basically, I just looked at the shavings, which appeared to be from a drill. Whenever you drill into wood it kind of spirals out, and that's what it appeared to look like to me."

"Thank you, I have nothing further."

Witness for the State – Don Perry
Questioned by Moore

Mr. Perry is an executive presbyter who covers forty-two Presbyterian churches in central Nebraska. He oversees the churches within a geographical area assigned to him and is a support to the churches and pastors, so they might best serve the Lord as they do their work. He provides resources when a pastor needs information and also is available to answer a pastor's questions regarding how a pastor might go about a certain task. He is like a pastor to a pastor because pastors don't have another pastor to go to, so he listens and gives them support.

Mr. Perry was going to be out of the country and would not be available to testify in person, so Judge Martin allowed the two parties to take his deposition earlier by way of videotape. He was placed under oath during this taping, just as if he were in the courtroom today and testifying in person.

Gregory Wilson objects to the use of this taped video testimony, based on the fact that comments made by his client to Mr. Perry were confidential and that those communications are privileged. Judge Martin overrules his objection and allows the State to proceed.

"Mr. Perry, how do you know the defendant?"

"Bill Guthrie was serving as pastor in the Christian Church in Beaver City, which is within the geographic bounds of our Presbytery. The pastor of the Beaver City Presbyterian Church knew Bill, liked him, and recommended to the Orleans Presbyterian Church, about twenty miles to the east of Beaver City, that they take serious consideration in calling him as their pastor. I became acquainted with Bill as the church became interested, and I was asked to do some reference checking and to facilitate the process of having him come to the Orleans church as its pastor."

"Since the defendant was not a Presbyterian minister, Mr. Perry, please explain what had to happen for him to become a pastor in the Presbyterian faith?"

"The pastor nominating committee from the Orleans Presbyterian Church had to request that he be their candidate. He was not ordained, but on June 1,1992, he was initially hired and began to serve, preach, and minister to the people. Later on, he took five ordination exams regarding Bible, worship, sacraments, theology, and church government. He passed the exams and was then accepted as an ordained Presbyterian pastor."

"What was your relationship like with the defendant?"

"We had a good relationship and we talked together frequently. He trusted me and I trusted him. As I recall, we would talk roughly once a month, either on the phone, at a meeting, or at his house."

"Did the defendant ever tell you about an incident that happened to him in Lincoln, Nebraska when he was assaulted?"

"Yes."

"Prior to the defendant telling you about this incident, Mr. Perry, had he mentioned anything about this to you before?"

"No, but he did indicate a few months before that he wanted to share something with me, but said he wasn't ready to share it yet. When he did share the assault with me, I asked him if this is what he wanted to talk to me about, and he said that it was."

"Do you remember approximately the time or date that he told you about this incident in Lincoln?"

"I can't be sure, but backtracking from the time Bill left Orleans, which was July 1,1996, it was approximately a year before that."

"After he told you about the assault, did you offer him any help or advice?"

"Bill told me that I was the second person to hear about this, so I suggested that he tell his wife and the session at the church in Orleans. I also suggested that he report it to the police because it was an assault and the police needed to know about it. I suggested that he should seek out counseling and support because he was obviously distraught about the incident. He said it was affecting his sleep, affecting all aspects of his life, and he had a hard time carrying on his pastoral duties."

"Do you know who was the first person that he told about the assault?"

"As I recall, the first person was Myra Conner. That's how I remember our conversation."

"Mr. Perry, did you do any follow up or talk to anybody about this incident?"

"I told Bill that I would talk to the chief of police in Lincoln because he said he felt uncomfortable talking to the police. I called Chief Cassidy and told him what Bill had told me about the incident."

"Did Chief Cassidy seem willing to sit down and have a conversation with you and the defendant?"

"Yes, Chief Cassidy was, but Bill said that he would go some time in the future with me to talk with him, or he would go by himself."

"Did the defendant take any other advice from you regarding the alleged rape?"

"Yes, he said that he had told the session and his wife and was also seeking and had received psychological counseling."

"Did you attempt to verify any of that information?"

"I talked to somebody from the session who indicated that Bill had shared the incident with them."

"Did you get names of any counselors from the defendant?"

"No, I did not."

"Mr. Perry, did you have a conversation with the defendant about the rumors of the alleged affair?"

"When I asked Bill, he indicated that there was no basis for those rumors --- that he did not have an affair with anyone in that church and that he was true to his wife."

"Did you actually go to the defendant and ask him about the alleged affair?"

"Yes, I asked him whether there was any truth in it, and Bill said there was not. He said he was impotent and could not have an affair. He said he was unable to perform sexually; therefore, any rumor regarding a sexual affair could not have basis."

"After you had this conversation with him, did that satisfy you to keep his position at the church?"

"Yes, I fully believed Bill and had no reason to doubt his integrity. He had not shown previously that I should have reason to doubt him."

"Did you make any recommendations to the defendant about staying at the Orleans church?"

"I recommended that he bring his résumé up to date and look for another position."

"Why did you do that?"

"Because there were concerns in the church. Bill was under a great deal of stress and the ministry was not going well. People were not coming to worship, the attendance was down, and the giving was down. There were problems in the church and Bill was feeling that."

"Did you continue to have contact with the defendant when he moved to Wolsey?"

"I might have talked to him once in the first six months or so, but not very much."

"What did you do after you received the information regarding Sharon's death?"

"I waited roughly a day or two, then I called Bill to extend my condolences."

"Mr. Perry, did you make this call prior to Sharon's funeral?"

"As I recall --- yes. One of my main purposes of calling was to find out if I could get permission to send out notices to all the clergy in the Presbytery to tell them that Sharon had died, so they could pray for Bill and send him notes of sympathy and support."

"When you spoke with the defendant, what did he tell you?"

"He told me that he was very distraught. He said that Sharon had been under medication. Approximately two weeks prior, she had gotten up in the night and overdosed on her medication, and he had taken her to the emergency room."

"What did he tell you regarding how Sharon had died?"

"Bill said he woke up and Sharon was apparently sleep- walking, and he decided to go over to the church building where he could pray and work on his sermon. And when he came back to the house roughly an hour later, the water in the bathtub was overflowing. Water was running out of the bathroom and down the stairs and he ran into the bathroom and found Sharon in the bathtub."

"Did he tell you that he tried to help her?"

"As I recall, he tried to resuscitate her, and then he called 911."

"Did the defendant tell you what time of night it was when he got up and noticed that Sharon was sleepwalking?"

"As I recall, he said it was about midnight."

"What did he tell about his relationship with Sharon?"

"He reassured me that his relationship with Sharon had been very good recently because it had not been good when he was in Nebraska. He said they have had a great relationship since coming to South Dakota."

"What procedure does the Presbytery have regarding a minister or pastor that is allegedly having an affair with a parish member?"

"If it becomes known to me, or even to another member, any Presbyterian can write to the state clerk who then is obligated to begin an investigating process. If the investigating process shows that there is enough evidence, an ecclesiastical trial begins."

"If that is found true, Mr. Perry, what ways would the pastor be punished?"

"There are different levels of punishment. A pastor could just be reprimanded, a pastor could be temporarily deprived of the pastoral privileges and not be allowed to function as a pastor, or a pastor could be permanently removed as a Presbyterian pastor."

"So, if it were true regarding this affair, how would this be detrimental to a pastor's job?"

"If a pastor would seek another job, he would have to sign that a sexual misconduct conviction was upheld, be up front, and disclose the information regarding the sexual involvement."

"Thank you, I have no further questions."

Cross-examine by the Defense

"Mr. Perry, as a pastor's pastor, where you consult and counsel pastors, do you also hear matters from them in confidence?"

"That is correct."

"Is confidentiality an important thing for a minister to maintain?"

"Yes, but there are certainly limits to confidentiality. As we have been told, ministers know and of course I know that..."

"Excuse me for interrupting, Mr. Perry, but I believe you have answered the question. Would it be fair to say, in your mind, that Bill was coming to you as his minister to talk about various matters and talking to you in confidence?"

"Yes."

"Mr. Perry, did you get to know Bill and Sharon fairly well?"

"I would say that I knew Bill a lot better than I knew Sharon."

"Would it be fair to say that they were both somewhat prone to embellishments --- adding real or imaginary details?"

"I --- I did not know that, and no, I would not say that was true."

"Is it your recollection that it was the day before Sharon's funeral that you talked to Bill on the phone about her death?"

"Yes."

"I believe that you were contacted by law enforcement some time in late June. Is that correct, Mr. Perry?"

"I believe that's the correct time frame."

"Wasn't that over a month after you talked to Bill?"

"That feels about right."

"Is it correct to say that you were recalling your conversation with Bill from memory?"

"Yes, I was --- I didn't take any notes."

"You stated your recollection was that Bill told you Sharon died in the middle of the night. Do you think that you could be wrong in that regard?"

"I can be wrong, but I think my memory of what he said is apt to be correct."

"At any rate, did Bill tell you about Sharon's apparent overdose incident that occurred several weeks prior to her death?"

"Yes."

"Mr. Perry, did he tell you that Sharon was having some sleeping problems?"

"In terms of getting up and walking while she was partly or all asleep --- yes."

"Bill told you that he and Sharon, prior to her death, had actually been getting along well. I believe the words you used were that he said his relationship with Sharon had become good or great. Is that correct?"

"Yes."

"Going back to the incident in Lincoln, did you state that you contacted a police officer by the name of Chief Cassidy in Lincoln?"

"That is true."

"Isn't it true that you had previously indicated you had talked not to a Mr. Cassidy, but a Mr. Crosby?"

"No, I don't know of any Mr. Crosby. The chief of police in Lincoln is Cassidy. Was, and still is, I believe."

"When you were previously interviewed by DCI Agent Lindberg of South Dakota, didn't you tell him that you had talked to a police officer by the name of Crosby in Lincoln?"

"I don't ever recall saying that --- no."

"Mr. Perry, just for clarification, when you talked to Bill the day before Sharon's funeral, did he tell you he had gone over to the church to pray?"

"Pray and work on his sermon. That is correct."

"Did he also tell you that when he came back to the house he found the water running, found his wife in the bathtub, and water in the tub was overflowing?"

"That is true."

"I have no further questions."

Redirect by the State

"Mr. Perry, why was Sharon's death unsettling to you?"

"Because Sharon was a good person and Bill is a good person, and I could identify with him losing his wife. Also, the story that Bill told me just didn't seem to make sense."

"As you can recall, when you spoke on the phone to Agent Lindberg a month or so after Sharon's death, was there any particular reason why you would remember this conversation that you had with the defendant?"

"Yes. After I got off the telephone --- after what Bill had said about them getting along great, it just clicked. I thought, 'Goodness gracious, this doesn't add up.' Bill told me before they went to South Dakota that the relationship was not good, and he didn't anticipate that they would be married much beyond the time he got there; he was just thinking about separation and divorce. Then to hear that she had died and hear him say that their relationship had been great since they had been in South Dakota. This just didn't make sense and that was unsettling."

"Is this what made it easy for you to remember?"

"Yes, sir."

"I have no further questions."

January 14

Trial Day Three

Witness for the State – Roger Mathison
Questioned by Moore

Mr. Mathison, a chemist at the State Health Lab in Pierre, S.D., was requested by Mr. Moore to conduct a series of taste tests. These tests were done to determine if the presence of Temazepam in chocolate milk would have any type of noticeable taste or texture which would give an individual consuming it a clue that there was something unusual with the chocolate milk.

"Mr. Mathison, do you recall how much chocolate milk was mixed with the contents of ten capsules of Temazepam?"

"Approximately six or seven ounces, which would be half the size of a large glass."

"Could you taste anything after you mixed the chocolate milk?"

"No, I didn't detect any change in flavor or texture and nothing that would be noticeable to the person consuming the chocolate milk. I also didn't notice any odor being emitted from the mixture."

"Mr. Mathison, please explain what I have here."

"Last evening we took this jar of chocolate milk and placed the contents of twenty thirty-milligram capsules of Temazepam into it, then shook it for a couple of minutes to properly mix it.

Today it is in the same condition as last evening. There is no visible evidence that anything was added to the chocolate milk."

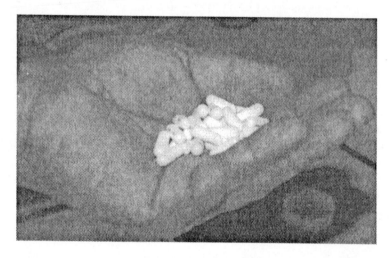

Mr. Moore produces two empty clean jars, a normal size quart canning jar and a quart size jar resembling a mayonnaise jar. He instructs the witness to pour the same amount of chocolate milk into each of the jars and put the lid on the canning jar. He then gives the witness twenty thirty-milligram Temazepam capsules, instructs him to open the capsules and pour the contents into the mayonnaise jar and then place the lid on that jar. He asks him to shake each jar, just as he did the prior evening, then label each jar. The canning jar is labeled as having no additives and the mayonnaise jar is labeled as having additives.

"Mr. Mathison, I also have here the container with chocolate milk that was mixed in your lab. How many Temazepam capsules are in this container?"

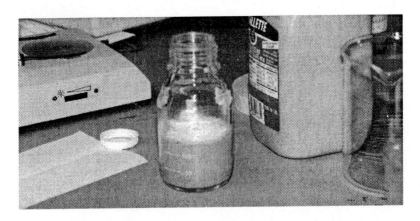

"Ten capsules."

"Thank you, I have no further questions."

Cross-examine by the Defense

"Mr. Mathison, would you say that it's fair to estimate it took you ten minutes to empty the capsules into the milk?"

"I wasn't keeping track, but I believe you could empty twenty capsules in no more than ten minutes."

"Was this the third time or the fourth that you have conducted this experiment?"

"The third time."

"Would it be fair to say, Mr. Mathison, that since there are thirty-two ounces in a quart, that there is approximately ten ounces of milk in these jars?"

"Yes, roughly."

"Can you explain the idea of a liquid saturation point as it pertains to absorbing a powder?"

"There will always be a point where the liquid will not be able to absorb, absolve or hold any more of the solid material depending on the nature of the liquid and the nature of the solid material you are placing in it and how soluble it is."

"What would happen at that point?"

"After a couple of minutes you would see residue forming at the bottom of the container and it would not be able to be held by the liquid."

"Do you recognize this photograph as being one from the first experiment conducted with Mr. Moore and Agent Lindberg present?"

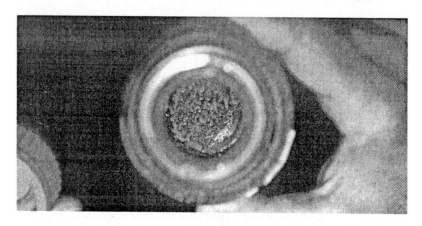

"Mr. Lindberg took several pictures while we were conducting the experiment and this photo appears to be one of the containers that was part of that demonstration."

"Would this have been after the Temazepam and the chocolate milk solution was dumped out?"

"Yes."

"Mr. Mathison, approximately how much chocolate milk and how many capsules were used in the first experiment?"

"Probably closer to approximately six or seven ounces and ten capsules."

"No further questions."

Redirect by the State

"Mr. Mathison, when we conducted the experiment in your lab, what was the method used in mixing the chocolate milk?"

"We relied primarily on stirring with a glass rod in a glass beaker. Later on we had a couple of containers that we shook, which works a great deal better than stirring. Within a couple of minutes of vigorous shaking you can get the contents to dissolve throughout the liquid, so it is totally unnoticeable and will not leave any sediment."

"When you did the stirring, which took a little longer, did you end up with the same results?"

"Yes."

"How long did you keep those beakers and observe them?"

"I observed them the following day and also for a couple days after that for a period of five days. They were kept in the refrigerator and at no time did we have a settling of any tablet material or capsule material that was noticeable."

"Thank you, I have no further questions."

Witness for the State – Suzanne Hewitt Questioned by Moore

Suzanne, the Guthries' oldest daughter, states that she and her mother had a very close relationship and phoned each other almost every day, along with frequent visits, since they only lived thirteen miles apart. She always spoke with her father when she and her family attended church in Wolsey.

"Ms. Hewitt, please tell us about the last time you talked with your father about his relationship with your mother?"

"In March, while he and I were fishing, he told me that he didn't love Mom anymore and was going to divorce her after my sister's wedding in June. I asked him why they had stayed together this long. He said it was because of his job and also he wanted to stay with Mom until my youngest sister was out of school."

"Had you ever talked to your mother about her relationship with your father?"

"I did, but she was very quiet about it."

"Did your mother ever tell you they were having troubles in the marriage and that she was planning on divorcing your father?"

"No."

"How did you find out that your father was having an affair?"

"When we lived in Orleans, Nebraska, I became suspicious. The people that I did daycare for would tell me about the rumors that he was seeing Myra Conner, but I didn't know for sure until after my mother's death."

"What reasons did your father tell you regarding his trips back to Nebraska?"

"He said that he was going there for counseling and also to continue his education."

"Do you know if your mother knew anything about this affair?"

"She was suspicious, but she said that my dad told her there wasn't anything going on."

"Did you know anything about your parents' sexual relationship?"

"Mom told me that he could not have sex because of an incident in Lincoln, Nebraska."

"Were you aware of any of your father's medical problems?"

"He had nightmares, problems with his heart, and migraine headaches."

"In March or April, prior to your mother's death, did your father ever complain to you that he was having problems sleeping?"

"Not that I can recall."

"Were you aware of any of your mother's medical problems?"

"I knew that she was taking something for hormones because when she took them she would tell my children they were *happy pills*. As far as anything else, she didn't tell me a whole lot."

"Did your mother ever tell you that she was sleepwalking?"

"She said that my dad told her she was sleepwalking."

"What did your father tell you about your mother's sleepwalking?"

"He said that she had started sleepwalking in March or April and would get up in the middle of the night. He would never know exactly what she was doing, but she would leave the lights on in the house and then go back to bed."

"Prior to March, did your father ever mention to you that she had been sleepwalking before in her life?"

"No."

"Had you ever seen your mother sleepwalk?"

"No."

"What medications did your mom take for her allergies?"

"She took things like Benadryl and Allegra."

"To your knowledge, was your mother allergic to anything around the house?"

"Yes, she was allergic to perfumes, different scents in candles, flowers, dust, and flour that you use for baking."

"Ms. Hewitt, please explain what your father's reaction was when you told him that your mother had spoken to you about the incident with the string across the stairway."

"When I called him on the phone, he was very angry that I knew about the incident. He had told Mom not to tell anyone because he was going to discuss it with the sheriff. The next day he told me that Mom had tripped on her shoelace."

"What happened when you got to the clinic the day that your mother was groggy?"

"I saw them bringing Mom down the hallway in a wheelchair; and I tried talking to her, but she was very out of it. She wasn't in any condition to talk, so I talked to Dad. He said that she had gotten up several times in the night; and he thought that she had taken Benadryl every time she got up."

"Did your mother ever talk to you about this incident at the clinic?"

"She told me that she didn't remember anything of that day."

"What did your father tell you about the time your mother stopped breathing?"

"He told me that he had rolled over in bed and that she wasn't breathing, so he yelled her name and did CPR on her, got her breathing again, and then they both went back to sleep."

"To your knowledge does your father know how to do CPR?"

"Not to my knowledge."

"Whom did you talk to first regarding the electrical incident in the bathroom when your father was allegedly shocked?"

"My mother called me on the phone the night it happened and said that Dad had been shocked and to meet them at the hospital. When I arrived at the hospital, Dad was yelling that he was in a lot of pain. Mom said she had been in the bathtub and he was helping her wash her hair --- that they were having a kind of romantic evening. The lights didn't work, so they put a lamp on the plant stand. The dog must have come into the bathroom because she heard Dad yell at Lady, and then she saw the lamp coming towards the bathtub. She jumped out and just as the lamp was hitting the water Dad grabbed it. She said at the time she didn't realize that he could have been shocked because he walked out of the bathroom while she let the water out of the tub; then he came back in the bathroom and collapsed."

"Did your mom tell you that she saw the dog knock the lamp over?"

"I don't remember that she did."

"Did you talk to your father about this?"

"He called me a few days later and said that he was in the bathtub and that Mom was leaning over the side of the bathtub, that he was helping wash her hair when Lady came in and knocked the lamp into the bathtub. He said they both jumped out, and when he was jumping out he got shocked and collapsed."

"At the hospital the morning your mother drowned, what did your father tell you?"

"He said he woke Mom up, then he got up and went over to the church. When he came back, he could hear water running; so he went into the bathroom and found Mom in the bathtub, pulled her out of the tub and called 911."

"So, he told you that he had gotten her out of the tub?"

"Yes."

"Did he tell you why he had gone over to the church?"

"He said that he was doing morning prayers."

"Have you ever seen your father go over to the church in the morning to do morning prayers after getting up?"

"Not that I can remember."

"In the months prior to your mother's death, did you notice any changes in her such as her mood, or did she seem stressed or tense about anything?"

"Other than normal day-to-day stuff, she was a little tense about things at work. More so, she was excited about my sister's wedding, which I wouldn't call stress. Lexi was going to wear Mom's wedding dress and it was going to be a large wedding."

"Did your father stay around after your mother's funeral?"

"The funeral was on Monday, and I believe it was on Thursday when he went out of town. He said that he was going to Wyoming and would meet us in Nebraska for Lexi's wedding.

"Why did your father ask you and your sisters to remove your mother's belongings from the house?"

"He felt like he didn't want to have her belongings around anymore."

"On July 26th of last year did you take a tape recorder with you to Wolsey and tape a conversation between you and your dad?"

"Yes, I did."

"I have here the tape recording of that conversation. After you listened to this tape, did it accurately show what transpired during that conversation?"

"Yes, it did."

"I have here a transcript of the tape. When you played the tape and looked at the transcript, did you make changes and add things if you thought something wasn't right?"

"Yes, I did."

"Does the transcript accurately reflect what is on the tape after the changes were made?"

"Yes, it does."

Gregory Wilson objects to the tape being entered into evidence, but is overruled by Judge Martin. Wilson again objects to the playing the tape and allowing the jury to have a copy of the transcript to follow along with the tape.

"Objection is overruled, Mr. Wilson. We will play the tape and the jurors will receive a transcript of the tape recording. Ladies and gentlemen of the jury, please note that in the transcript the speakers in the conversation are identified. You are permitted to have the transcript for the limited purpose of helping you follow the conversation as you listen to the tape recording. However, remember the transcript is not evidence. Whether the transcript correctly or incorrectly reflects the conversation or the identity of the speakers is entirely for you to decide. Based on what you have heard about the preparation of the transcript in relation to what you hear on the tape recording, the tape recording itself is the primary evidence of its own contents. If you decide that the transcript is in any respect incorrect or unreliable, you should disregard it to that extent. When there is a difference, you should rely on what you hear rather that what you read. Please hand out the transcript to the jurors. When the tape recording is completed, we will collect the transcripts."

July 26, 1999, after leaving Deputy Sheridan's office, Suzanne drives to the manse in Wolsey to visit with her father. At 11:45 a.m. she parks her car, reaches into her purse and turns the tape recorder on, then proceeds to the front door of the house. She knocks on the door a couple of times, then slowly opens it calling out to her father.

"Hello --- who's there?"

"Dad, it's Suzanne. I came to talk to you."

"About what?"

"About you."

"What about me?"

"Dad, I want to know what's going on."

"Sit down. What do you want to know?"

"I need to know what's going on with the case."

"Nothing."

"Dad, I've talked to quite a few people now and I need to know some answers."

"Okay, ask."

"Were you having an affair?"

"No --- where did you hear that?"

"I've heard it from everybody."

"No --- not in the terms of what they say."

"Dad, she has admitted it --- you admitted it."

"Where did that come from? Who did she admit it to?

"She admitted it to Deputy Sheridan, the State's Attorney, and everybody else --- you admitted it, too."

"Yes, but it was just so that they wouldn't continue on that."

"Dad, why do you call her so much?"

"I haven't called her so much."

"Why does she call you all the time?"

"She calls me --- yes. I don't call her."

"Dad, why did you tell Les and me that you were calling from Sheridan when you were not at Eddy and Karen's?"

"Where did you get that?"

"It was on my caller ID the day after Father's Day. You told me you were standing out at a store in Sheridan or Buffalo, Wyoming."

"No!"

"Yes you did! You told Danielle and me that. And on my caller ID, you were at Eddy and Karen's."

"I was there and went back."

"So --- why didn't you just tell me you were there?"

"Because I didn't want even more coming out of that."

"What's going to come out of that, Dad?"

"God knows --- anything."

"They have a lot on you, Dad. A lot and I need to know the truth. All of it --- I have to know Dad. I have to stand behind you, okay? I'm on your side. I don't want to think that you've done the things that you've done."

"What do you think that I did?"

"They think you did Mom?"

"Who thinks I did?"

"The sheriff, everybody else I've talked to! There's medicine missing! I mean just everything, Dad. I need to know."

"I don't know anything about the medicine that's missing."

"There were sixty pills of yours. There's fifty-four of them that's unaccounted for. They're gone --- you had six left."

"Six left? Where ... where was ... where did they come up with fifty-four?"

"Cuz, there should have been sixty. There were six left and fifty-four are gone. Where did you go Super Bowl weekend, Dad?"

"Super Bowl weekend? I was in, uh...."

"Bassett for the hunting thing?"

"No. That was when I went to --- the --- to a meeting in Hastings."

"Super Bowl weekend you guys met --- you and Myra."

"When did the State's Attorney talk to you?"

"I talked to Mike Moore this morning. I got tired of hearing what everybody was telling me and you weren't answering me --- I have to know, Dad!"

"I told you I did."

"Told me you did what, Dad?"

"With Myra --- I told you that. That everybody thinks it was more than it was. It wasn't! She saw me twice after --- we helped each other."

"Why did you both admit to it? That makes things that much worse. For goodness sake, Dad, the admission is a motive."

"Of what?"

"Of killing Mom!"

"How did you get a motive to ... "

"So that you can be with Myra."

"I haven't been ... been with her. I haven't seen her."

"But, you told them you were. You told me you had a sexual affair with her. She told them she had a sexual affair with you. That's motive, Dad. Do you see what they have?"

"Yeah."

"Now, you've got to disprove that. You've got to go tell them the truth. She's going to tell them the truth. What the hell are you going to do if they send you to jail, Dad? I don't want that --- I don't want the kids to go through that. They've lost their grandma and I don't want them to lose you. Do you see that?"

"Yes."

"I don't want to lose you. I lost my mom, for goodness sake. They told me she took the drugs into the bedroom --- she couldn't have gotten to the bathroom. So, Dad, how did she get all the medicine in her system?"

"I don't know."

"If she would have taken that much in the middle of the night, she would never have gotten up. I don't see her committing suicide and what does that leave? Do you see where I am at?"

"Yeah."

"I can't do this --- I'm going nuts! I want to prove that she committed suicide, but I don't want to prove that she committed suicide! So what did she do? What was she doing that morning? What did she do the night before?"

"I don't know. She was really complacent the night before. I don't know what she took --- I don't know."

"Dad ... she took your medicine. Your medicine was in her system."

"My medicine was in her system?"

"Yes, she had one of her meds in her system, that was it. The rest of it was yours."

"I don't know how she got my meds."

"Did you have them put up?"

"Yeah. They were in that --- in the medicine cabinet. I don't know how they can say that I had fifty whatever ... whatever pills."

"Because you got a prescription and Patricia wrote it down on paper, right? She had you go fill it. You called Mom to say you lost that piece of paper, so Mom got it refilled."

"I never called your mom and told her I lost that."

"Dad, this is the way it is --- this is what I've been told. They said you had that one. You got those refilled ---those four prescriptions for that one medicine, which makes sixty pills."

"I went ... "

"Mom picked up one prescription and you picked up the other three."

"Uh --- no. I picked up one ---- I picked up only..."

"Dad, you signed for three."

"No, I didn't!"

"You signed for three; your signatures are there. So there should have been sixty pills. If you would have taken fifteen, that leaves forty-five. There were six in her system. That leaves thirty-nine. So they have accounted for that many, which leaves thirty-nine to fifty something left.

"I've been taking that prescription."

"They said that if you would have taken the fifteen, cuz it was from the 1st and the 15th."

"But, ever since I've been taking it."

"Right, so you got a different prescription. Didn't you have a different prescription filled after you came back?"

"Yeah, but I haven't used those."

"Hmm. I don't know, Dad, but that's what they are saying. There's that many left."

"Oh, man."

"There's got to be things you can do to prove your innocence, Dad. There's got to be things we can do to prove your innocence. You need to get with Myra. You need to get this story taken care of. What do you want me to do?"

"There were six pills in her system?"

"There were --- what'd they tell me? Fifteen you took ... six that were left makes thirty-nine. And we don't know how much exactly was in her system. I don't know if there were thirty-nine of them in her system or six, but the biggest thing is, it was your prescription, not hers, plus you not being here. You said you were at the church."

"I was at the church!"

"I know ... that's what you said. Don Perry said you told him that it happened at 1:30 in the morning."

"No, I didn't tell him that! I don't know where he got that."

"I'm just telling you the little tidbits I've heard. Paula and Rich called; Larry and Bonnie called. All of them are wondering what's going on. They have all been questioned."

"Dad, has Joan talked to you since Friday?"

"Why?"

"Cuz they talked to her on Friday, and they said she didn't believe anything they told her. So, can we go talk to them and let them know what's going on?"

"I can't do that without my lawyer."

"If you haven't done anything wrong, why do you need a lawyer?"

"Because ... because Presbytery asked me to get one."

"We need to get this straightened out, Dad."

"So, just take me!"

"That's not what you want --- that's not what I want to happen, Dad!"

"I know it."

"Dad, you've got to make a stand one way or the other. You can't let this go, so what are you going to do?"

"Wait until I can get my lawyer. Let's call him and see what he says. Where did you hear all these rumors from?"

"Everybody in town. People called me from Orleans. Nancy's called me, Linda's called me, Paula and Rich called. Paula and Rich were questioned --- Myra has been questioned. If they are questioning people, telling them you were having an affair, people are going to think that now. People do think that now. Me, I'm stuck out in limbo cuz I don't know what to think."

"I wish I could wake up from this nightmare."

"That won't happen, Dad. I keep expecting to call your phone number and have Mom answer the phone. Dad, did you tell them you think Mom committed suicide?"

"Why?"

"Because, that's what they said that you thought."

"I was ... there were times ... when she tried it."

"I don't see her doing that to Lexi, not that soon. I really don't think she'd been caught dead naked. I really don't. Tell me what you're thinking."

"Hmm?"

"Tell me what you're thinking, Dad."

"I don't know where she --- I would not --- the only place I got that one prescription was out at K-Mart."

"And Dad, she picked one up from Statz. I don't know where the others came from."

"I picked up so many prescriptions for her at Statz and K-Mart and ..." The phone rings. "Hello ... Hi ... yeah ... No ... yeah ... huh, yeah ... okay ... okay ... all right. Bye, Karen."

"Oh, does she plan on coming up?"

"I don't know."

"Have you heard anything back on Grandma's tests?"

"No."

"She was pretty grouchy Saturday night, Dad."

"You saw her on Saturday night? She said she hasn't seen you for two weeks."

"I saw her --- I think that was Monday afternoon, cuz she asked me how come I didn't tell her that Mom was caught in the bathtub with all her clothes off and that's how she died. I asked her who she heard that from and she said that's what they said at the nursing home."

"Dad, are you going to let me know what you decide? I feel I need to know what's going on."

"Yeah."

Suzanne left her father's house in Wolsey and returned to Huron to deliver the taped conversation to the sheriff's office.

"Ms. Hewitt, would you please tell the jury what you observed about your father during this conversation?"

"He seemed very nervous and wouldn't make eye contact with me."

"When was the last time that you talked to your mother before she died?"

"The night before she was found in the bathtub we spoke on the phone between 10:15 and 10:30 p.m. I had left a glue pot at the church and asked her if she would bring it to work the next day."

"What was your mom doing when you called her?"

"She was in bed."

"Did she sound stressed out or depressed?"

"No, she said she would be more than happy to bring it to me the next morning."

"What did your father tell you regarding your mother's reactions when he told her about the affair?"

"He said they had gone to supper the night before she died; and when he told her that he was having an affair and going to divorce her after Lexi's wedding, she was quite upset."

"Did he say anything about her having an anxiety attack, shaking, or anything?"

"No."

"When you were talking to your mother on the phone about returning the glue pot, did she tell you that your dad had told her about the affair?"

"No."

"Did you talk with your father later on in the week after the taped conversation?"

"Yes, he came to where I worked and admitted to me that he had had an affair, said he told my mom about the affair the evening before her death and that he was going to divorce her."

"Isn't it correct, Ms. Hewitt, that your father had denied the affair to you earlier that same week?"

"Yes."

"Did he mention anything about suicide?"

"Yes. He said he felt that Mom had committed suicide."

"On May 15th, after your mother's death, when you went to the house in Wolsey, do you remember if there was any chocolate milk in the house?"

"I didn't check that day, but I did the next day. There was part of a half gallon, a full gallon, a pint or quart, and a smaller paper carton in the refrigerator."

"Was any of that chocolate milk thrown away?"

"Yes, we threw away the one in the smaller paper carton. It smelled bad, and it was past the due date."

"Thank you, no further questions."

Cross-examine by the Defense

"Ms. Hewitt, did your mother ever express any concerns to you about her work?"

"Yes, she felt there were financial problems at work."

"Was she stressed about them?"

"I would say that she was mildly distressed."

"Did she tell you that they were ready to close the doors at the clinic?"

"Yes, she thought that could be a possibility."

"You said that your mother had an allergy to flour and under certain circumstances flour would make her sneeze. Nonetheless, your mom and dad did have flour in the house. Is that correct?"

"Yes."

"How about baking powder, baking soda, and pancake mix?"

"Yes, all of them."

"Any number of things that would be a white powdery substance, correct?"

"Yes."

"Did your mom bake and use flour?"

"Yes."

"But, if she happened to catch the dust from the flour just right it would send her into a sneezing fit. Correct?"

"Yes."

"Describe your parents' dog for me, would you?"

"She's not real big, but not small, blind in one eye, and she's very hyperactive."

"She's hyperactive?"

"Yes."

"Does your mom use a computer at work?"

"Yes, she does."

"On the morning of your mother's drowning did you notice any damp spots on your father's clothing?"

"He had one damp spot on his knee."

"As though he had knelt on a wet floor?"

"Yes, on one knee."

"You testified that your father told your mother the night before she died that he planned to divorce her after the wedding. Correct?"

"Yes."

"You also testified that before your mother died your father told you that he planned to divorce her. Did you ever discuss that with your mother?"

"No, she was pretty private about those things."

"Your father told you that your mother had started sleepwalking some time in March or April. Would that correspond roughly to the dates that your mother started complaining to Patricia Minor about having difficulty sleeping?"

"Yes."

"Regarding the incident on the staircase, did your mother tell you what she tripped on?"

"No.'

"There has been evidence admitted into this trial regarding pill bottles. Exhibit 3 is a plastic bag full of pill bottles retrieved from your parents' home. Were those the only pill bottles that were in your parents' home?"

"No, I also have a bag of probably twenty to thirty bottles of medications."

"Are they a combination of your mother's and your dad's?"

"I don't know."

"Do you know what your mother's typical position was when she washed her hair?"

"She was usually on her knees, leaning over with her head under the faucets."

"Does it seem logical to you that in the time it took for her to see the lamp falling that she could leap from the tub before it could hit the water?"

"If she was on her knees, yes."

"Ms. Hewitt, you said that you weren't familiar with your father going to the church in the morning. Approximately how many years has it been since you lived with your parents?"

"Fifteen or sixteen years."

"Did you know that it was your parents' practice to go to coffee in the morning before your mother left to go to work in Huron?"

"Yes."

"What time would she arrive at work?"

"8:30 a.m."

"How far is Wolsey from Huron?"

"It's about a twenty minute drive."

"Presumably, she had to leave Wolsey by ten minutes after eight. Correct?"

"Yes."

"Do you have any idea how long they would spend having coffee together in the morning?"

"No, I don't know that."

"Is it correct that your mother would be dressed for work and leave for work from the coffee shop?"

"Yes."

"Ms. Hewitt, do you agree that a wedding doesn't come about without a little bit of nervousness?"

"Yes."

"In fact, your mother may have had a little more reason than normal to be nervous about this upcoming wedding. Correct?"

"I am sure she was."

"I don't have any further questions. Thank you."

Dr. Rick Hensley shares office space with Reed Clinic. He attended Sharon the day Bill brought her to the clinic when she was groggy. Testifying for the State, he states that Sharon responded when spoken to and would answer him, but she didn't know what happened. Bill filled him in on the details, stating that there was some history of sleep apnea, but that was not investigated because of her excessive snoring. A CAT scan was done; they drew blood and did an electrocardiogram, but could not find anything medically wrong with her. A urine toxicology screen was also done, which didn't show any drugs present, but there wasn't a test done for Benadryl.

Cross-examine by the Defense

"Dr. Hensley, I have here a copy of the office note that you dictated on the day Bill brought Sharon to the clinic. You made reference to Sharon consuming Benadryl and codeine. Did you have reason to believe at some point that Sharon was consuming both of those drugs?"

"I was told that both of those drugs were in the medicine cabinet. When she was in her sleepwalking episode, she had been in the medicine cabinet, but exactly what she took was not clear."

"Were the symptoms that you observed in Sharon consistent with someone who had taken too much of one or both of these drugs?"

"Could be, yes."

"No further questions."

Redirect by the State

"Dr. Hensley, does Benadryl come in tablets or capsules?"

"I believe it comes in both."

"No further questions."

Witness for the State – Danielle Guthrie
Questioned by Moore

Danielle, the Guthries' youngest daughter, testifies that she has been away from home approximately two years prior to her mother's death. The relationship with her mother was distant when she was younger, but they had grown closer as she grew older. They would communicate by phone at least once a week and see each other in person at least once a month. She would spend all of her vacations from school at her parents' home in Wolsey. She says that when she was younger, she looked up to her father as a role model; but as she got older and grew closer to her mother, the relationship with him grew distant.

"Ms. Guthrie, what was your father's disposition like when you lived at home?"

"He had a very bad temper. Once, when I was in seventh grade, I went for a walk with a friend and stayed out a little later than I was supposed to. He was worried and looked all over for me. When I came home, he slapped me across the face and knocked me to the ground."

"How often would you contact your father in the months prior to your mother's death?"

"Mostly I called Mom at the clinic, but when I was home I would talk to him quite a bit."

"What was the relationship like between your parents during the years prior to your mother's death?"

"Dad told me several times that he hated Mom. He said she was fat and ugly and disgusted him so much that he couldn't force himself to touch her. He said there were several times that Mom wanted him to hug or kiss her, and he acted as though that was the worst thing possible. He just didn't really have anything to do with her."

"When would he tell you these things?"

"Constantly, since I was in the seventh grade. Whenever we were fishing or going somewhere or at home when my mother was in another room."

"Did he ever talk to you about his divorcing your mother?"

"Yes, the first time was when I was in the seventh grade. I was very upset when he said that, and he told me that I shouldn't feel upset or sad about it. From then on he constantly mentioned it."

"Did you ever talk to your mother about your parents' relationship?"

"Yes, every once in awhile, from seventh grade on."

"Did this continue up until her death?"

"Occasionally ... yes."

"Who would talk about the relationship the most?"

"My father."

"Did your mother ever tell you that she wanted to leave your father or get a divorce?"

"No."

"Why did you leave the house the day of your high school graduation?"

"I wanted to get away from the tension and the problems in the household, but it never got any better."

"Did your mom ever talk to you about suicide?"

"Yes, when I was in the eighth grade after my parents had an argument my dad told me to go talk to my mom. When I spoke to her she said that it was my fault they were having marital problems. She said that when she commuted half an hour to work both ways, there were several times she had thought about driving into the other lane of traffic."

"What did you do after she told you that?"

"Suzanne came the next day to get me and I stayed at her house for awhile. I also went to see my other sister in Oklahoma; then I went back to Suzanne's."

"What happened between you and your father when the two of you were together on a backpacking trip to Wyoming?"

"I was very upset with everything that was happening at home, and I did not want to be on that trip. I refused to speak to my dad the entire time that we were there, which made him very upset. One morning when I woke up, I saw a noose hanging over a tree limb near my tent; and I told him that I wanted to go home. On the ride home I told him that I wanted to go back to Suzanne's. He would never let me use the phone to call her. He would always dial and then tell me that they weren't there. He said if I did not go home with him that he was not going to make it home --- that he would kill himself, so I went home with him."

"When you were living in Nebraska were you aware that your father was having an affair?"

"I knew that Myra loved him and I knew that he loved her as a friend, but I did not allow myself to think that they were having an affair."

"When you lived in Nebraska, your father asked you to lie for him. Tell us what happened."

"There was a rumor that Myra had been at the dog kennel or out in the country with him. He said that if anybody asked me if she was out there that I was to say I was out there and that she had never been out there."

"Did you ever find anything in your parents' house from her?"

"Yes, I found cards and letters."

"Did you ever receive a gift from Myra?"

"I received a graduation present. My father kept it hidden from my mother until I came home. He gave it to me and told me to hide it and not to tell her about it, but I left it out and Mom found it. She was very upset, so she went to my father and asked him why I hadn't told her about the gift. Dad told her that I didn't want to upset her."

"When you moved to Wolsey, did your father go back to Nebraska periodically?"

"Yes, he would go back a couple times a month. As the years went by it was less, but he still went there."

"Did he tell you why he was going back to Nebraska?"

"He said that he was going there to hunt, to continue his education, to conduct church business, to get counseling, and to sell dogs."

"To your knowledge did your mother know about this affair?"

"Mom had strong suspicions, but she stated that she would never know for sure unless she caught them in bed together."

"In the months prior to your mother's death were you aware of any medical problems that your mom was having?"

"She said the doctors told her that she had sleep apnea. I believe that she had a hernia and a recurring cyst on her arm and severe allergies."

"Was your mother allergic to flour?"

"Yes. The flour was always kept in sealed containers. If it was in an open bag, it was put towards the back of the pantry."

"To your knowledge would flour ever be left lying around on the counters?"

"Not to my knowledge."

"Were you aware that your mother was allegedly sleepwalking?"

"Yes, my father told me that she had been sleepwalking for a couple months and that it had something to do with the medicine that she was taking."

"Did your mother ever tell you that she was sleepwalking?"

"She said that my father told her she was sleepwalking."

"In all the years that you lived with your parents, did you ever see your mother sleepwalking?"

"No. The farthest that she would go at night is to the bathroom and back to bed."

"The nights that you slept at your parents' house, did you ever hear your mother in the kitchen?"

"No, but every once in awhile I would hear my dad in the kitchen."

"Ms. Guthrie, when you lived in Nebraska, did you hear the rumors going around about this affair between your father and Myra Conner?"

"Yes."

"Did you ask him about the rumors?"

"He offered a lot of information, so I never had to ask. He said that he was not having an affair with her, that they were just good friends, and he was helping her through a hard time."

"Were you aware of the time that your father went in front of session at the Orleans church?"

"Yes. He had to wait at the manse until they called him, but I was not allowed to go with him. He told me how it was impossible for him to have an affair with Myra because he was impotent. He said that a doctor had signed a paper or written a note about it, but I didn't see the note."

"What did your father tell you about the incident that happened in Lincoln?"

"He said that he had nightmares and couldn't stand to be around my mother because of being raped and that was the reason they had separate beds."

"When you were living at home, what was the normal routine at bedtime?"

"My mother would go to her room somewhere between eight and ten o'clock and would watch television until she fell asleep. My father would stay up until at least midnight watching television in the living room; then he would go to the bedroom, either watch television in the bedroom or go right to sleep."

"What was their morning routine?"

"My mother would get up and get ready for work. My father would stay in bed until she was dressed and then they would go for coffee. After coffee, Mom would go to work and he would go over to the church. Several times I was at the church finishing school work when my dad came in and I was late getting to school."

"Did you ever see your father get up when your mother got up and then go over to the church?"

"I don't recall that ever happening."

"The day of your mother's drowning what did you hear your father telling others regarding what had occurred?"

"I heard him tell several different stories. The first part was always the same --- his going over to the church while Mom was taking a bath. When he came back, he noticed there was water on the floor; so he opened the door and found Mom face first in the water. Then the stories varied from his checking her and calling 911 to taking her head out of the water, getting her out of the tub, and trying to do CPR. It varied from him not doing anything to him trying to save her."

"Was there a computer at the house?"

"Yes, an older one. I'm not real sure, but I don't think it had been used for several years."

"Do you know if the computer in the office at the church had Internet access?"

"Yes, I think it was hooked up in January or February of 1999."

"Did you have the opportunity to use the Internet on that computer?"

"Yes, I would do searches for school papers when I came home from college, and I also used it to e-mail."

"Did you ever do any searches for any kind of drugs or bathtub accidents?"

"No."

"Do you remember the password that your father used to get on the Internet?"

"Yes, it was *tabernacle*."

"When you observed your father using the computer, did he know what he was doing?"

"Yes. During my senior year of high school I had shown him several times how to use the computer that was in my room which is now with me in Brookings."

"Did you ever show your mother on your computer how to use the Internet?"

"I tried, but she didn't really show any interest."

"Did you use the computer in the church office with your mother?"

"Yes, I helped her open a hot mail account and tried to show her how to do searches, but she always relied on me to do those for her."

"Did you ever see her on the computer by herself?"

"Without me being present or without me asking her to go there, no."

"How would you rate her proficiency on using the Internet?"

"Fairly low. She sent me a few e-mails and I think she sent some to my sisters, but they were very few."

"What did your mother use the computer for at work?"

"She used it for insurance claims and financial things. Other than at work she didn't really have any knowledge of the computer."

"In the months prior to her death, did you notice any changes in her, such as being depressed?"

"Only that she was very excited about Lexi's wedding. When I was home she was always showing me what she was going to put on the tables and how she was going to arrange things. She was stressed about work, but she had been stressed about work for several months and things weren't any better or worse than what they had been."

"What incidents were you aware of that happened to your mother in the months prior to her death?"

"I didn't know about the string incident on the stairs, but I was aware of the bathtub incident with the lamp. I also knew about the time that she went to the hospital when she wasn't coherent."

"Did you see your mother the day she wasn't coherent?"

"Yes, I did. I had brought my nephew back to Huron from a concert in Brookings, and I stopped to see her at work. They said that she was having tests done; so I waited for her to return and when I finally saw her she looked like some of the people that you see in a nursing home. She looked like she'd had a stroke or something. Her body was there, but it looked like she wasn't there mentally."

"Who told you what had happened to her?"

"My father told me that he had woke up in the middle of the night and Mom wasn't breathing. He said that he performed CPR on her; and when she started breathing again, they went back to sleep. In the morning he said she got up to get ready for work, said she wasn't feeling well, so he told her that she should stay home from work. He called the clinic to tell them that she wouldn't be coming in, but they said to bring her in, so he took her to the clinic."

"What did your mother tell you about the incident with the lamp falling into the bathtub?"

"She said the lights were not working in the bathroom, and Dad put a lamp in the bathroom so she could take a bath and wash her hair. The lamp fell into the tub, and Dad caught it right before it hit the water. She jumped out of the tub, and he walked out of the bathroom. Then he fainted and she called 911."

"What did your father tell you?"

"He said he went into the bathroom to talk to Mom when she was taking a bath, and their dog Lady came in and knocked the lamp over. He said he caught the lamp before it hit the water or right when it hit the water; then when he went out into the hallway he fainted, then went to the hospital."

"When was the last time that you saw your mother alive?"

"On Mother's Day, the weekend before she died."

May 9, 1999, Sunday church services are about to begin at the Wolsey Presbyterian Church. There is a fan at the front of the church circulating the air and making faint clicking noises, as if rebelling.

Dr. Bill Guthrie and his wife portray an outstanding couple, as he escorts her down the center aisle. Mrs. Guthrie, dressed in a black dress trimmed with a white collar, compliments Dr. Bill's black suit and tie and white shirt. Sharon's short medium brown hair is very stylish with lots of curls. Dr. Bill's hair, which he usually keeps colored, exhibits a hint of graying around the ears.

They pause at the third set of pews from the front of the church. Sharon sits down and Dr. Bill proceeds to the lectern.

Several members of the congregation are a bit stunned as they witness Dr. Bill escort Sharon to her pew. Normally she seats herself after he is at the lectern, but being it's Mother's Day, they conclude that it's an admirable gesture.

Dr. Bill, now having reached the lectern, picks up a mobile microphone from a shelf under the lectern. The cord is tangled slightly. With hands trembling, he proceeds to straighten it, and then attaches the microphone to his shirt. He opens a Bible lying on the lectern. Noticing that the Bible is upside down, he picks it up, slowly turns it around, and lays it back down. He then opens the church bulletin, also lying on the lectern. With his head down, hands resting, one on each the side of the lectern, he slowly taps his fingers, one at a time, as if impatient for the pianist to finish.

"Good morning!" Dr. Bills shouts in a boisterous voice as the music ends. "Happy Mother's Day. The children will be on the hot seat this morning." Pausing for a second, he looks around; then loudly states, "And believe me --- I can do it!" He chuckles. Laughter erupts from the pews.

"I'd like to call your attention to today, not only being Mother's Day, but it is also Confirmation Sunday. We have eight young people here who are going to be confirmed during --- during Sunday School --- ah --- during church, dah, da dat, dah, dah … " The congregation explodes with laughter at his error. " … and we are glad that they are here."

As Dr. Bill reads the announcements, regarding upcoming church events, at times he seems somewhat confused. With the assistance of members of the congregation, which is fairly common in a small church, he manages to finish; then leads the congregation in the Call to Worship printed in the bulletin.

Quietly and more subdued, he looks down at his notes and speaks a prayer of confession. "Heavenly Father, we look to your word. And in it, we find that you forgive us of our sin. As far as the east is from the west, so far you have removed our sin from us. Amen."

Before speaking again, a frown appears on his face, and he pauses. Then in a very loud disgruntled voice, he shouts loud enough to wake the dead, "How many of you watched the movie *NOAH'S ARK* this past week?"

Pausing again, he tones down the volume of his voice, but with authority continues, "That was the most pathetic piece of material I have ever seen in my life. When people take license like that, they view things that are very reprehensible to our concern because they confuse our children. And when they confuse our children they've damaged us! And that's exactly what that piece of trash did."

Dr. Bill pauses. Much more in control now he reads the scriptures, then asks that the young people come forward for the children's sermon. As the young children proceed to the front of the church, he seats himself behind the lectern.

Mrs. Guthrie rises from her pew, steps forward, and removes the microphone stationed on the lectern. She sits down on the top step as six children gather around her. Using a puppet she has with her to portray her message to the children she tells the children that Lambchop needs to tell his parents what he wants, such as a hug.

"How many of you have told your mom Happy Mother's Day this morning?" she asks.

One child raises her hand.

"How many of you have already been in trouble this morning?" she asks.

Heads down, three children raise their hands. Behind the lectern, Dr. Bill's hand appears. The congregation laughs.

Sharon becomes very serious. "This morning I want to tell you about an ordinary lady that would get up every Sunday morning, help her children get dressed, take them by their hands, and walk them to Sunday school. She would drop them off at their classrooms, and then go into her own classroom to teach Sunday school. She would then go with them to church services and then walk them home. She worked the other days of the week, so Sunday was their time together.

"The day came when she had to find a new job, which was cleaning motel rooms. Her job required her to work on Sundays. She told her boss that it wouldn't work because she had to teach her Sunday school class. Her job was about twelve blocks from the church, but she would get up, get her family ready, put dinner in the oven for her family, walk to work, and then she would leave work long enough to teach Sunday School. She walked the twelve blocks, was never late for Sunday school, and then would walk the twelve blocks back to work. She loved God and her family so much that she wanted to be with them for Sunday school.

"This lady that I am talking about was my mom. She gave me the greatest gift of taking me to church and to Sunday school. I want you to respect your mothers whether you are just a youngster or in junior high or even in high school."

Sharon smiles as she produces a small bag. The children already know that there is something in the bag for them because she always gives them a small gift to take home.

"I have a rubber ball for each of you today, but if you play with it in church, your mothers are going to be after me," she proclaims. The children and the congregation join together in laughter. "Remember, when you look at your ball, that no matter what happens in your life, God will be with you, and you will bounce back."

Mrs. Guthrie ends with a prayer, then hands each child a piece of candy as they rise from the floor. She tells them to find a mother that does not have her children here with her today, or a grandmother, or anyone else, and give them a special hug.

"Also," she quickly adds, "when you get back to your seat, I want you to give your mom a big hug." Sharon rises, places the microphone back in the holder on the lectern and retreats to her seat.

Dr. Bill, now facing the congregation, begins, "When I was in high school, I went with my girlfriend to her church. Her pastor didn't even open the Bible. All he did was take the newspaper and read the headlines. Well, I've already done more than that because I have read to you from Proverbs, and I am not going to read to you from the newspaper --- I'm going to read to you from the funny papers." Holding the folded paper high in the air, Dr. Bill waits for the laughter to subside, then opens up the paper, and explains one of the comics. There's a little boy named Billy and another little boy named Joseph. Billy has drawn this card and he's taking flowers to his mother. The card says, Happy Mother's Day. Love, and kisses, Billy. Joseph says, 'That's a nice card, Billy, do you want to see mine? It says Happy Mother's Day to my mom. I love you very, very, very, very, very, very, very, very much!' It was signed Joseph and he added lots of X's and O's. Billy asks, 'Why all the **very's**?' Joseph says, 'Cause she's very special to me … I'm adopted.'

"When I looked at this, I was looking for an introduction to my message this morning because it's about a mother who was a slave, and during that time the number of her people grew to such a great number that it scared the Pharaoh. In fact, it scared him so much that he ordered all the male children a certain age and under to be killed.

"This mother could not stand this kind of loss, so she hid her child in such a way that no one could find him. As the child grew, and as the child began to cry louder, she knew she had to do something, so she made an ark out of bulrushes and covered it with tar. She placed her baby in the ark and set the child adrift. She didn't just put it anywhere; she put it adrift where she knew the Pharaoh's daughter would find it. She put it in the water at just the right time. What a coincidence! God was working through all of this. Pharaoh's daughter was looking for someone to nurse the baby and her sister said she knew of someone. The mother that had given up her baby was able to receive him back for a period of time to nurture him, until she was dismissed.

"Now this mother didn't know the overall picture of where this child was going or what this child would become. But she knew in her heart that this child was special. For forty years, this child grew up with the greatest instruction in the world, and yet the goodness that was in his heart didn't come through the Pharaoh's family, but it came through his mother's. As he was walking one day, he saw the monstrous things that were being done to the slaves, so he killed the man that was abusing the slaves. He was sent into exile for another forty years, but during that period of forty years --- guess what? He learned who God was. When he went on the mountain, God spoke to him three times."

Dr. Bill hesitates for a moment. His voice becomes very boisterous. "WIVES! Have you ever had to tell your husbands more than three times that you have something that needs to be done?" He pauses. His voice becomes more restrained. "This is a typical male. I know - it happens to me. My wife tells me to do something, and maybe after the thirteenth or the fourteenth time, it sinks in. And if after a little anger … anger on her part, I realize, hey --- this better be done! And so the job gets done," he adds, chuckling. "It's not just a male thing ladies. We are not going to pick on you today because you are moms.

"I think about my childhood --- I think about my mom a lot. I love her a lot. She's been a tremendous inspiration to me. When I was struggling in Bible College, my mom would always send a little help. And that help was a sacrifice, but I know she did it because she loved me. She saw me through my graduate college --- my graduate school. I couldn't afford to go, but she paid my tuition. I've never said this about her before, but she was a tremendous help to me. You know, some people say that everything they are and everything they will be, they owe it their mother. Well … this is very true.

"You know, I had a father, that if he were here in this present day and if I went to school with some of the marks he left on me, he would probably be called a child abuser." Dr. Bill pauses for a moment, then speaks in a loud robust voice, "BUT, I would never, never call him that! NEVER!"

Dr. Bill becomes more restrained, but only for a moment. With one finger pointing at the congregation and shaking, he begins to talk very fast. "Every single time I got it, I deserved it. Every time I went to school my father said, *'You get spanked at school you can just expect to get it back when you get home. If you don't get it back when you get home, and when I do find out about it you'll get it even worse. So if you get it in school you'd better come home and tell me you got it because if I find it out some other way you'll get it worse.'* That's the way I went to school."

Dr. Bill pauses and becomes more serene. "Sharon has told me that when she was growing up, her father's favorite instrument of corporal punishment was the razor strap. How many of you have ever had the razor strap?" Hands rise in the congregation.

"Yardstick?" Hands go up.

"Switch?" A few hands rise.

"Ping-Pong paddle?" No hands rise.

"Wooden spoons?" Several hands rise.

"Did your generation of children ever kill children? Not mine --- not yours. Do you know what's happening in this country? Nothing! That's just it ... nothing! Superintendents in schools are scared of children, teachers are scared of children, and parents are scared of children. You know why?" He pauses. "Because everything is really messed up."

Dr. Bill pauses again, then continues. "I know there are children who have been abused. There's a very thin line between abuse and correction. I will stand behind any child if that line has been crossed, and I have. But, I'll always stand behind the parents' right to discipline. We --- must --- have --- the --- right to correct children ... not abuse them!

"I took a guy to blows one time because he abused his child. I'm not proud of it, but I'll stand behind our right to correct because I think our world is in dire need of correction ... in dire need of discipline. Not abuse ... discipline.

"Any child that I have in confirmation class, I can see if they are disciplined. You know the scripture says to honor your father and your mother. It doesn't say *maybe* --- it doesn't say *perhaps*. That doesn't mean talking back to them, that doesn't mean screaming back to them. That means listening to them and honoring what they have to say.

"Do you think that my father was always right? NO, SIR! Did I think he was always right? I had better." Dr. Bill smiles as he waits for the congregation's laughter to subside, then continues.

"My father's gone now, and there's no man that I adored on the face of the earth more. There's a couple of times when I know I got it when I didn't ask for it. You know what happened in school? I got into trouble twice and one time he never did find out. The teacher reprimanded me by slapping my hands with a ruler. I didn't say anything to my father because I didn't want any consequences at home --- I'd had enough already.

"Sometime down the line we have to pull things back together again. We have to have the respect, but we must also warrant that respect.

"We have a class with us here today that we are going to conform --- confirm them." The class joins him up front as the congregation chuckles at his error. "These eight young people that I present to you for confirmation will lead us in the Apostles' Creed."

Dr. Bill asks the class to recite the books of the New Testament in unison. When they finish, he goes to each one individually, places one arm around them, and holds one of their hands. "Do you believe in Jesus Christ, Son of God, and take Him as your personal Savior?"

Each answers, "I do."

Dr. Bill approaches his grandson and gives him a good squeeze. "This is kind of the pride in our house and he's also ... I'm not going to say it." Derrik blushes as everyone chuckles.

"Before you sit down, class, being today is Mother's Day, you are not going to be conformed --- confirmed until you give your mothers a kiss." Dr. Bill points his finger sternly towards the congregation. The class depart to the pews to find their mothers.

Dr. Bill walks to a pew where his mother is sitting, gives her a kiss, then joins the class who is again at the front of the church.

"You know, our mothers have done a lot of things for us, and our wives have done a lot of things for us, and ah, --- my wife has not always been thanked as much as she should be." Dr. Bill walks to the pew where Sharon is sitting. "The only time I have kissed her in church was when I married her." He chuckles, then leans over, and gives her a quick kiss, then walks back to the front to join the class.

"I present to you this class with pride. I hope that they will live up to their responsibilities, stay true to the church, stay true to each other, and stand up for one another when one is being chastised in school by others. We've made a special covenant.

"This class has reached a high of joy and irritation," smiles Dr. Bill, "but they all have learned the lessons and have done it with pride." He gives each of the class a Presbyterian cross, then presents one classmate with a special award. The students walk to the pews and sit with their families.

The offering is taken, the Lord's Prayer and the benediction are spoken, and the last hymn is sung. Dr. Bill takes off his microphone, leaves the lectern to meet up with Sharon, and escorts her down the aisle of the church. The congregation follows behind.

"Ms. Guthrie, during Mother's Day weekend, did your father tell you that he was having trouble sleeping?"

"No."

"Did he ever tell you that?"

"No."

"Did you witness him sleeping on Mother's Day weekend?"

"He had a habit of sleeping in his chair in the living room, but that weekend the normal routine had changed. Dad went back to his room earlier to go to sleep, while my mom stayed in the living room with me."

"Do you remember if your father got up in the morning and went over to the church to do prayers and devotions when you were home on Mother's Day weekend?"

"I don't recall him doing that."

"Did your father talk to you that weekend about divorcing your mother?"

"Yes, when we were alone, he told me that he was going to get a divorce after the wedding because he didn't want to upset Lexi's wedding."

"I have no further questions. Thank you."

Cross-examine by the Defense

"Ms. Guthrie, would you say it's fair to state that your mother was prone to being melodramatic?"

"Yes."

"Did you ever talk about the affair with your mother?"

"Occasionally. She would get very upset whenever Myra's name was brought up and would often comment about how much she disliked her."

"You stated that on Mother's Day weekend that your father told you he was going to divorce your mother. Assuming that he told her he wanted a divorce, wouldn't that have been something quite upsetting to her?"

"I think that would be upsetting to anyone ... yes."

"Referring to the incident in Orleans when your parents had a fight, what would your mother do when there was a fight or disagreement?"

"At the end of the fight she would get to the point in the argument where the argument couldn't go any further, so she would usually get in her car and drive away."

"Did you talk to her after this particular argument?"

"Yes, right after. My dad told me to go upstairs and talk to her."

"So, is it correct at least that time, there were some hard feelings expressed by your mother?"

"Yes."

"Is it correct that the comment made by your mother to you when you lived in Orleans was along the lines of --- there are times when I'm driving to or from work when I just think about driving into the oncoming traffic?"

"Yes."

"Is it correct that your mother wasn't threatening you with suicide trying to get you to do something, but was saying this is how she felt sometimes?"

"To understand how my family was I would have to explain the context."

"Ms. Guthrie, was your mother trying to get you to do something?"

"She was trying to lay a guilt factor on me."

"Wasn't she saying, 'if you don't do this right now, I'm going to kill myself'?"

"No."

"Have you lived with your parents since you graduated from high school?"

"No."

"Did you use the bathroom closest to your bedroom when you lived at home?"

"Yes."

"Did your mother keep her things in that bathroom also?"

"Things that she used for her hair she kept in my bathroom."

"What items did your mother keep in the bathroom located off your parents' bedroom?"

"Mainly things for bathing."

"Did the bathroom off your parents' bedroom have a tub/shower enclosure?"

"Yes."

"Were you familiar with your mother washing her hair on her knees and holding her head under the faucet?"

"Mom preferred baths to showers, and as far as I knew, that's the way she was raised."

"Would it be fair to say, Ms. Guthrie, according to your observations, that your parents' relationship deteriorated after you left home?"

"Yes."

"You stated that when you were at home your mom would not sleepwalk, but would get up at night and go to the bathroom. Which bathroom would she use?"

"The bathroom closest to my parents' bedroom."

"Approximately what time would your parents leave for coffee in the morning?"

"I would say sometime after seven thirty."

"What time would your mother routinely get up in the morning when she was working?"

"About seven, seven-fifteen --- sometime in there."

"She didn't spend much time getting ready for work before she left, did she?"

"No."

"Do I understand correctly, that after you left home there was still a computer in your parents' house that didn't work?"

"It worked, but they didn't use it."

"Do you think they would have used it for writing letters or anything of that nature?'

"Not that I am aware of. My nieces and nephew basically used it to play solitaire."

"You testified that your mother did have some interest in utilizing the Internet and you tried to teach her how to do searches, but didn't have much luck. Did you try to teach her more than once on the computer over at the church?"

"Initially it was on my computer in my room and the second time it was the one in the office."

"Ms. Guthrie, regarding the fact that your mother did know how to use e-mail and would e-mail you, do you know if that e-mail would have originated from work or the church?"

"From the church."

"No further questions."

Witness for the State – Larry Provance
Questioned by Moore

Sharon's brother states that he and his wife were in Wolsey to see Sharon and Bill only one time, but would take mini vacations with them, along with his sister and her husband. He said that he normally communicated with Sharon quite often, but the communication had occurred more frequently regarding the plans for Lexi's wedding.

"Mr. Provance, did Sharon tell you about any medical problems that she was having?"

"She told me that they thought she might have sleep apnea like I had. When I told her that I didn't have sleep apnea, she was surprised. We talked about my blood pressure problems, and I told her that mine was under control. She said that her blood pressure was also under control, but her allergies seemed to cause her the biggest problems."

"Did she talk to you about her sleeping problems?"

"She said Bill kept telling her that she was sleepwalking and wasn't resting well, but she couldn't remember any of that."

"Mr. Provance, do you remember having any episodes with sleepwalking?'

"Everybody tells me that I used to sleepwalk when I was six or seven years old, but I don't remember sleepwalking in my adult life."

"Were you aware of any of the incidents that took place prior to Sharon's death?"

"She mentioned the string incident to me and called my sister to tell her about the lamp in the bathtub. I called her as soon as I found out about it."

"So, Sharon kept you pretty much informed of what was going on?"

"Yes."

"When you were at the house in Wolsey, did you hear the defendant talking about what happened to Sharon?"

"Yes, he received a lot of phone calls. I could hear him explain to each caller what had happened, and it seemed like with every phone call the story changed a little bit. The details seemed to change back and forth like it was a different story."

"What part of the story seemed to change in particular?"

"How he found her, what he did, where the water was, that he took her out of the tub, that he couldn't get her out of the tub."

"Did the defendant at any time say that there was water running down the steps?"

"Yes."

"Mr. Provance, what happened on Sunday, the day after Sharon's death?"

After spending Saturday night in Huron at a motel, Larry, Thelma, Bonnie, and Vic drive to Wolsey to attend church services. They stop at the manse and invite Bill to go with them. Bill says that he doesn't want to go ... that he doesn't feel like seeing people.

"We can sit in the back of the church and leave before anyone notices," prompts Larry.

"I don't think so," Bill replies. Then unexpectedly, without taking a breath, he adds, "Oh, all right." He leaves the foursome sitting in the living room and retreats to his bedroom to change into church clothes.

The five walk next door to the church and seat themselves in the back row. Bill, sitting beside Larry, rests his head on Larry's shoulder throughout the hour and from time to time, Larry hears Bill whimpering.

The organist begins to play the last hymn. Not sure if Bill is listening, Larry leans over and whispers, "Bill, the last song is being played. We should leave now if you want to beat the crowd."

Bill hesitates for a time and mutters something, which Larry can't hear. As the end of the hymn approaches, Bill suddenly shoots out of the pew like a bullet and walks briskly down the aisle to the front of the church. Now, very composed, Bill faces the congregation, pulls out a piece of paper from his suit pocket, and begins to read a letter regarding Sharon's accident.

Larry, having the distinct impression that Bill didn't want to talk to anyone, is totally stunned. "What gives?" He listens as Bill finishes the letter, then watches him walk back down the aisle to join them again. As they leave the church, Larry notices that Bill is again crying and whimpering.

"Mr. Provance, at the house after church services there was some discussion among the family members regarding having an autopsy done on Sharon. What was the defendant's reaction?"

"Bill was against it. Said that he couldn't afford to have one done. Later, law enforcement ordered an autopsy done."

"At the funeral did Bill tell you that the reason for Sharon drowning in the bathtub was due to a large amount of Temazepam in her system?"

"No, he never mentioned it. I found this out through conversations with other people."

"One thing that stayed consistent in the defendant's story was that he had gotten up and gone over to the church to do his prayers and devotions. Mr. Provance, had you ever witnessed him doing that?"

"No, I did not."

"When you were with the defendant and Sharon, what would you witness as their morning routine?"

"If they were at our house or if we were at their house, Sharon would be up doing her things in the morning and Bill would still be in bed."

"Mr. Provance, what did you do when you found out that the large amount of Temazepam found in Sharon's system was a medication prescribed for the defendant?"

"I felt as if I was not getting the whole story. There were a lot of unanswered questions, so on August 22nd, Jack, a neighbor of mine, rode with me to Wolsey to confront Bill. I was not sure if Bill would let me in the house, so I sent Jack to the door ahead of me."

"Please tell us what happened that day."

Bill hears a knock at the door. "Hang on. I have somebody at my door," he tells the caller on the phone, then grabs the handle and swings open the door. "Hi, can I help you?"

"I have someone here who wants to see you," Jack replies and moves aside.

Larry steps into view. "Hello, Bill."

Bill's face pales as he motions them in. "Be with you in a second… I have someone on the phone." He walks into another room, bids the caller goodbye, and then joins his guests in the living room. Bill points to the couch for them to be seated.

Larry introduces Jack to Bill. "We need to talk," Larry says. "There are just too many changes in your story about Sharon's death."

"Whaatt … doo … you mean?" Stammers Bill.

"When I was here for Sharon's funeral I overheard you say several different things to lots of people on the phone about her death."

"I didn't do anything to Sharon," Bill begins rattling. "You know --- I found her --- I went over to the church --- came back and found her in the bathtub."

"What about this business of the affair?" Larry asks.

"What do you mean?" Bill wrings his hands and looks away from Larry.

"I mean the affair with that woman in Nebraska." Larry answers sternly.

"Oh that. Yes, I did have an affair."

Larry, attempting to hide his anger, takes a deep breath. "Did Sharon know about this affair?"

"We talked about it in March."

"Bill, what happened in Lincoln?"

"How do you know about that?" Bill asks in surprise.

"I know about the incident, Bill. What happened?"

Bill rises from his chair and begins pacing back and forth. "I don't want to talk about it."

"Did you call 911 after that happened in Lincoln?"

Bill hangs his head and pauses for a time. "Yes, but the lady laughed at me, so I hung up and went back to Orleans."

"Do you know that they keep a recording of 911 calls, Bill? Did you ever talk to anyone in law enforcement?"

"A lady."

"Why do you think that Sharon was suicidal?"

"Everybody knew that."

Larry's voice rises. "Tell me somebody that does know?"

Bill becomes silent and doesn't respond.

"What's the deal with these pills that Sharon took?" Larry asks.

"They were Sharon's *happy pills.*"

"That's not what they were --- they were sleeping pills."

"Larry, I picked up those pills for her for over three years. I didn't know they were sleeping pills --- I thought they were her *happy pills.*"

"You signed for those sleeping pills."

"So ... I always signed for Sharon's pills."

"How about the lost prescription, Bill?"

"Sharon must have found it and filled it."

"Why did you guys need sleeping pills?"

"There were difficult things going on."

"Like the affair?"

"No --- other things."

"When did Sharon take those sleeping pills?"

"The Thursday night before ..."

"On May 13th, Bill?"

"Yes."

"How many did she take?"

"One."

"How about the night when she was getting up and taking pills?'

"She got up during the night and took them."

"Bill, you just said that the usual thing to do was take one before you went to bed."

"Well, she ..."

"Are you going to change the story again? Bill, tell me about the lamp incident."

"I was in the bathtub and Sharon was leaning over the side of the tub. We were having an evening of washing her hair. Things were going good --- we were having an evening together."

"What did you tell Don Perry?"

"I don't remember what I told him."

"Thank you, Mr. Provance, I have no further questions."

Cross-examine by the Defense

"Mr. Provance, did you sleepwalk as a child?"

"That's what I've been told, but I don't remember."

"So, if Sharon was sleepwalking, wouldn't it certainly make sense that she couldn't remember it?"

"Yes."

"You wouldn't be sleepwalking, Mr. Provance, if you remembered it and were awake, correct?"

"Right."

"Did Sharon tell you about her heart racing when she went to bed, that she wore a Holter monitor first and later an event monitor and that neither of those devices detected any abnormalities with her heartbeat, even when she sensed there was a problem?"

"Yes."

"You stated that you didn't remember Bill and Sharon's morning routine the way Bill described it. When was the last time you stayed at Bill and Sharon's house?"

"A year prior to Sharon's death."

"How long did you stay there?"

"Probably two or three nights."

"Was that over a weekend?"

"Yes."

"Presuming that Sharon wasn't working, it would make sense that their weekend routine would be different than their weekday routine, correct?"

"Correct."

"What time of day would you usually call Sharon?"

"In the early morning around six thirty."

"There was earlier testimony that Sharon didn't get up until seven or even closer to seven thirty. Would that be incorrect then?"

"I don't know. Anyhow, I would talk to her before I went to work."

"Mr. Provance, was it your impression that Sharon was already awake when you called --- that you weren't waking her up?"

"Yes."

"I have no further questions, Your Honor."

Redirect by the State

"Other than the months prior to Sharon's death, Mr. Provance, had you ever heard about Sharon's sleepwalking?"

"No."

"Had you ever observed her sleepwalking?"

"No."

"I have no further questions, Your Honor."

Redirect by the Defense

"Isn't it correct, Mr. Provance, that approximately two months prior to her death was when Sharon started complaining to Patricia Minor that she was having difficulty getting to sleep?"

"I understood that Bill was telling Sharon that she was sleep walking."

"We will let the jury remember what they think Patricia Minor's testimony was. No more questions, Your Honor."

Witness for the State – DCI Agent Jerry Lindberg Questioned by Moore

"What was Sharon's position in the tub?"

"According to Nancy Holst, Sharon was face up with her head at the faucet end of the bathtub."

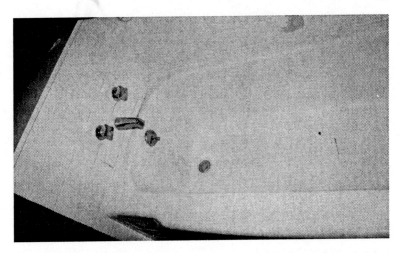

"How did you find out that the defendant was having an affair?"

"Basically, I was just doing a normal background check to find out if Mr. Guthrie had a criminal record. I talked to a dispatcher from a nearby community in Nebraska where the Guthries had lived. It was gossip, but she relayed it to me as a possibility and gave me the individual's name as being Myra Conner."

"What did you find out when you interviewed Ms. Conner?"

"She admitted that she had been involved with Mr. Guthrie."

"Who told you what had transpired that morning and how Sharon came to be in the bathtub?"

"We talked with Suzanne Hewitt. Her story was quite different from what the first responders had told us. She said that her father told her he found her mother in the tub, that he pulled her out of the tub and attempted to do CPR."

"Agent Lindberg, what did you do when you received the information on May 17th that Sharon had a large amount of a controlled drug called Temazepam in her system?"

"I found out that the Temazepam was prescribed for William Guthrie, so I obtained records of where the prescriptions were picked up, how many were filled, on what dates, and who had signed for them."

"Was the area between the vanity and the bathtub in the bathroom where Sharon was found a tight area?"

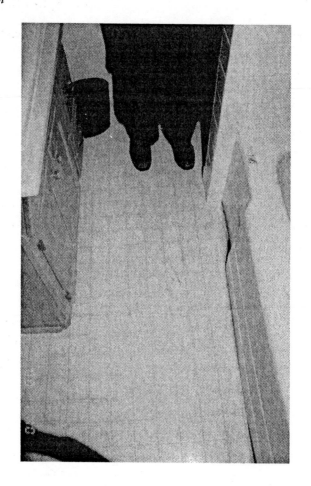

"Yes, very tight."

"Do you remember how many lights there were in the bathroom?"

"There were two fluorescent lights on either side of the bathroom cabinet mirror."

"Was there an outlet in that bathroom?"

"Yes, as you faced the sink, there was one attached to the underside of the medicine cabinet."

"When these photographs of the Guthrie bathroom were taken on Monday of this week, is it correct that this bathroom is the same as during the time of the search, but only minus a few items?"

"Yes, it is."

"What did the defendant tell you when you interviewed him on June 9th regarding Sharon's sleepwalking incident?"

"He said there were three glasses of chocolate milk and that she must have gone to the kitchen during the night to get a drink or something, and he just couldn't get her awake the next morning."

"What did the defendant tell you that he saw the next morning in the bedroom?"

"He said there were five empty Benadryl bottles beside the bed on the nightstand. He said that she was kind of hooked on Benadryl; and he had tried to get her to leave it alone, but she kept taking it. When he tried to hide the Benadryl from Sharon, she would get irritated and go buy another bottle."

"Agent Lindberg, what did the defendant tell you regarding the night before Sharon's death?"

"He said that Sharon had been having anxiety attacks and she had a really bad one. She was having pain in her chest and down her left arm and was shaking. He asked her if it was severe enough to go to the hospital and they decided it wasn't, so they went to sleep. He also added that he really slept hard that night."

"After the defendant made the statement that he was sleeping hard, did he tell you that he did notice Sharon getting up during the night?"

"He said he assumed that she had gotten up during the night when he noticed four or five red glasses on the nightstand."

"Did you specifically ask him about his morning routine?"

"He said his regimen in the morning was to get up and go to his office at the church to do prayers and devotions, so Sharon would have time to take her bath; then he would get in the bathtub and take his bath."

"What did he tell you regarding the morning of the drowning?"

"He said that he came in and noticed the carpet was a little wet, then he broke down momentarily, but went on to say that he opened the door and found her lying down in the water. He said he got her out of the water as best he could and tried to get as much water out of her as best he could and then called 911 as soon as possible. That's basically the way he put it."

"Agent Lindberg, did the defendant tell you that he wasn't able to get her out of the bathtub?"

"He said he tried to get her out; but she was too heavy, so he couldn't."

"Did you ask the defendant what Sharon drank when she took her medications?"

"He said that she took her medications with chocolate milk."

"Did you ask him what medications he was taking?"

"He said Toradol, Tylenol 2 or 3 with codeine, a muscle relaxer. He said that Dr. Reed had prescribed a sleeping pill to help him sleep because of some past problems, but didn't know the name of it."

"Was there any discussion regarding suicide?"

"He said that as far as he knew Sharon had never tried, but she did threaten suicide about four years ago when they lived in Orleans."

"What did the defendant say when you asked him about the affair with Myra Conner?"

"At first he indicated that he was only involved in counseling her; and when she would come to his office for counseling, he would leave the office door open. When he said that he never touched Ms. Conner, I told him there were some lively rumors. Then he admitted to the affair, but said that it happened three years ago. He said that it was a sexual relationship and that the last time he saw Ms. Conner was in January of 1999."

"Did you ask the defendant if Sharon was aware of his affair?"

"He said that she was aware of the affair. When I asked him if this was recent information that his wife had just discovered, he answered no."

"Did you ask him if Sharon had made suicide threats as a result of this news?"

"He said that he thought she did. I asked him to give me some idea of what she said or did. Sharon told him if it wasn't resolved that she was going to do something about it. I then asked him if he was trying to tell us that Sharon was going to take her life if he didn't stop and he said yes."

"Did you ask the defendant if he had been in contact with Ms. Conner since Sharon's death?"

"He said she called him when she learned of Sharon's death."

"What did the defendant say regarding the night that Sharon quit breathing?"

"I asked him if he was trained in CPR and he said no. He said he started hollering at her and she took a breath."

"What did he say when you asked him about the string incident?"

"He said that there wasn't any string across the staircase, that she had tripped on her own shoe lace, and he had grabbed her."

"Did you ask him about any specific drugs that were found in the house?"

"We asked him what the Prilosec was for, and he said it was for his stomach, that he had an ulcer. When we asked him about the Biaxin, he said it was an antibiotic and was prescribed for him by a Dr. James."

"What was his reaction when you told him that you were going to Nebraska to check his story?"

"He again mentioned that the last time he had seen Myra Conner was at the end of January."

"Did the defendant tell you that he had also seen her in late February or early March?"

"By the time we finished the interview, I had the distinct impression that he had seen her the end of January or first part of February for the last time."

"Is that what he told you?"

"Yes."

"I have no further questions."

Cross-examine by the Defense

"Agent Lindberg, is it correct that you never started interviewing or doing any other investigation until May 17th, three days after the drowning incident?"

"Yes, that's correct."

"Is it also correct that you never went to the Guthrie residence to look for any evidence until the end of July, even though by Saturday, May 15th, at least some authorities knew that there was a drug overdose involved?"

"That's correct."

"Did Mr. Perry tell you that he had contacted a law enforcement officer in Lincoln, Nebraska?"

"Yes, he did."

"In your interview with him, did he twice refer to this officer as Chief Crosby?"

"Yes."

"When Mr. Perry testified earlier, he referred to a Chief Cassidy in Lincoln, Nebraska. Did you ever mention the name Cassidy to him that you can recall?"

"I may have --- I don't know. I only spoke with Mr. Perry once on the phone and once in person."

"Is it correct that Mr. Perry used the name Crosby, not Cassidy?"

"Yes, he did."

"I have here Sharon's death certificate. Is this the original death certificate?"

"I guess it is --- yes."

"Is this something that you include as part of your report?"

"Yes."

"Agent Lindberg, I'm not sure that I understand your earlier testimony. Your investigation determined that Bill Guthrie had obtained a written prescription for Temazepam from Patricia Minor, a physician's assistant at Reed Clinic. Is this correct?"

"My understanding is that the defendant had a prescription and he had his wife ask for another one saying that he had lost the original one and the second one was issued to another pharmacy, so he was able to obtain four bottles of medication instead of two. His wife picked up one and he picked up three."

"Did you know that the original prescription was written for sixty pills, one bottle of fifteen pills, plus three refills?"

"No, I didn't know that."

"Agent Lindberg, you said that Bill asked Sharon to have another prescription issued. I believe that's a fair way of stating what you just said, isn't it?"

"Yes. I was told that he called her, said that he lost the prescription, and asked her to go to the physician's assistant and get another prescription. She was able to obtain a second one --- which I believe was called I in to Statz Drug."

"In other words wouldn't it be fair to say that Sharon Guthrie caused this second prescription to be issued?"

"That would certainly be fair, but there is no way to know."

"In fact, assuming that Bill already had one prescription for sixty pills, in essence one bottle with fifteen pills in it plus three refills, he already had access to sixty pills, right?"

"I thought the prescription was for one refill of fifteen, so he got thirty at each place."

"Okay, Agent Lindberg, we will let the jury rely on their recollection of Patricia Minor's testimony. Regarding the photographs of the bathroom that you took on Monday of this week, do you have any idea what the bathroom looked like on May 14th?"

"I assume that it was very similar except for what might have been removed. I understand there was a plant stand in there at the time."

"So there's really no way of knowing because there wasn't any physical evidence gathered on May 14th was there, Agent Lindberg?"

"No."

"How about on the 15th?"

"No."

"Isn't it a fact that there wasn't any physical evidence gathered in the months after Sharon's death until you executed the search warrant in July?"

"Correct."

"Did Bill tell you that when he left the house to go over to the church for his morning devotionals that Sharon was in the bathtub with the water running?"

"He said the water was running, but I don't recall if he said that Sharon was in it."

"Did you do some investigating in the bathroom regarding how long it took for the tub to fill?"

"Yes, I did."

"How long was Bill gone?"

"Approximately ten minutes."

"Mr. Lindberg, how long did it take you to fill the tub when you did your experiment?"

"If there is no one in it and mixing the waters together so that you have a temperature that you can stand or sit in, it takes about eleven minutes for it to overflow. If you add a person to that equation it would overflow much faster."

"Would the bathtub overflow faster if a large person was in it?"

"Yes."

"Did you also check to see how long it would take to drain the water from the tub?"

"Yes, I did. According to my notes, two minutes, forty-five seconds."

"So, in July the water drained quite quickly. Is there anyway of knowing how quickly it would have drained in May?"

"No."

"Basically because nobody bothered to check --- correct?"

"No."

"I have a photo here that shows the lever that is pulled up to drain the bathtub. If someone was going to reach in to drain the water from the tub, would he get all wet while doing that?"

"I assume not."

"Going back to how quickly the tub filled, Bill's statement to you was that it filled to overflowing in the time that he was gone to the church. Is this consistent with what you found?"

"Yes."

"Thank you. I have no further questions."

Redirect by the State

"Agent Lindberg, I have here a certified copy of the death certificate of Sharon Guthrie where it says amended at the top. What is the date that it was amended?"

"June 14, 1999."

"Did you ask the defendant where he had worked previously?"

"He said that he had worked in security and also for the Sinclair Sheriff's department in Carbon County as a deputy."

"Did you attempt to verify that information?"

"Yes, we contacted authorities in Carbon County, Wyoming. There wasn't any record of his employment as an officer."

"I have no further questions."

January 18, 2000

Trial Day Four

Witness for the State – Dr. Alan Berman
Questioned by Moore

Dr. Berman, a clinical psychologist, has a practice in Washington, D.C. He is also the Executive Director of the American Association of Suicidology, a national organization of professionals and nonprofessionals interested in the study of suicide in order to prevent suicide where possible. Dr. Berman is often called to testify as an expert witness when there aren't any witnesses to the death. When the medical examiner or coroner cannot determine without a behavioral science investigation whether the death was a suicide, an accident, or homicide, it's called an equivocal death case.

"Dr. Berman, please give us the definition of a suicidologist."

"A suicidologist is someone who, by virtue of professional experience and training, has done research in the area of suicide. He studies suicidal death primarily in terms of learning about the character of individuals who are suicidal and those that complete suicide and the circumstances that surround suicidal death. The research is primarily designed to help clinicians better treat suicidal people and better understand suicidal behavior. Also, by virtue of those studies, they hopefully devise strategies to help prevent the next suicide if possible."

"Has the federal government recognized the study of suicide, Dr. Berman?"

"Yes, in a number of ways. Beginning in 1989, the Department of Health and Human Services produced a major report on youth suicide, which involved a massive study and a number of contributors. Last July, the Surgeon General presented a major report advocating a national strategy for suicide prevention based on better research."

"The research that has been done by you and others has revealed what are called risk factors. Dr. Berman, please explain what a risk factor is."

"It is a characteristic, a trait, or an attribute regarding some aspect of the individual in terms of his or her personality, or experience associated with suicidal behavior and less associated with non-suicidal behavior. When the coroner or medical examiner has affirmed that an individual has completed suicide, we would study common characteristics of those people, the manner of their death, and the circumstances of their death. We then compare them to non-suicidal people, either other forms of death, or healthy living people to look at those attributes that are more common among the suicidal group. This research has been going on for forty to fifty years, and there are a large number of risk factors involved."

"Will you please tell us what research you did and your findings regarding the investigation of Sharon Guthrie's death?"

"I reviewed a large body of materials in terms of documentary evidence and interviews that were sent to me by your office. I then independently conducted interviews with some of Mrs. Guthrie's family members. After reviewing the documents provided to me and also interviewing the family members, I basically found that she had no history of what we describe as predisposing risk factors. Predisposing risk factors are those conditions that make us more vulnerable to be suicidal. They show no clear evidence of any acute risk, which is something happening currently that would create a suicidal behavior. Mrs. Guthrie had no history of suicide risk, no history of suicidal behavior, and no history of mental disorder with her or her family. In ninety percent or more of all completed suicides, significantly depression, alcoholism, or other forms of mental disorders are found. There wasn't any record of a family history with mental disorder, which is also a risk factor for suicide. There wasn't any history of family suicidal behavior and no prior treatment for mental health problems. There simply wasn't any record provided to me that described any vulnerability to be suicidal by virtue of her history. We did find that she did have a record of problems sleeping, but that is not a risk factor for suicide. Mrs. Guthrie was described as being stressed out, but she never behaved in any suicidal way. According to family members, she would typically get in her car and go for a drive when stressed. Mrs. Guthrie had no particular reason at this point in time, no motive if you will, to become acutely stressed other than what has been recorded as the affair that her husband was involved in, which allegedly she had known about for some period of time. She had reason to look forward to the upcoming wedding of her daughter, which was reported that she was quite excited about and had reason to be concerned that her wedding dress needed to be fixed so that her daughter could wear it. It was also reported that she was very intent on trying to lose some weight, so she had several reasons to stay alive. Typically, a female who is suicidal will most likely use a gun, particularly if she owns a gun. Mrs. Guthrie did own a gun. Less than two percent of American women drown themselves in suicide, and very small proportions of those drown themselves in a bathtub, so if she were suicidal, the method of drowning herself in a bathtub would be quite unusual. Typically, a female would go to a large body of water. Most powerful, it's very unusual for someone to drown himself or herself face down. Typically, if one were to drown oneself in a bathtub, he or she would be sitting up and would essentially sink under the water. There was nothing in Mrs. Guthries' predisposition to be suicidal, there was nothing dramatic to describe her intent to be suicidal, and there wasn't any behavior described that was consistent with what we know to be suicidal deaths."

"Dr. Berman, you prepared a risk analysis for Sharon Guthrie. What does predisposing mean?"

"Predisposing risk factors are chronic long term risk factors for suicide. In our studies of completed suicide, we go back and look at a person's history to see if there were signs and symptoms of a mental disorder. In our research, those studies have shown that over ninety percent of people that complete suicide had a mental disorder, a significant psychological or a psychiatric condition. The most significant ones are depression or a bipolar disorder called manic depression. Others are alcoholism, drug abuse, or other significant mental disorders; such as schizophrenia or psychosis. I listed half a dozen or more in my report that I looked for in this case. Mrs. Guthrie had no evidence of those significant risk factors."

"Did Sharon show any evidence of physical disease?"

"Using examples such as AIDS, multiple sclerosis or diabetes, she did not."

"What did you find under prior suicide or prior suicidal behavior?"

"Women in particular have histories of suicidal behavior prior to completing suicide, but I couldn't find any evidence that Mrs. Guthrie had made any suicide attempt in the past or had begun an attempt."

"Did she show any evidence of prior suicidal ideation?"

"Ideation means thinking. There wasn't any significant evidence that Mrs. Guthrie had thought about suicide. Her daughter stated that once several years ago her mother talked about suicide to make her feel guilty, but that was not significant evidence. According to the daughter, she also stated that several years ago her father also had used the same kind of mechanism on her to control her behavior."

"Dr. Berman, in your report you noted the word *acute*. What does that mean?"

"Acute refers to current and severe evidence that there is something going on right now, which would increase the risk that she could act without vulnerability in the present in some suicidal way. Mrs. Guthrie showed no evidence that she had expressed thoughts of suicide or had written any thoughts of suicide."

"What is meant by current death fantasies?"

"There are some people that do not directly communicate that they are thinking about killing themselves. They might declare that they would be better off if they weren't living; or perhaps they have a loved one in Heaven that they would like to join, but I found no evidence of that in Mrs. Guthrie."

"What is meant by recent rehearsal behavior?"

"Not all, but some people who complete suicide will prepare themselves to act in a suicidal way. Figuratively speaking, they may go to a bridge and scout it out or walk up to the ledge and get a sense of that. It's sort of a way to reduce stage fright and convince themselves that they can do it. Some people will take a gun, sit with it, and sit with it, and sit with it, and maybe even put a bullet in the gun. Mrs. Guthrie showed no evidence of engaging in any of that type of behavior."

"Dr. Berman, please explain the meaning of recent termination behavior?"

"That is where there is evidence by their behavior. For example, they may tell someone, *'I'm not going to need this anymore,'* and give away something of value. There wasn't any data to show that Mrs. Guthrie had done that."

"What does social isolation absence supports mean?"

"When people attempt suicide, or complete suicide, they have no attachments to other people of any significance. They withdraw from people, most likely live alone and most likely do not have significant others in the world that matter to them. Mrs. Guthrie was not socially isolated, was not unattached to others, and she did have people around her that she could turn to if in trouble."

"You have listed negative emotional state. Please explain."

"When we can't document a mental disorder, we will, on the other hand, have a number of very significant symptoms by virtue of emotional expressions, which describe the inability to keep control over one's emotional life. For example, some people will be out of control in their expression of rage, and there will be many expressions of being significantly angry with other people where they can't contain that feeling and panic. There would be evidence, as an example, that they would not be functional to go to work. Also, they would be overwhelmed by symptoms of major anxiety and guilt. None of that was found in regards to Mrs. Guthrie."

"Dr. Berman, what are significant specific symptoms?"

"In a similar sense, we would look for evidence that there were some symptoms that she wasn't totally together. The only specific symptom that is mentioned with any repetition is the fact that Mrs. Guthrie was having trouble sleeping. There were a couple of other symptoms that were mentioned here and there, but nothing over time and nothing that made her not functional, such as work and involvement with others."

"Did you find any significant behavioral problems in regards to Mrs. Guthrie?"

"An example of behavioral problems would be if someone wasn't an alcoholic, but went on a drinking binge, or if someone who is generally very calm all of a sudden is very agitated and becomes out of control. We did not find any behavioral problems."

"You have listed exposure to another's suicide. What does that mean?"

"This is called contagion. When there is a death in one's immediate world, as in one's family or among one's peer group, a friend for example, or a reported death, the suicide risk goes up for people who are vulnerable to be identified with or associated with the person that completed suicide. Mrs. Guthrie was not exposed to anyone else with suicidal behavior."

"Please explain the factor called acute loss."

"We would look for some evidence of something within hours or days of her death that would be the motivating force at that moment to make her kill herself. Examples would be loss of a job, loss of one's financial status, or the loss of a relationship. There wasn't any evidence of acute loss. There were clearly some statements about relationship problems regarding her husband's affair, but she allegedly had known about that or had wind of that for quite a period of time."

"Please explain the one listed as other significant acute problems."

"In a similar sense, there are people who become suicidal when they are under tremendous emotional strain or tremendous stress. An example for internal would be those struggling with their sexual identity, such as being gay, but haven't come out and are terrified about becoming public that they are homosexual. An example for external could be a legal charge and having to go to court. None of this was found in regards to Mrs. Guthrie."

"Dr. Berman, did Mrs. Guthrie show any evidence of hopelessness as a risk factor?'

"No, she did not. Depression usually signals not feeling good about one's self or having negative thoughts that turn to hopeless thoughts, such as *I'm an awful person. Nobody cares about me. Nothing will ever get better.*'"

"Please explain problem solving deficits."

"All of us are faced with problems in our lives and are able to think clearly and rationally to deal with those problems, but suicidal people operate as if they have blinders on. They can see their pain, but they don't see any alternative strategies to solve their way out of the pain and they get very rigid in their thinking. We describe this as black or white thinking, where there is no gray area or middle ground. We have acquired a lot of research that says suicidal individuals, whether those who have made an attempt or those who have completed suicide, give us evidence that they have deficits in the way they solve problems. There was no evidence that Mrs. Guthrie had any deficits in problem solving."

"So, Dr. Berman, is it correct that the only thing present of any significance was that Mrs. Guthrie had insomnia?"

"That's correct."

"You have demographic high risk group listed under the category called *other*. Please explain briefly."

"There is a lot of data that tells us that certain groups of people are higher risk versus lower risk for suicide. The older white male is most at risk for suicide, while the highest risk for females is the middle-aged female, between the ages of forty-four and fifty-five. You could say that Mrs. Guthrie was in that group. People who lose their jobs, who are chronically unemployed, or who are fired have a higher risk of suicide in the period of time after their unemployment, but that factor did not pertain to Mrs. Guthrie."

"You have listed contraindications. What does that mean?"

"Women who own firearms significantly are more likely to use a firearm if they are going to kill themselves. Mrs. Guthrie had a firearm available to her and did not use it."

"Dr. Berman, I have here data from the Centers for Disease Control and the National Center for Health Statistics. What was the data in South Dakota from 1994 to 1996 pertaining to female suicides that used a firearm to complete suicide?"

"It shows within those three years that over half of the total of forty-nine females that completed suicide used a firearm. Using a firearm is the leading method of suicide by women in this state and also nationally."

"You also state in this report significant reason for living and future anticipation. Please explain."

"I mentioned earlier that Mrs. Guthrie was looking forward to her daughter's wedding. People who use suicide as a means of a way out get tunnel vision on their pain. There was data obtained from several people to document that Mrs. Guthrie was excited and looking forward to her daughter's upcoming wedding."

"What did you find out about the method of death?"

"The data that I reviewed suggested that Mrs. Guthrie had ingested a number of a prescribed drug called Temazepam, and that she drowned in her bathtub, face down and unclothed."

"Was it a significant factor, given the fact that Mrs. Guthrie was unclothed?"

"Her daughters, in particular, mentioned that their mother was very conscious about her appearance, and if, indeed, she was going to kill herself, it would be very unlikely that she would want to be found naked."

"What was significant to you about the fact that she was facedown in the bathtub?"

"I personally have never seen a suicide case of a bathtub drowning where the decedent was found facedown."

"Dr. Berman, in all your years of experience based on your research, your investigation, and the information that you have gathered, were you able to form an opinion of whether you feel Sharon Guthrie's death was a suicide?"

"In my opinion, Sharon Guthrie did not die by suicide."

"Thank you, doctor."

Cross-examine by the Defense

"Dr. Berman, would it be fair to say that the majority of women in South Dakota who committed suicide during that three-year span did not use a firearm?"

"That's correct."

"Doesn't that make it more likely that Sharon did commit suicide?"

"No --- the point I was making is that the most common method is by firearm, and it is even more significant that if one owns a firearm, one would most likely use that firearm to complete suicide. The fact that Mrs. Guthrie died by some other manner or method doesn't make it more versus less."

"What is the second most likely method of suicide among women on a national basis?"

"Nationally, it is between drug overdoses and hangings."

"Doesn't the fact that drug overdose makes it more likely that Sharon committed suicide?"

"Mrs. Guthrie did have an overdose of medication in her system that could have occurred in a variety of ways, but her cause of death was from drowning."

"Dr. Berman, the fact that Sharon didn't use a firearm, but considering the fact that drug overdose is the second most common method of suicide and a drug overdose being present in this case, wouldn't that be an indication of suicide?"

"It's true that it doesn't rule out suicide, but again, it's not an indication of suicide because Mrs. Guthrie's cause of death was drowning."

"Dr. Berman, isn't it certainly possible that if Sharon intended to commit suicide, her drowning in a bathtub had nothing to do with the suicide attempt?'

"I don't understand how that could be possible. She did ingest medication or have medication in her system, and she did get into the bathtub."

"Isn't it possible that the medication overtook her more quickly than she anticipated, and that's how she happened to drown in the bathtub?"

"I don't believe so, but it's in the realm of possibility."

"You also stated that since Sharon's position was face down in the bathtub that it would make it less likely to be a suicide, but would make suicide more likely if she was found face up in the bathtub."

"It would have increased the possibility, yes."

"Doctor, regarding your risk factors, how many have to be present before you would find the death to be a suicide?"

"An analysis isn't done in that fashion. This isn't an issue of having a checklist with a cutoff point. It's only a matter of describing more versus less on the basis of the presence or absence of risk factors, so there is no specific number."

"I believe you testified that psychological autopsies have been used for awhile. Dr. Berman, are you saying that there is no set criteria for conducting a psychological autopsy?"

"No ... there are criteria, but there is not a cutoff score. This isn't a scale to predict suicide. It is a listing of risk factors common to suicidal people and an evaluation of whether these risk factors were indeed present or absent. It's an overall view of how these things work together or do not work together to suggest suicide or not."

"You bring up a good point. Is it then correct that these risk factors were established with the goal in mind of preventing suicides, not doing psychological autopsies?"

"These risk factors were established by studying suicides and comparing them to people who are not suicidal. The primary purpose of doing research is to better understand individuals who are suicidal. Risk factors are used in order to better understand a manner of death, such as in this case with Mrs. Guthrie."

"Dr. Berman, I'm still not sure I understand how many risk factors need to be present in order for a psychological autopsy determination of suicide. Am I understanding correctly that there is no set number?"

"That is correct. There are no set numbers where you have a cutoff score --- it just doesn't work that way."

"Would it be fair to say, Dr. Berman, that the predisposing risk factors carry less weight than the acute risk factors?"

"No, sir. As I said earlier, the most significant risk factor from the research is the presence of a mental disorder."

"What are some of the shortcomings of the psychological autopsy process?"

"There are a number of shortcomings. First of all, it is a retrospective analysis. Therefore, we do not have absolute evidence that validates the opinion that is derived because the person is dead, and there is no way to go back to prove that the opinion is absolutely correct. It is a probabilistic statement, which means I can say to you that from my perspective, and on the basis of my analysis, that this person was quite likely to be suicidal or quite likely not to be a suicidal or somewhere in between. Unless the evidence is overwhelming and includes witnesses that state how the person died, I can't say with absolute certainty."

"Isn't one of the shortcomings of the psychological autopsy the fact that you depend on interviews of third parties for part of your assessment?"

"Well, I'm not sure I would describe it as a weakness or limitation. We do multiple interviews because any one interview may have distortions in what the third parties remember. They may remember some things and not others. With this procedure, involving interviews with a variety of people, we can look for common evidence, which dramatically suggests a risk factor or not."

"I don't mean to disregard what you just said, Dr. Berman, but as I understand, somewhere in there you are acknowledging that individuals whom you interview, all have their own personal biases or prejudices, correct?"

"That's absolutely correct."

"I would also assume that a common problem you encounter in doing psychological autopsies, for example, is someone not wanting to offer evidence that supports a suicide theory because there is life insurance involved. Would that also be correct?"

"That is also true. Again, that is why we do multiple interviews."

"Dr. Berman, was there any life insurance involved in this case?"

"I don't know what the life insurance status was in this case."

"Would another common reason for someone coloring statements to you be that he or she might not want you to think that the friend or relative committed suicide because it's contrary to one's religious beliefs?'

"That's possible, yes."

"So, then, Dr. Berman, people may have many reasons for coloring their statements to you, if I may use that term."

"That's the nature of interviewing respondents --- yes."

"Would that be considered one of the shortcomings of a psychological autopsy?"

"Yes, but it's also one of the shortcomings of a homicide investigation as well. This is what we do when we retrospectively analyze a case."

"To the extent that you don't have correct facts, you can't render a valid opinion can you, Dr. Berman?"

"I can still render an opinion on the basis of my reading of multiple interviews and a large body of evidence that has been provided to me."

"Isn't it a possibility that the facts you have collected are wrong and could affect the validity of your opinion?"

"Again, sir, I can't give my opinion with absolute certainty; but I can surely render an opinion that the death was more likely to be a suicide versus less likely."

"The more facts you have wrong the more likely you are to be wrong, correct?"

"Sir, it all depends, as well, on how many facts I have right."

"Dr. Berman, going back to the risk factor regarding mental disorder, are you talking about a diagnosable mental disorder or one that is not diagnosed?"

"In this case I didn't find any diagnosed mental disorder. The issue here was, were there signs and symptoms that weren't picked up, but would give evidence that Mrs. Guthrie could have had a significant mental disorder were not found."

"Dr. Berman, do I understand that you don't believe a diagnosable mental disorder was present in Sharon Guthrie?"

"That's correct."

"However, didn't she display some physical symptoms that had no organic cause, such as the sleeplessness and the racing heart at bedtime?"

"Those do not describe a mental disorder; however, they could be due to any number of factors."

"Did Patricia Minor and the other medical doctors attending to Sharon's sleep problem and her heart racing problem eliminate physical causes for those problems?"

"No, they treated it as a sign of anxiety and insomnia, but it could well have been a side effect of the Temazepam."

"I assume, Dr. Berman, that you reviewed Patricia Minor's office notes. Did you also review Patricia Minor's testimony before the Grand Jury?"

"Yes."

"Patricia Minor recorded in her medical records that Sharon complained of sleep problems and her heart racing back in March, months before the Temazepam was issued. Wouldn't that have been long before the Temazepam prescription was available to Bill or Sharon Guthrie?"

"I believe that's correct."

"Doctor, Patricia Minor also testified that they eliminated the possible physical causes for these problems, so wouldn't that leave only mental problems or mental causes?"

"I didn't read anything in her medical records that a thorough physical evaluation was conducted to eliminate all sorts of possibilities, but for the sake of discussion that still doesn't describe a mental disorder."

"Does it describe a disorder that's not brought on by physical problems?"

"It describes where we have a symptom of insomnia, which could be a result of her racing heart, but unto itself that is not a mental disorder and is very unlikely to be associated with a mental disorder. Insomnia is a common symptom of depression; but if there were a symptom of depression, we would have a number of other symptoms that would be in evidence and none of those are described."

"Do you know, Dr. Berman, if a full psychological evaluation was done on Sharon?"

"That is also not in the record."

"Did you see where the records indicated that she had hypertension?"

"Yes, but that is not a significant risk factor for suicide."

"What is the significant risk factor for suicide in terms of diseases?"

"The major medical diseases that have been investigated to document the odds of becoming suicidal are multiple sclerosis, AIDS, and cancer. The odds of becoming suicidal are greater for one having these diseases than not."

"Is it correct that, again, we are talking about odds?"

"Yes, that's the way we do our research."

"Dr. Berman, isn't it true whether I perceive a problem to be significant is dependent at least as much on my perception of it as it is on a third party's objective perception of it?"

"That's often true, yes."

"You talked about rehearsal behavior and stated that you didn't think that was present in Sharon's case. Wouldn't the April 15th overdose on Tylenol or some other drug that was documented in her medical records reflect that behavior?"

"There is no evaluation of that as a suicidal behavior."

"Again, I ask you, Dr. Berman, was there any psychological evaluation done on Sharon?"

"No, there was not."

"Wouldn't it have been a good idea at the time of that April 15th overdose to seek some consultation from a mental health professional?"

"Possibly, if someone was concerned about her mental health at that point, but clearly she wasn't concerned and no one else was."

"Dr. Berman, what kind of things can termination behavior include?"

"That would involve a person giving away prize possessions, completing a will out of context, and acting as if in the near future that they will be dead."

"You stated that you didn't think social isolation was a factor in Sharon's case. Even though she was a very private person and didn't share her problems with people, she would go off on her own to think about her problems. Don't you see that as an issue of isolation?"

"Being private is not an issue of being socially disconnected. Social isolation refers to not having an available support system and evidence that one does not use a support system when in significant trouble."

"Well, Dr. Berman, if someone didn't complain or didn't seek medical or mental health help and tended to keep things to himself, wouldn't that be a risk factor that you would want to acknowledge?"

"It might be a risk factor, but would have to have a context for significant psychological problems, which there were none in evidence regarding Mrs. Guthrie."

"Isn't it true that one of the reasons to commit suicide is to preserve identity?"

"That's true."

"Going back to your statistics, are you saying that Sharon couldn't have committed suicide because she is female?"

"No, sir, I'm not saying that she couldn't have completed suicide. I'm saying that in my opinion she was very unlikely to be a candidate for suicide."

"Dr. Berman, if the data would have said there were five or six times as many suicides in South Dakota as there were homicides, would that make it more likely that it was a suicide?"

"No, it would still reflect a very small proportion of those suicides as female, and that data would not affect my opinion at all regarding Sharon Guthrie."

"Isn't it true that a certain percentage of suicides are completed with little, if any, warning to others?"

"Twenty to twenty-five percent do not give overt warnings at the time of the suicide. There are ninety-plus percent of cases where there are a variety of signs and symptoms that are in the form of risk factors."

"Dr. Berman, what is the percentage of the general population that do have diagnosable mental disorders?"

"Depending on the specific disorder, it falls within the range of five to fifteen percent."

"Can you tell us how many are actually diagnosed?"

"Roughly twenty-five to thirty percent."

"Let's say that Sharon had only five pills in her system instead of twenty. Would that make it more likely that this could have been a suicide gesture gone wrong?"

"Not in my mind. The implication would be that Mrs. Guthrie was planning on getting into the bathtub to wait for her husband to leave to do his morning prayers, then to be found by him in the ten to twelve minutes or so that it took for him to do that before returning. The implication is that this was a planned behavior, but I find nothing to suggest that it was planned. I don't believe it was suicidal, and there is equally nothing to say that this would have been planned behavior."

"Dr. Berman, people that make suicide gestures don't necessarily display a significant number of these risk factors, so wouldn't it be correct to say that a suicide gesture is by definition not a sincere attempt?"

"No, that's not the definition. A suicide gesture is an initiating behavior, which is meant typically to influence another person. If I follow your logic, Mrs. Guthrie would have had reason to try to scare her husband or to provoke his sympathy by doing something. She had the pills available if that's want she wanted to do, so she didn't need to get in the bathtub. She also had a gun available, so she didn't need to get into the bathtub, which makes me believe that this was not a suicide."

"Do you acknowledge, Dr. Berman, that you were told Sharon had on previous occasions told her daughter that sometimes she thought about driving her car into oncoming traffic?"

"I don't recall that as a plural statement, but yes, she did."

"If it was a plural statement, would that make it more significant in your mind?"

"It would depend on the number of times and the number of circumstances. In my interview with the daughter, it was not described in those terms. It was described as when Sharon wanted to make her feel guilty about something."

"Let's assume, Dr. Berman, that this happened about five years ago and now the daughter is twenty years old. In essence, aren't you telling the jury that you are accepting a then fifteen-year-old daughter's interpretation of her mother's statement?"

"To the extent that the daughter was the only reporter of that statement, I have to accept her view of that statement. I'm not specifically going on her interpretation other than the description and the context of the statement."

"Again, aren't you relying on the daughter's information in that regard?"

"That's correct."

"Doctor, would it be a significant risk factor in your mind if we speculate that Sharon had been told by the defendant that he was going to divorce her after her daughter's wedding?"

"That would add to her potential motive for suicide, but again one would have to wonder why tonight and why this day versus whenever he is threatening divorce."

"Are you saying that there would be a lack of a triggering event?"

"One would describe that as a triggering event in the context that she had a vulnerability to be suicidal."

"Wouldn't being told by Bill that he was going to divorce her be a triggering event?"

"Triggering events can't trigger behavior unless there is a potential to be vulnerable to that. For example, if I ask you if you are thinking about suicide, I can't make you become suicidal simply by raising that in your mind. You have to already be in the ballpark to be moved towards suicidal behavior. Again, she didn't have the predisposing likelihood to be suicidal."

"Dr. Berman, what pattern did you observe regarding Sharon's case?"

"Every suicide is unique and there is no particular pattern. There are common risk factors that are in, or are not in, any particular suicide. There is no one pattern; suicide comes in a variety of forms. Invariably, there are signs of suicide risk; but if you are speaking to a particular pattern or typical suicide, there is no such thing."

"How often would you find the characteristics you observed in Sharon's case in a homicide case?"

"I don't have any specific numbers. My approach in this case was to answer the question of whether this was a suicide or not a suicide and what my opinion was about it being a possible suicide. It was not to address other manners of death."

"Just so there is no doubt about it, is it correct from your investigation of this case, that Sharon herself reported to Patricia Minor the sleep problems, the heart racing episodes, and the difficulty of falling asleep at night?"

"Yes, sir."

"Isn't it correct that Sharon wasn't telling Patricia Minor that Bill was telling her that she was having heart racing episodes or that Bill was telling her that she was having problems getting to sleep?"

"I believe, according to Patricia Minor's testimony, that's true."

"Dr. Berman, if the facts that you were given or the facts that you determined in your investigation were wrong, your opinion is bound to lose validity, correct?"

"Well, I imagine if a large number of facts that I have reviewed are not right, then my opinion would change."

"No more questions."

Redirect by the State

"Dr. Berman, you testified that in your career you have never seen a person in a suicidal drowning that was face down in a bathtub. Also, in that thirty-plus years of research, have you seen where the head was at the faucet end of the bathtub in a suicidal drowning?"

"I have not."

"What is significant about the ten-minute time frame when the defendant allegedly left the house to go over to the church to pray and do devotions?"

"If you were to think of this as a suicide, you would have to assume that Mrs. Guthrie specifically waited for her husband to leave the house to get into the bathtub, to lie face down and to drown herself. She had already taken, or had been given, a large number of pills and to the extent that those pills were doing what they do, she would have been perhaps in a stupor or even comatose at some point in time. If her intent were to take those pills to complete suicide, the bathtub would not be in the story. None of it makes sense as to why she would go to the bathtub in this ten-minute period to kill herself."

"You testified that one of the side effects of the drug Temazepam is heart palpitations. Is that a common side effect for benzodiazepines?"

"Yes."

"Dr. Berman, was there anything that indicated to you that Sharon had planned this as a suicide?"

"I found no evidence of that."

"Did you find any evidence that she was thinking about suicide?"

"No, sir."

"I have no further questions."

Recross by the Defense

"Dr. Berman, isn't it true that if a person has significant depression issues that benzodiazepines can trigger suicidal thoughts?"

"It would be very difficult to conclude that suicidal thoughts are triggered with involvement of any medication. That would be very unusual."

"Assuming that you have done research on benzodiazepines, isn't there a caution stating to be careful when giving this to people with depression issues because it could trigger suicidal thoughts?"

"I haven't seen that particular sentence, but I do know there is a caution about depression and also about drinking."

"Dr. Berman, you stated that the bathtub doesn't figure into this scenario in terms of suicide, that it just doesn't make sense; so are you saying that people who commit suicide think rationally, logically, and with common sense?"

"No, sir, I have said that they do not."

"No further questions."

Michael Moore announces that the State will rest. Judge Martin states that a recess will be taken. He meets with the defendant, and counsel in judge's chambers outside the presence of the jury. Gregory Wilson makes a motion for a judgment of acquittal on the grounds that the State has failed to state a prima facie case. His motion is denied.

Gregory Wilson requests five minutes to confer with his client and to speak with Mr. Moore. When the attorneys return to chambers, Moore informs Judge Martin that the State has just received information from the defense regarding a document that they just presented. Moore states that he doesn't have the original document and has not had the opportunity for any of the State's experts to review this document. Moore further states his objection to the defense offering an expert fingerprint testimony regarding this document.

Mr. Wilson explains that what Mr. Moore is talking about is a note and a report from a latent fingerprint examiner that the defense has just provided to the State.

"Mr. Wilson, when was this document discovered?"

"Your Honor, the testimony would be that this document was discovered in early June of 1999, approximately three weeks after Sharon Guthrie's death."

"Are you at liberty to tell me who discovered it?"

"Yes, Your Honor. The testimony would be that the defendant discovered it."

"Mr. Wilson, since you have had this note for six months, why wasn't this turned over to the prosecution by January 5th?"

"Your Honor, my first thought when I received the note was authenticating it by way of computer or disproving it by way of computer. I simply never considered fingerprints until reading an article in the newspaper about Cindy Orton, a latent print examiner expert. Honestly, I can say that this is the first time for me in twelve years where fingerprints were a factor in a case. Myself, along with the other lawyers in our office, agreed that we never considered fingerprints to be a factor in this case until reading that article."

"Why would it take that many months to authenticate this note if it was found in June, Mr. Wilson?"

"Your Honor, I would gladly present the testimony that the first consultation I had with Cindy Orton was the morning of January 5th. I phoned her after reading the article in the paper on December 27th, but she was out of state, so I left a message on her answering machine. She arrived home on the evening of January 4th at approximately 9:30 and returned my call. She met me at my office the next morning, and I filled her in on what I needed her to do."

"Where was this note found?"

"Your Honor, the testimony would be that the note was found printed in the office area at the Wolsey Presbyterian Church. The Guthries' youngest daughter testified that her mother had utilized the computer in the church office."

"Mr. Moore, does the State have anything to add?"

"Yes, Your Honor. Assuming that Mr. Wilson calls the defendant to testify that the note is authentic, I would bring to the Court's attention that this will be a waiver of the defendant's Fifth Amendment right. We will then have the opportunity to cross-examine the defendant on any relevant or probative material in the case."

"I'm still puzzled, Mr. Wilson, as to why you have waited months to bring this to light."

"Your Honor, if I would have given that document to the prosecution without authentication in terms of trial tactics, without knowing for certain what it is, or knowing as best I can what it is, I would have given them more ammunition to use against my client. I couldn't deduce any way to protect my client from repercussions from incriminating evidence by disclosing it prior. In order to create a solid defense for my client, I felt I simply had no choice but to protect it until now. The State's case has been to use everything against the defendant on what he has said or commented about regarding this case. We would most likely never have gotten here if the note was in Sharon Guthrie's handwriting and signed by her, but since it is a computer-generated note without handwriting on it, I had to have some method of authenticating it before I could disclose it as evidence. By the afternoon of January 5th, I knew that there were fingerprints on the note, so I asked myself three questions. A – If the fingerprints are my clients, I don't use it.

B – If they are Sharon's, I do use it. C - We don't know whose they are. I believe that Mr. Moore will confirm the fact that I contacted him on January 5th asking for Sharon's fingerprints and was told that there weren't any available. If I would have had fingerprints of the deceased, I would have either met the discovery deadline or missed it by very little. Cindy Orton has handled in excess of sixty various items that were handled by Sharon, which I will introduce into evidence. At this point I can definitely exclude my client as the source of the fingerprints in question, and we also took the precaution of excluding my fingerprints.

Yes, Your Honor, I should have considered fingerprints being a factor much earlier than I did. Had the State retrieved fingerprints from the deceased, which they should have, then I have no doubt that we could have disclosed this document on January 5th. Nonetheless, I didn't know what we had; and until we did, I couldn't use it."

"Well, Mr. Wilson, let me think about this and when we reconvene here in chambers at 1:15, I will give my ruling," Judge Martin replies. Martin enters the courtroom to announce that a recess will be taken for lunch and that court will resume at 1:30 p.m.

At 1:27 p.m. Judge Martin, the defendant, and counsel are back in judge's chambers. "Mr. Wilson, I understand that you want to make record of an incident that you advised the Court of during the break. Will you please tell the Court and Mr. Moore about this?"

"Yes, Your Honor. I have here an original document inside a hastily gathered plastic bag. While we were in recess for lunch I was speaking with Mitch Rivers, one of the sons-in-law of the Guthries'. He asked me if the fingerprint expert had gotten anything off the note that was handwritten by Sharon. He, along with the other son-in-law, Les, and the two older daughters, Suzanne and Lexi, had previously assisted me in collecting items that they knew had been handled by Sharon. I told him I didn't know what note he was talking about, so he described it. I then had Cindy Orton go with me to the location of the items that were collected and we searched through them. After a thorough search it was apparent that the note he described to me was not in the items that had been sent to her to examine. Mitch called his wife to ask where the handwritten note on the napkin from Sharon was that was supposed to be sent with the fingerprint expert. Apparently someone had removed this note, and just ten minutes ago it was brought to me. This is the first that I have heard of it or seen it. Mitch is waiting out in the hallway and is prepared to offer testimony regarding the disclosure of the note."

"Have the State seen this handwritten note, Mr. Moore?"

"Yes, Your Honor."

Dear Bill
My love for you is as strong as ever and I feel even stronger. But, I know now that you can't & will never feel love for me again. I relieve

you from your commitment to me. It's not enough for you. I know that note to "your sweet Darling" was not written to me. And it is not fair to you or her to have me in the way.

It's time (past) for the truth. I do know what name was in it & know that person graduates in 1½ years. So set your goals & know you don't have to wait. It need not be hard any longer. I bow out. I will begin looking for a new home. Do what you have to do to make things right for the other person in your life. You and your "sweet Darling" need to be together. I want nothing I take nothing. You may tell your girls & I know then you can spend time with them.

Thelma told me you asked her to go on your and Danielle's camping trip so I knew then I was out of the picture this summer. Have a good life.

I'm sorry I called out to hold you, but you deserve nothing but the best & I am the lowest. It may take me awhile to get things straightened out. I will stay out of your way, but I need to stay in Orleans for a little while longer. I will stay away from Choir and Church. That will be easier for you.

"Does anyone here want to have this note in the bag analyzed and processed?"

"I don't, Your Honor," replies Mr. Moore. "Looking at this note written on a napkin, it looks as if Sharon hand wrote it when they were living in Orleans, Nebraska, which was over three years ago. It's fine if the defense wants to do it, but I feel that at this point there aren't any prints that would last three years."

"Mr. Wilson, any comments?"

"You know the thought occurs to me, Your Honor, that it may be a source of latent prints that could be attributed to the deceased. I consulted with Cindy Orton briefly and she said that it's a possibility. She said only processing and time would tell, but how much time she couldn't tell me. I know she has had some documents processing in excess of a week and still has not yielded anything. May I have time to consult with her again?"

A brief recess is taken. Mr. Wilson leaves judge's chambers to consult with his fingerprint expert and within three minutes he is back. "Your Honor, I am prepared to go ahead with testimony on the computer-generated note that we discussed earlier today. I spoke with Cindy Orton and she advised that there certainly is the possibility that fingerprints could be on it. She said that it would take her a maximum of twenty-four hours to process it, which would mean she would not know anything until Thursday. If she gets home this afternoon and starts the processing, she might have something tomorrow afternoon; and yet she might not. That is about all the more specific that she could be."

"Okay, Mr. Wilson, let's cut to the chase. If there are fingerprints on this napkin, are there some undetermined fingerprints on this note?"

"That's correct, Your Honor."

"Would it be of some great significance if the two matched, Mr. Wilson?"

"Yes, Your Honor."

"Are you trying to say that you don't want to have that done?"

"No, Your Honor. I'm prepared to offer testimony that this was basically hidden from our efforts and I would like the opportunity to have it examined, but I just don't know what to tell the Court in terms of how much time it's going to take. Ms. Orton has had some materials under examination for days, and she says that even old fingerprints will develop if they are there."

"Mr. Wilson, with respect to this note that is typewritten, I want to get something clear. When you refer to this note as being computer generated, are you are saying that it came off the office computer?"

May 13, 1999

Dear Suzanne,
I'm sorry I ruined your wedding. Your dad told me about
Your concerns of my interfering in Lexi's and the possibility
I might ruin hers. I won't be there so put your mind at ease.
You will understand after the wedding is done.

I love you all Mom.

"No, Your Honor, I meant that it has come off a computer. My computer expert would be able to testify that it was printed on an ink jet printer not presently connected to the computer that was seized from the church office."

"Mr. Wilson, going back to the computer-generated note. When I look at the order for discovery and the reciprocal order for discovery, I really feel that the State should have had this long before they received it. From what I have heard from you, the defendant apparently discovered the note in the church office in early June. There are some fingerprints on the note, but allegedly the note does not contain any fingerprints of the defendant, so we simply don't know if they may or may not match Sharon Guthrie's fingerprints."

"Your Honor, excuse me for interrupting. I have one other factor I think that should be considered. I expect that Cindy Orton would testify that the fingerprints that were left on the typewritten note were there as a result of someone under stress, since a person under stress generates a lot of perspiration. This would find the prints to be consistent with the type of prints that she has found on notes written by someone who has committed suicide."

"Mr. Wilson, it's still a bit astounding to me that it would not have registered with someone to try to find out if this typewritten note that you have had since June had any fingerprints on it and to try to identify them. As I see it now, with this late revelation the State is put in a heck of a bind, as well as the Court. The State doesn't have the opportunity to have their computer expert determine whether this was on the hard drive and possibly when it would have been put on the hard drive if, in fact, it was done by that computer.

"Plus, once more, suicide has been one of the issues in this case from its onset. Mr. Wilson, I remember, in your cross-exam of the State's computer expert you asked him if he had tried to use the words *good-bye, sorry, love mom,* or anything like this to try to trigger some kind of message on that computer. Depending on a lot of different circumstances, the note could, in fact, be interpreted as being a suicide note; yet the defense has had this note for several months.

"23A-13-17 provides as follows: 'If, at any time, during the course of a proceeding, it is brought to the attention of the Court that a party has failed to comply with an applicable discovery provision, the Court may order such a party to permit the discovery or inspection, grant a continuance, or prohibit the party from introducing evidence not disclosed, or it may enter such other order as it deems just under the circumstances. The Court may specify the time, place, and manner of making the discovery and inspection and may prescribe such terms and conditions as are just.'

"In fairness to everybody, even if it means a continuance of the trial for a few days, the State should have an opportunity to have its own examiners take a look at the typewritten note and conduct whatever investigation they need to do regarding this note.

"Also, Mr. Wilson, this will give you time to have your latent fingerprint expert look at the hand written note on the napkin and offer her opinion. If she can get a fingerprint off the napkin, you can try to match it up with something else.

"We are here to find out what the truth is, so I am giving both the State and the defense an opportunity to do some more work on this. The typewritten note is what I would call a surprise, not only to myself, but also to the State; and apparently the second one, the handwritten note on a napkin, is a surprise to both parties.

"The only thing I am going to hold in abeyance is what the terms and conditions may be by virtue of the defense failing to turn this document over. I have some further research to do, but I will grant a continuance. My suggestion is that you take some time right now, call your experts to find out what it's going to take, and then come back here in chambers. I will then address the length of the continuance."

"Your Honor, I would like to make a record on two things before we do that. I understand the Court's feelings that we should have disclosed this note earlier. However, I still maintain that I could not disclose that note until I knew what it was, and I was not obligated to disclose the note under the Court's order unless I was going to use it in my case and chief. I don't mean to argue with the Court; but in other words, pulling from memory, I believe the Court's order says to disclose such documents as will be utilized in the case and chief."

"Mr. Wilson, do you expect to introduce this in your case and chief or not?"

"I do now, Your Honor."

"Okay, Mr. Wilson, according to the discovery order, it says that you were to turn over the books, papers, documents, photographs, and tangible documents or copies thereof which are in the custody or control of the defendant, which he intends to introduce as evidence in chief. I will do some legal research with respect to what your obligation is."

"Your Honor, I just hope the Court appreciates my situation, whereas I had this note. I couldn't tell the Court, I couldn't show this note to the State; and I needed an indefinite delay to see if some new evidence developed, which I didn't know how long. So, I got ready for the trial and when the day came, which is today, I looked at what I had and made my assessment that this evidence could help my client. My client gave me his consent to utilize that evidence and we will use it. Do I understand that the Court will not allow me to put on any evidence of the note at this time?"

"That is correct." Judge Martin replies. "Let's get back in the Courtroom."

Judge Martin addresses the jury, "Ladies and gentlemen, my apologies to you for not starting exactly at 1:30. We try to do that, but sometimes there are things that come up in chambers that have to be dealt with. I will try to move the case along as quickly as possible. The State has rested its case, so the defense will be calling its witnesses."

Witness for the Defense – Dr. Michael McGrath

"Dr. McGrath, were you present when Dr. Berman testified?"
"Yes, I was."
"Are you a suicidologist or an expert on suicides?"
"No, I am not. I am a clinical psychologist."
"Do you have any knowledge and experience in research studies?"
"Yes, I have published a number of different studies, the earliest being in terms of behavioral treatment of smoking, then research related to the functional properties of sleep, and more recently I have been involved in research related to neuropsychology."
"Dr. McGrath, is research an established method of testing the validity of the theory when a psychologist or some other expert has a theory or an idea?"
"Yes, there are a variety of ways to do research. In this particular case a psychological autopsy can, in fact, provide valid information

concerning whether a person committed suicide or whether h
victim of homicide."

"What is meant by validity?"

"Validity is a term which means the extent to which an indicator measures the property that you are interested in. For example, a ruler is a valid technique for measuring height; whereas a weight scale is not valid. If you want to draw conclusions from any type of technique you use in a psychological autopsy, you have to make sure it's a valid technique for drawing those conclusions."

"Doctor, what other techniques would be utilized in a study to determine the validity of a psychological autopsy?"

"A technique has to be reliable. Reliability refers to the fact that if the same technique is used over and over and used by more than one person, you will come to the same conclusion. Using a ruler to measure can be a reliable way of measuring length, but if you use hand size to measure length it will not be considered reliable because people have different lengths and sizes of hands. You have to have validity and reliability."

"Dr. McGrath, what information would be needed to test the validity of psychological autopsy as a tool?"

"You would have to have some kind of research showing how accurate your predictions are when coming to the conclusion that a person did or did not commit suicide. In this type of case you would basically do a study on a group of completed suicides and a group of homicidal victims."

"Are there specific terms for both of those concepts?"

"Yes. One term is sensitivity, which means basically the frequency with which an indicator occurs in the population that you are interested in. If you want a sensitive indicator of whether a person is a male or female, you come up with a number of different indicators. If I were asked to come up with some indicators that would be sensitive to identifying females, I would find a number of indicators that would occur very frequently among females. For example, I could guarantee you that these indicators would be ninety-five to ninety-eight percent accurate; therefore, it would seem that if a given person didn't have these indicators they wouldn't be female, which sounds pretty good to you I imagine. It wouldn't sound so good though if I told you that my indicator was the presence of two legs, two arms, two eyes, a nose, and two ears, which features occur in ninety-five to ninety-eight percent of females. That would be sensitive to identifying females, but not a very good predictor of whether a given person is a female or a male because it isn't a specific measure."

"Dr. McGrath, how about if we use names such as the female name of Angel?"

"That would seem to be a very specific indicator. Specificity is the scientific name, which is the degree to which the indicator is unique to the population that you are interested in. The name Angel hardly ever occurs in the male population, at least in the United States, but being that it does occur among females it wouldn't be very sensitive. Whenever you would hear the name Angel, you would most likely refer to them as female, at least in the United States. Angel is a common masculine name in Mexico, so the name doesn't have specificity there."

"Dr. McGrath, Is there a term for identifying the population that you are interested in?"

"Yes. It's called base rate, which means the frequency with which the group you are interested in occurs among the entire population. For example, if you have one hundred people in this room and sixty of them are female, the base rate of females would be sixty percent. The base rate of any observation or any behavior is very important in determining how accurate your predictions are going to be."

"Doctor, let's get a little more specific to this case. If we were going to do a validity study on this case, would you need to know how sensitive the criteria was for determining suicide and how specific it was for eliminating homicide?"

"We would need to know how specific they were to suicide and how often this criteria shows up in suicide and not homicide."

"Have you found any such studies that study the validity of psychological autopsies?"

"With respect to comparing suicide to homicide there are no studies."

"Doctor, do we know what sensitivity or specificity rate there is for such a study?"

"When Dr. Berman testified, he mentioned ninety percent of completed suicides have a diagnosable psychiatric disorder, so out of one hundred suicides, ninety of them are going to have a diagnosable psychiatric disorder. That's great, but it gets back to my example of the two-legged kind of thing where my indicator shows ninety-five percent. You thought that was great when I said if it doesn't show up, it must not be female. If a diagnosable disorder doesn't show up, then it must not be a suicide, because ninety percent of them have a diagnosable disorder. You saw how wrong that conclusion was. The reason that it could be wrong is to say fifty percent of the homicide victims have a diagnosable disorder and say there's ninety suicides for every homicide. You take ninety people who have completed suicide and ten people who have been victims of homicide, you will find that diagnosable disorder shows up in ninety percent of the suicides, which would be eighty-one of the suicides with nine of the suicides that did not have a diagnosable disorder. When a diagnosable disorder shows up in fifty percent of the homicides, fifty percent of ten would be mean that five of them would have a diagnosable disorder, and five would not. So when I say this person did not have a diagnosable disorder, there are nine suicides that didn't, and five homicides that didn't. If I use that as my predictor, I would be wrong nine out of fourteen times --- wrong more often that I am right."

"Is it correct that sensitivity and specificity are expressed in terms of percentage?"

"Correct."

"When there is a relationship, Dr. McGrath, do they get higher together or lower together?"

"In general there is an inverse relationship. That is the more sensitive a measure is, the less specific it is, in general or vice versa. The more specific it is, the less sensitive, like the name Angel. In the United States that's a fairly specific indicator of females, but it's not very sensitive. If I use that as an indicator, I'm not going to identify very many females."

"Dr. McGrath, do we have a base rate for homicides and suicides in South Dakota?"

"Yes, we do. The most recent information taken from the *National Vital Statistics* published June 30, 1999, reports that there were one hundred twenty-seven suicides and twenty-two homicides in South Dakota in the year 1997."

"Does this information give us our base rate for our study?"

"Yes. In fact, if you did those in percentages, eighty-five percent were suicides and fifteen percent were homicides, which would give us the base rate of eighty-five percent for the South Dakota population."

"Are these risk factors accumulated by studying a group of people?"

"Yes, sir."

"Doctor, does that present any problems in applying those general risk factors to specific individuals?"

"The statistics that Dr. Berman presented, though they are valid, that ninety percent of completed suicides have a diagnosable psychiatric disorder are not necessarily useful in predicting an individual case. They may lead to a very erroneous conclusion where you are wrong more than you are right."

"Dr. McGrath, since your involvement with this case, have you done some research on psychological autopsies and reviewed what has been written about them, particularly with regard to cautionary notes?"

"Yes, I have."

"What are some of the examples of the information that you found?"

"One of the problems, which I believe was touched on somewhat in Dr. Berman's testimony, was doing interviews with survivors where they may conceal information for a variety of reasons. Suicide is perhaps frowned upon, and they don't want to make it look like suicide, or they don't like the defendant, so they try to shape the information to look like the defendant did, in fact, commit a homicide. People can purposely distort things or unconsciously, not distort, but conceal information. Also, sometimes a person who is being interviewed may feel that suicide is a sacrilegious act and the person who committed suicide is deemed a bad person; therefore, unconsciously they may try to present information to suggest that this person didn't commit suicide. As Dr. Berman pointed out, you try to compensate for that by doing a lot of interviews. How many is a lot I don't know; it's an ill-defined term. It would be important that you would interview people from both sides, not just the prosecution. Another shortcoming is that fixed procedures for psychological autopsies have never been established. There are areas that you cover, there are various how-to manuals to make sure you cover this area or that area; but how precisely you go about covering those areas, there is no established or uniform way of doing them. Dr. Berman may do it one way, another doctor may do it a slightly different way, and if I would get into it as a novice, I would probably do it a lot differently than either of them. It's not objective or uniform. Maybe the most important thing pointed out is that often times psychological autopsies terminate inconclusively. You can't make a decision whether the person committed suicide or did not commit suicide. There are no pre-established criteria for identifying a death as a suicide or accident. When Dr. Berman was asked how many of those risk factors in Mrs. Guthrie's case were needed by him before he could conclude it was a suicide, he didn't answer that question. He couldn't answer because there isn't any established criteria. It's left to the clinician's intuition whether it is a suicide or not a suicide. There are no criteria of how many things you need to have, or how convincing the checklist of risk factors have to be, before you can say it is suicide. It's meaningless information."

"Dr. McGrath, what comments about psychological autopsies did you find that were significant?"

"The term psychological autopsy was coined by a well-known doctor, who is obviously a very well-respected individual in the area of suicide. The frequent error in this field is to confuse statistics with individual events and then to argue that because this individual does or does not have certain characteristics of a group, suicide must have or must not have occurred. They are saying you can't do it. Also, statistics are made up of individual cases and an individual case is not controlled by statistics."

"Dr. McGrath, would it be fair to say that Dr. Berman's opinion is just that --- an opinion?"

"That's being diplomatic."

"Can a psychological autopsy be demonstrated to be accurate to any degree by any studies that you are aware of?"

"No, it can't even be demonstrated that he is more likely right than wrong. He could be more likely wrong than right using the psychological autopsy because we don't know how often those characteristics or lack of characteristics show up among homicides."

"Dr. McGrath, in the end would Dr. Berman, no matter how good he is, be limited by the facts that he has available to him?"

"Yes. Dr. Berman is very well published in the field and is very knowledgeable about suicide. I would never argue that fact; but unfortunately the information that he has, he cannot use to make predictions in an individual case. You just can't use it logically."

"Thank you. No further questions."

Cross-examine by the State
Questioned by Moore

"Dr. McGrath, is your purpose here today to tell the jury whether Sharon's death was a suicide or not?"

"Absolutely not --- I have no idea."

"Then, your only purpose here is to say that Dr. Berman doesn't know what he is talking about?"

"That's being undiplomatic. My purpose here is to say that the research does not exist for him to draw a conclusion that Mrs. Guthrie did or did not commit suicide. It just doesn't exist."

"Do you recognize the field of suicidology?"

"Sure -- it exists."

"Do you recognize that Dr. Berman is a leader in that field?"

"Yes, he is one of the bigger names in my review of the literature."

"Would you agree that suicidal people display common risk factors?"

"Yes."

"Do you see suicidal people on a regular basis?'

"Yes."

"You've made a decision and locked people up, haven't you?"

"Correct, but I think we are getting a little carried away. I haven't locked them up. I make a recommendation that they go into the hospital."

"Dr. McGrath, aren't you then making a prediction on their future behavior?"

"Exactly."

"Isn't that even harder than making a retrospective analysis, which is what Dr. Berman did?"

"I don't know if it's harder --- actually it might be easier. When you make a prediction of suicide, there is a study. I believe it's in one of the books that Dr. Berman edited using four thousand patients, and they tried to predict who was going to commit suicide. Their predictions were right 2.8 percent of the time, but they were wrong ninety-seven percent of the time."

"Dr. McGrath, don't you lock up people 2.8 percent of the time and are wrong ninety-seven percent of the time?"

"I suggest that they be hospitalized, I don't lock them up --- I am not a jailer. You are right though. When somebody comes in, and I think that for some reason they are going to commit suicide, I am going to be wrong on the side of having them come into the hospital because of the consequence. If it's one of those three percent where I'm wrong, it's going to have very dire consequences because the person has committed suicide and I didn't take measures to prevent it. I am quite willing to make mistakes in that respect."

"Are the risk factors that Dr. Berman talked about in his testimony some of the things you look at?"

"Sure."

"Dr. McGrath, are you saying that based on mathematics that Dr. Berman can't do what he is doing?"

"Based on logic and mathematics and lack of research, we don't know how often those characteristics show up among homicides, so you can't do it."

"Based on mathematics, would you say that forty-two percent of the time that Dr. Berman would be right?"

"Yes, it's not just mathematics --- it's logic."

"So, if you took ten people and locked them in a room by themselves, gave them rope and they hanged themselves, and then Dr. Berman came in and said, 'Well, they all committed suicide,' would you say that he is only right forty-two percent of the time?"

"No, I would not."

"Isn't that what you just said, Dr. McGrath?"

"That's not a psychological autopsy. I'm not saying that nobody can predict suicide. Of course, people can predict whether someone committed suicide if they use a very sensitive and a very specific measure. If a video camera was placed in a room for twenty-four hours, with only one door into that room, and the camera showed that only one person had gone through that door into the room, that would be an example. Then when you came back and found that one person was dead from hanging by his neck from the ceiling, that would show a very specific measure of suicide. I can't think of how a homicide could occur under those circumstances. It's not very sensitive since not very many suicides will occur in that fashion. Those are the facts. Obviously, it was a suicide, but a psychological autopsy doesn't show that fact, so we don't even know what specificity it is. I am just granting Dr. Berman eighty percent --- it could be fifty percent."

"So, we have this guy locked in a room and he hangs himself. What if the person is at home and he hangs himself. Will you ever know if he committed suicide?"

"It would depend on other information, I guess."

"Wouldn't that depend on the risk factors, Dr. McGrath?"

"Risk factors wouldn't matter too much to me in that particular case. I don't really know the pattern that Dr. Berman uses to say this is a suicide or not a suicide, so we don't even know how sensitive it is. To come here and say this wasn't a suicide, I don't know how often that does or does not occur among suicides and I don't know how often that does or does not occur among homicides. Therefore, you can't say how accurate the prediction is."

"Dr. McGrath, what else would you want to know about that person hanging in his house to determine if he committed suicide?"

"You're kind of getting me out of my area of expertise. I said earlier that I am not a suicidologist, so I would be real speculative to start talking about stuff like that."

"Doctor, isn't it important that we know if the person committed suicide or not?"

"Of course, it's important to know."

"Are you saying that you wouldn't want any other information to help you determine that?"

"No, I'm saying I wouldn't try to make the determination based on psychological autopsy. You can't do it --- that's what I am telling you."

"Wouldn't you rely on risk factors that have been researched for over thirty years?"

"Not unless I knew how often those risk factors occur in the other alternative. Are we talking about this person as a homicide? Is that the decision we are trying to make in your example? Is this a suicide or a homicide? I definitely wouldn't use psychological autopsies because there isn't any information on how often those risk factors occur in homicides."

"Isn't it correct that the only thing Dr. Berman testified to was whether this was a suicide?"

"He testified that it was not a suicide."

"That is correct, but he didn't try to decide if it was a homicide, he didn't try to decide if it was a natural death, and he didn't try to decide if it was an accident."

"Yes, sir, you are right; however, it happens to be that Mr. Guthrie is not on trial for his wife dying accidentally; he is on trial for homicide, so we have to compare suicides to homicides. When Dr. Berman says that he considers in his opinion, with a high degree of certainty, that Mrs. Guthrie did not die of suicide we are then left with the conclusion that it must be homicide because that is what Mr. Guthrie is on trial for."

"Dr. McGrath, is it correct that we are looking at an individual case and that all Dr. Berman did was decide if Mrs. Guthrie was more or less likely to have committed suicide?"

"Yes, and he may have been right forty-two percent of the time."

"Would that be based on mathematics?"

"Based on logic and mathematics."

"But not on real life, Dr. McGrath?"

"Based on real life there were one hundred twenty-seven suicides and twenty-two homicides."

"You testified earlier about males and females and their height. Will you please briefly explain that again?"

"I was using that as an example of how group means can be misleading. It was noted that you can't use group statistics necessarily to make individual predictions."

"Didn't it say that you should look at an individual case?"

"No, it doesn't say that."

"Wasn't that what Dr. Berman did --- look at an individual case?"

"Right."

"So, Dr. McGrath, if you are using the example on the height of people and give them one factor that everybody above sixty-nine inches is a male, anybody below is female and actually two were females, would you be right twenty percent of the time?"

"Yes."

"Now if I gave you twenty-six more factors in that example regarding whether they are males or females, I bet we could be right one hundred percent of the time, couldn't we?"

"Research would show that you are wrong, and the reason is that it looked pretty impressive when you have all those risk factors. One thing that was not pointed out is that many of those risk factors go hand in hand. For example, a diagnosable psychiatric disorder and a family history of psychiatric disorder means that if you have one you are most likely to have the other, so those two are not independent predictors. There are a number of them that go hand in hand, so there really aren't as many risk factors that are implied. Even if there are, it doesn't matter because it's how sensitive when they are all put together."

"My question again, Dr. McGrath. If I gave you twenty-six more factors in that group, could we be right a hundred percent of the time?"

"No, absolutely not. I guarantee you that."

"What if we had the height, two had breasts and a vagina, then could we be right in determining that they are females?"

"Sir, if you can come up with a psychological measure which is a hundred percent sensitive, the vagina, and a hundred percent specific, bingo --- you can use that in a psychological autopsy. It would be perfect. In fact, there would be no sense in having a trial."

"So, Dr. McGrath, we would be right a hundred percent of the time?"

"You can't come up with it. Research shows you can't come up with anything with that kind of sensitivity or specificity. It just doesn't happen."

"I have no further questions."

Witness for the Defense – Joan Colby

Not only a member of the church, Ms. Colby was also a close elderly friend of the Guthries' and knew Bill and Sharon personally. She has been a member of the Wolsey Presbyterian Church for sixty-five years and served on the governing board when Bill was hired as pastor.

"Ms. Colby, did you ever participate with Sharon and Bill in any functions for the church?"

"Oh, yes, many times."

"Will you give us an example?"

"One of the first things I helped Dr. Bill with was the decorating of the church at Christmas. We had a surprise birthday party for him on December 29th. He didn't see the balloons or our sign at the back of the church that said *Happy Birthday*. Sharon had to poke him to see them ... he didn't know he was having a birthday party."

"Did you do formal things with Bill such as distributing communion?"

"Oh, yes, a good many times. Usually I would help on Sundays. Then during the week we would go to the nursing homes. They liked the communion, as much as the visitation."

"When you arranged for the delivery of communion, did you ever have an occasion to contact Bill in the early morning?"

"Yes. I knew that if I called him at 7:00 o'clock at the church office I could catch him there to find out what I was needed to do."

"Did you find him there at 7:00 o'clock in the morning on more than one occasion?"

"Oh, yes. There was more than one occasion that I was there opening the church for funerals, so the ladies could bring in the sandwiches, cakes and other food. If I saw a light in the study, I would knock on his door to say something to him and let him know that I had been there. I would also go into the sanctuary and open the east door, so the funeral director could come in. I'm on the worship committee and since the janitor quit, I would volunteer to do the cleaning."

"Ms. Colby, how many times would you estimate that you were able to catch Bill by phone or in person when he was over at the church office at 7:00 o'clock in the morning?"

"Two dozen, maybe."

"To your understanding was this his routine?"

"To my understanding --- yes."

"You took a road trip with Sharon several weeks prior to her death. Where did you go?"

"We went to Aberdeen to look for a dress for Sharon to wear to her daughter's wedding in June. I knew of a nice dress shop where I get my clothes, so I suggested that we go there and see what they had."

"On the drive home from Aberdeen, what did Sharon tell you about her retirement account at the clinic?"

"We talked about several things, but she said something about buying their youngest daughter a car because she needed transportation to get home from college. She first said they had thought about borrowing money from me, but then she said, *'I think I will cash in my retirement fund --- what the heck.'* That's the very words she used, *'what the heck.'*"

"Did Sharon ever talk to you about having problems sleeping?"

"Well ... I can't say that it was Sharon that told me herself. I had heard that she was having anxiety attacks and problems and I know what anxiety attacks are. I've had them myself. You don't die, but wish you could."

"Ms. Colby, when did you go to the Guthries' house to help do some cleaning?"

"The funeral was on Monday, so it was possibly the following Wednesday."

"Who went with you?"

"At first I was there by myself, then a friend came along because she didn't want me to be there alone. I am a little bit lame in one hip, so she helped me that day and came back the next day again to help. On the third day, another church lady came to help, and the fourth day I was there alone. A carpet cleaning service was there and I thought someone should be there."

"Did you see any prescription medications in the house when you were there those four days?"

"I can't name them, but there were lots and lots of them. I remember two boxes of Allegra, which I presumed was an antihistamine of some sort. They were in little boxes and the pills were in cardboard that you punch out to get the pills out. They were like the doctor would give a patient --- just samples that are not to be sold."

"Professional samples."

"Yes."

"In your opinion, Ms. Colby, would Bill have been fired on the spot if he would have announced to the members at the Wolsey and Bonilla churches that he was seeking a divorce from Sharon?"

"I don't think so."

"There has been some testimony regarding the Presbytery enacting some recent guidelines regarding divorce. Are you familiar with that information?"

"No, I'm not, but I do know that the minister from Pierre has been married twice and a minister from Brookings has a second wife. I don't know about divorce in the Presbyterian Church ---we've not had that situation."

"In your opinion, was Bill secure in his position at the church in Wolsey?"

"I'm sure that he would have been as far as the older people were concerned. We have had the best sermons that we have ever had."

"Ms. Colby, you told me about a suicide affecting some families in the Wolsey area that occurred around the time of Sharon's death. Approximately when would that have been?"

"Possibly two weeks before Sharon's death. A young lad, the grandson of our neighbors that lived next to us when we lived in the country, drove his car into some water and blew his head off."

"No more questions. Thank you."

Cross-examine by the State
Questioned by Moore

"Ms. Colby, you stated that you were on the session in your church. What special requests did the defendant make before he took the minister's job in Wolsey?"

"I don't remember that he made any special requests."

"Do you remember the defendant asking for some time off to go for counseling?"

"Yes, there would be times that he would want off."

"Specifically, Ms. Colby, do you remember the defendant requesting time to go to Nebraska for counseling once a month or every other month?"

"Not specifically. I knew that he went there for some seminars for further education; and, as a result, his name was put on a national committee."

"You testified that the defendant getting a divorce wouldn't really affect his job at the church. Would it have been more detrimental if you found out that the defendant was having an affair with a parish member?"

"That might have --- I don't know."

"Did you know that he was actually going to Nebraska to see Myra Conner?"

"I didn't know that."

"Would that maybe change the opinion on how secure he was in his job at the church if you knew that he was going there to see her?"

"Well, seeing is believing --- hearing is not."

"Did you and Sharon have plans to go back to Aberdeen shopping again?"

"Yes, she wanted to get some table liners and I told her that we could get them at a store in Aberdeen."

"Wasn't that trip to Aberdeen actually planned for the Saturday after Sharon's death?"

"Yes, I think so. They had brought the van over to my garage to keep it there for the wedding. They had it cleaned professionally and wanted to keep it inside."

"So Ms. Colby, the first trip was to get a dress for Sharon and the second trip was to get some tablecloths for the tables. Were these trips to Aberdeen pertaining to Lexi's wedding?"

"Yes."

"I have no further questions. Thank you."

Witness for the Defense – Mitch Rivers

Mitch married Lexi, the Guthries' middle daughter in June of 1999, and has known the Guthrie family for twelve years. As a paramedic

RN and a critical care paramedic, he also directs emergency services and responds to emergency calls.

"Mr. Rivers, have you been present throughout the testimony that has been given in this case?"

"Yes, I have."

"Have you ever done intubations?"

"Yes, being a paramedic for over twenty years, I have done thousands of them."

"Will you explain intubation?"

"Intratracheal intubation is when you take a patient's head, tip it back into the sniffing position and insert a laryngoscope into the right side of the mouth by sweeping the tongue to the left. You then look into the mouth using the light that is on the laryngoscope to find the vocal cords. As you are looking for the vocal cords, you take a tube that has a cuff on the end of it and place that tube into the vocal cords. In some cases, we will use a metal manuable wire that goes inside the stylet to allow us to reach up in case we have difficulty in getting the stylet into that location. We then place the tube. One of our most difficult intubations is when a patient doesn't have much of a neck. Frequently we ask someone to provide the Sellick maneuver, which is where pressure is applied to both sides of the trachea around the Adam's apple and pushed down. That pushes the trachea and the vocal cords into better view so we can insert the tube into the trachea. Using this procedure also reduces gastric regurgitation that frequently happens, and we don't want the contents of the stomach getting into the lungs."

"In your experience, did Sharon have the type of neck structure that would have required the Sellick maneuver to be used?"

"Absolutely.'

"I believe there has been some reference in one of the reports that Sharon's intubation was not a traumatic intubation. Mr. Rivers, would the manipulating that you described be considered a traumatic intubation?"

"I think that no matter what you do, you are going to be exerting some force, when you are lifting up, pulling forwards and outwards on the tongue and lower jaw, and pushing down on the neck."

"Would the type of bruising that Dr. Randall described be what you would expect in an intubation, even if the person who did it described it as not traumatic?"

"Yes."

"Were you present the day law enforcement officers contacted Les Hewitt regarding collecting prescription drugs from the Guthrie house?"

"Yes, I was."

"Were all of the medications in the house collected?"

"The search was very brief. We checked specific areas where we believed we would find medications, such as, above the cabinet in the kitchen, in the bathroom, in Bill's bed, and in the bedside containers. We collected all of the ones that we could find at the time."

"While visiting Bill and Sharon's house did you ever see any prescription drug samples?"

"Yes, I did. Frequently when visiting I would find different antihistamines and other medications. In some cases Sharon would give the antihistamines to Lexi and me because we also took those medications. On one particular occasion, I did notice a medication called Prozac."

"Mr. Rivers, was the Prozac a sample or was it in a prescription bottle?"

"It was a sample."

"Thank you, I have no further questions at this time."

Cross- examine by the State
Questioned by Moore

"Mr. Rivers, would bruising on the neck be caused by pressure to the neck or by the tube during intubation?"

"Perhaps within reason --- a little bit of both. You have to understand that in the trachea itself, around the mouth, and the neck is connective tissue, a lot like the areas around your gums. If you poke your finger into your gums they will bleed, so in many cases during an intubation, therefore, there is bleeding and bruising."

"Do you agree with Dr. Randall's testimony that the bruising could have been caused by the intubation?"

"Yes, it's my belief that it is very consistent with intratracheal intubation."

"Is it correct, that Dr. Randall also testified, that the bruising could also be caused by pressure to the neck?"

"As I remember, yes."

"I have no further questions."

Witness for the Defense – Lexi Rivers

"Ms. Rivers, have you been present in the courtroom throughout your father's trial?"

"Yes, I have."

"Did your father work for the sheriff's office in Sinclair, Wyoming?"

"He worked for the city of Sinclair in April of 1986, the year I graduated. They had their own police department and the sheriff's office oversaw them."

"Is it correct to say, that for part of this time when your dad was working for the Sinclair Police Department, that you were still living at home?"

"Yes, that's correct."

"Did you see your father go off to work with a uniform on?"

"Yes, I did."

"Did he sometimes stop at home for lunch in a patrol car?"

"Yes."

"Is there any doubt in your mind that your father did work for the Sinclair Wyoming Police Department?"

"No doubt."

"Did he work for the Carbon County Sheriff's Office?'"

"No."

"Thank you, nothing further."

Cross-examine by the State
Questioned by Moore

"Ms. Rivers, is Sinclair in Carbon County?"

"Yes, it is."

"How close is that to Rawlins?"

"About six miles."

"Is Rawlins also in Carbon County?"

"Yes, it is."

"Ms. Rivers, are you sure that it was Sinclair, Wyoming?"

"Yes."

"I have no further questions."

January 19, 2000

Trial Day Five

Witness for the Defense – Dr. Howard Burns

Dr. Burns, an emergency physician and assistant director of the emergency department at McKennan Hospital in Sioux Falls, does toxicology consultation. Toxicology is a study of the negative effects and poison effects of various substances or drugs.

"Dr. Burns, what materials did I ask you to review concerning the death of Sharon Guthrie?"

"I reviewed various toxicology texts and the poise index, which is a micrometics production that lists data on various toxins, poisons and drugs. I also did some review of the medical literature."

"A blood sample was drawn from Sharon Guthrie on May 14, 1999. Dr. Burns, did you review the toxicology report, which yielded information regarding certain prescription drugs found present in Sharon's bloodstream?"

"Yes, I did."

"Do you recall what time that blood sample was drawn?"

"It was drawn shortly after her arrival in the emergency department."

"What were the results of her toxicology report?"

"It showed an elevated level of Temazepam, one thousand eight hundred forty nanograms per millimeter."

"Dr. Burns, would that amount of Temazepam be considered a therapeutic dose or an overdose?"

"It would be an overdose --- not necessarily a lethal dose, but more than a therapeutic dose."

"Would that be considered an overdose in the neighborhood of three times?"

"Yes, in that neighborhood."

"Regarding Sharon Guthrie, can you state what the effect would have been on her?"

"It would definitely have been an intoxicating effect, but not necessarily a lethal effect."

"Dr. Burns, what range of effects could you have expected to see on Sharon from that concentration in her blood?"

"Depending on Mrs. Guthrie's tolerance, she could have a moderate intoxication and still be partly arousable to a deep comatose state, possibly even death, if she was more susceptible to that type of medicine."

"Can you explain the time frame regarding how quickly drugs are absorbed into a person's system?"

"That varies according to the drug, but regarding Temazepam, there have been enough studies for us to know that generally after it is ingested orally on a relatively empty stomach you can reach a peak level within about one hour after ingestion."

"Dr. Burns, how quickly would a person ingesting Temazepam begin to feel the effects from it?"

"It could be as soon as fifteen to twenty minutes if it was a large ingestion and was taken on an empty stomach."

"Temazepam is in the category of benzodiazepines. What effect do benzodiazepines have on a person's blood pressure?"

"They could potentially lower the blood pressure."

"Going back to the level of Temazepam found in Sharon's blood. Can you tell us how many pills she would have had to take to reach the level of one thousand eight hundred and forty nanograms per millimeter?"

"Assuming a hundred percent absorption and fairly immediately, it would be around five pills. Five pills would be the minimum ingested to reach that level, but in all likelihood it was more than five pills."

"Dr. Burns, is there any way to determine how many more pills?"

"There is no real way to know unless one knew the actual volume of the entire stomach contents and the concentration of the drug."

"You say concentration? Does that mean that we are not talking about a large quantity of Temazepam, but a large concentration of Temazepam?"

"There is no way of knowing whether this is one pill that was in a particular area of the stomach with a volume leading to a large concentration or multiple pills, more dilute, in a large fluid filled stomach."

"Using an analogy, would it be correct that a packet of sugar in a small cup of coffee might make it very sweet, but a packet of sugar in a large pot of coffee wouldn't yield the same concentration?"

"Exactly."

"Dr. Burns, there has been some testimony that no gel cap pieces or pill fragments were found in Sharon's stomach contents. What can you determine from that information?"

"That's not very helpful because it was a small bore lavine tube used to suction the stomach. True stomach washing wasn't done where we put in a large bore tube and wash out the contents. Mrs. Guthrie was in a near cardiopulmonary arrest situation, so for obvious reasons they didn't pump out her stomach. With that small of a caliber tube, it wouldn't have removed any pill fragments or gel capsule fragments through the smaller holes."

"Can you explain how long it would take gelatin capsules to dissolve in the stomach?"

"Most of the time a gelatin capsule will be fully dissolved within an hour or less."

"How often do you personally deal with drug overdoses?"

"I work in a relatively large hospital with a psychiatric acute care unit; so when I am working, I see overdoses on a daily basis."

"Lorazepam and Oxazepam were also found present in Sharon's blood and stomach contents. Dr. Burns, in your experience with dealing with drug overdoses, is the presence of multiple drugs consistent or inconsistent with what you would find in an overdose?"

"It's more common for overdoses to be multiple drugs."

"When you talk about overdoses, are you talking about intentional self-administered overdoses?"

"Yes."

"Are the benzodiazepines Lorazepam and Oxazepam that were found in Sharon's system available in capsules or tablets or both?"

"They are available in both."

"What were the therapeutic levels regarding the Lorazepam and the Oxazepam?"

"Those were lower levels and would generally be considered subtherapeutic."

"Doctor, regarding the presence of those two drugs in Sharon's bloodstream, can you tell us whether that subtherapeutic level would give you any indication of when the drug was consumed?"

"It would imply that it was consumed recently, but you are going to have a low level of drug at the beginning of absorption and also at the end, so you can't say for sure."

"How about the presence of those same drugs in her stomach contents?"

"The fact that she had those drugs present in the stomach and not absorbed would imply that it was acute ingestion and that the low levels were early on in absorption."

"Dr. Burns, can you give us a time frame as to when the Lorazepam and the Oxazepam might have been taken?"

"I would estimate that all of the drugs were most likely taken within a four hour period before she developed the problems."

"For what types of symptoms might a doctor prescribe Lorazepam and Oxazepam?"

"Most commonly for anxiety, various psychiatric disorders usually involving anxiety, panic attacks, for sleep, and for depression."

"Would it be common to prescribe those two drugs to be taken together?"

"Since they are in the same class and generally have the same effect, normally I would say they would only be prescribed one drug at a time. It is possible that one might be used for anti-anxiety and the other for sleep, but that wouldn't be the usual case."

"You noted earlier, Dr. Burns, that one of the side effects of taking benzodiazepines is that it could reduce a person's blood pressure. If an individual was taking medication for hypertension or had high blood pressure, would that add anything to the equation?"

"It would be hard to predict. It could have an addictive effect or even more than addictive; but with somebody with high blood pressure, it might not have any effect."

"Is it possible that someone who has taken the benzodiazepines would be subject to decreased blood pressure, to faint if he would lean over, lower his head and sit up quickly?"

"Yes, it's possible that a person on those types of medications would be more susceptible to that type of a faint."

"There has been some testimony regarding bruising around the larynx of Sharon's neck. In your opinion, Dr. Burns, would that be consistent with intubating someone with a short, thick neck?"

"It's quite possible to get bruising from the method called the Sellick maneuver because you have to push quite firmly."

"Dr. Burns, because you have utilized this procedure, would that necessarily be considered a traumatic intubation?"

"Not necessarily traumatic --- no."

"Going back to the benzodiazepines. Are there any known side effects regarding patients suffering from depression?"

"They can have the potential to aggravate depression."

"Thank you, I don't have any further questions."

Cross-examine by the State
Questioned by Moore

"Dr. Burns, you referred to the one thousand eight hundred and forty nanograms per millimeter as a significant intoxication and that the range would be from awake intoxication to possibly death. Didn't you call this an acute overdose."

"Yes."

"Does using that formula to determine that there were at least five capsules of thirty milligram capsules of Temazepam in Sharon's system take into account what was left in the stomach?"

"No, it does not. Working backward from the level in the blood led me to the minimum amount that she ingested, and it was fully absorbed immediately."

"Did you find a large amount of pills still in Sharon's stomach?"

"There was more substance in the stomach, but we don't know how much?"

"Did you conclude that this was an intentional overdose?"

"I don't think that can be determined for sure by the data we have."

"Are these drugs that Sharon had in her system what caused her to drown in the bathtub?"

"It could potentially cause someone to drown in a bathtub."

"Dr. Burns, in Sharon's case, was there any other reason for her to drown in the bathtub that day?"

"Not that I know of."

"I have no further questions."

Judge Martin, the defendant and counsel retire to judge's chambers to address the late discovery of a typewritten note presented earlier by the defense to the State. Michael Moore and Gregory Wilson verify that this is the true and correct copy of the note. Judge Martin asks for any objections to receiving the note into evidence for the purpose of this hearing. No objections are given. He proceeds to enter into evidence a newspaper article dated December 27, 1999, regarding Cindy Orton, the fingerprint expert. No objections are given.

Judge Martin addresses counsel. "Mr. Wilson, in all fairness to the defendant, since you wanted to investigate the matter to make sure as to whether the typewritten note was going to be beneficial or detrimental to your client, I am going to allow this note into evidence. I will later on ask for a further hearing to determine what costs were incurred by the State by virtue of this document not being turned over by the discovery deadline.

"Regarding a South Dakota case entitled *State versus Dace*, I want to advise counsel that it deals with a situation where the defendant took the witness stand and wanted only to be cross-examined on certain items that he testified to during the course of his questioning with defense counsel. According to *State versus Dace*, cross-examine should be limited to matters covered on direct examination; however, it is within the discretion of the trial judge to allow questioning into all other additional relevant matters as if on direct examination. Counsel, I will allow the inquiry to go beyond the scope of the direct examination. I will grant the State the right to ask the defendant any additional relevant questions about any relevant issue in this case. I wish Mr. Guthrie to fully understand that when he takes the witness stand in this matter that he will be opening himself up to matters beyond what he has testified to. Now, let's get back into the courtroom."

Witness for the Defense – William Guthrie

"Bill, I am going to show you Defendant's Exhibit K. Please explain what this is?"

"This is a note typewritten by Sharon that I found in my office at the Wolsey Presbyterian Church on or around June 10, 1999."

"I have no further questions."

Cross-examine by the State
Questioned by Moore

"Mr. Guthrie, where did you find this note?"

"It was in a liturgy book that Sharon and I used to prepare bulletins for church."

"What did you do with the note after you found it?"

"I gave it to my attorney on June 15th."

"Mr. Guthrie, was the note folded when you found it?"

"Yes, it was."

"Did you unfold it and read it?"

"Yes, I did."

"Will you please read it to the jury?"

May 13, 1999

Dear Suzanne
I am sorry I ruined your wedding. Your dad told me about
your concerns of my interfering in Lexi's and possibly I
might ruin hers. I won't be there so put your mind at ease.
You will understand after the wedding is done.

I love you all Mom.

"Mr. Guthrie, did you tell law enforcement that you found this letter?"

"No, I didn't."

"When did the State or law enforcement find out about this note?"

"Yesterday."

"Am I correct that you kept this note hidden all this time?"

"My attorney had it --- yes."

"When you talked to Suzanne in June about what happened to Sharon, did you tell her about this note?"

"No, I didn't."

"Mr. Guthrie, on June 9, 1999, during the interview by law enforcement, did they specifically ask you if there was anything that would indicate that Sharon may have committed suicide?"

"Yes, they did."

"Did you tell them about this note when they interviewed you?"

"No, I didn't."

"What was your answer when Agent Lindberg asked you if your wife made any suicide threats as a result of your relationship with Myra Conner?"

"Yes -- I think she did."

"What was your answer when Agent Lindberg asked you to give him some idea of what Sharon said?"

"She said that if it wasn't resolved, she was going to do something about it."

"Again, Mr. Guthrie, when you were asked about Sharon making suicide threats, did you mention this typewritten note?"

"No, I did not."

"How was the note folded when you found it?"

"It was folded in half and I folded it again after I read it."

"When you talked with Suzanne in July when she came to your home with the tape recorder, didn't she beg you to give her a reason that her mother would have committed suicide?"

"Yes."

"Mr. Guthrie, were you aware of this note at that time?"

"Yes."

"Did you go to Suzanne's place of employment four days after the taped recording and admit to her that you were having an affair with Myra Conner?"

"Yes, I did."

"Did you also tell Suzanne that day that Sharon was suicidal?"

"Yes, I did."

"Did you tell her about this note?"

"No, I didn't."

"Mr. Guthrie, is this note conveniently dated at the top May 13th?"

"That's what it says."

"Is the note signed?"

"No, it's not."

"Is there any handwriting on the note?"

"No."

"Mr. Guthrie, is the note addressed to you?"

"No, it's not."

"Had this affair with Myra Conner lasted for a long time?"

"Yes."

"I understand that the affair was broken off in January of 1999. Is that correct?"

"Yes."

"Does the note say anything about the affair?"

"No."

"When talking with law enforcement regarding what happened to Sharon on the morning of the drowning, did you tell them that you tried to help Sharon?"

"Yes, I did."

"When you got back to the house after being at the church, did you say that you felt some wetness on the floor, and then went into the bathroom?"

"Yes, I did."

"Mr. Guthrie, when you tried to help Sharon, did you turn the water off first or did you pull the plug in the bathtub first?"

"I know there was a series of things --- but I don't recall."

"After you did those things, did you try to help her?"

"Yes, I did."

"Was that before or after the water had drained out of the tub?"

"I was holding her up while the water was draining out of the tub."

"Didn't that take about two minutes?"

"I don't recall --- it seemed like a long time."

"Did you try to get her out of the tub by pulling on her arms?"

"I just grabbed a hold of her and tried to pull her out. I don't recall grabbing an arm or a leg, whatever --- I was just trying to get her out."

"Mr. Guthrie, did you put your arms around her shoulders?"

"No."

"Did you put your arms around her body?"

"Yes."

"Did you get her out of the tub?"

"No, I couldn't."

"Did you try to swing her feet out of the tub and stand her up?"

"I tried to get her out."

"Did you get her feet out of the tub?"

"I tried, but I couldn't get her out."

"Did you get in the tub?"

"Yes."

"Did you have a hold of her in the tub?"

"I tried to get her out."

"When you couldn't get her out of the tub, did you then clean her airways?"

"I tried to force the water out of her lungs."

"Did you do that by pushing on her chest?"

"No --- on her back."

"Was Sharon face down in the tub Mr. Guthrie?"

"Yes."

"Did the water come out of her mouth?"

"Yes, it did."

"You did all of this and you didn't get wet, did you?"

"Yes, I did get wet."

"Peggy Stevens testified that you weren't wet. Either she is mistaken or lying?"

"I would say so."

"Mr. Guthrie, did you hide this affair from your family?"

"Yes, I did."

"Did you deny the affair to Suzanne during the taped interview?"

"I did."

"Even when Suzanne pleaded with you, not wanting to believe that her mother committed suicide, you still didn't respond to that, did you?"

"No."

"Even having this typewritten note, that you claim is a suicide note from Sharon, you still didn't respond, correct?"

"Yes."

"Four days later you talk to Suzanne again and tell her that her mother committed suicide?"

"No, I said I had suspicions."

"But, according to this note --- if this note is real, isn't it right that you knew that's what it was supposed to be?"

"I would suspicion that --- yes."

"But, yet, you didn't tell anyone about it and specifically Suzanne when she was begging you for an answer. Isn't that correct?"

"That's right."

"The day that you saw Suzanne at work, didn't you tell her that you told Sharon about the affair the night before she died?"

"Yes."

"That's not true, is it Mr. Guthrie?"

"What do you mean it's not true?"

"Didn't you tell Sharon about the affair before that night?"

"Yes."

"Mr. Guthrie, didn't you lead Suzanne on to believe that her mother had committed suicide because you had told Sharon about the affair the night before her death?"

"No."

"Did you know that Suzanne had talked to Sharon on the phone the night before the drowning?"

"Yes."

"Was Sharon upset while she was talking to Suzanne on the phone?"

241

"No."

"She wasn't having an anxiety attack like you said she was, was she?"

"Yes, she was."

"Did you tell law enforcement that you had told Sharon about the affair in January?"

"No, I don't recall that --- maybe it might have been, yes."

"Mr. Guthrie, didn't you tell law enforcement that you and Sharon had been getting along and that you were working things out with her?"

"We were trying."

"When your brother-in-law, Larry Provance, came to your home on August 22nd, didn't you tell him that you had told Sharon about the affair in March?"

"I may have told her --- yeah."

"Did you tell Mr. Provance that you and Sharon were praying about it and decided to go on?"

"We did."

"Isn't it correct, Mr. Guthrie, that you told Suzanne on July 30th at her work place, that you had told Sharon about the affair on May 13th, and that's why she committed suicide?"

"I did not try to put any guilt on Suzanne."

"Did you request special considerations of the church in Wolsey, telling them that you would have to go back to Nebraska periodically for counseling?"

"Yes."

"Mr. Guthrie, isn't it true that you were really going there to see Myra Conner?"

"Yes."

"Did you get up in front of the Orleans church and deny the affair to the congregation?"

"Yes."

"Did you also deny the affair to the session at the church in Orleans?"

"Yes."

"Did you claim that you weren't having this affair because you were impotent?"

"Yes."

"Did you actually have a note from a doctor, Mr. Guthrie?"

"Yes."

"You told law enforcement and your brother-in-law that you and Sharon were getting along quite well, yet didn't you tell Les, Danielle, and Suzanne that you were going to divorce Sharon after Lexi's wedding?"

"That's not all the facts."

"Isn't that what they testified to?"

"Yes, I know it."

"Are they mistaken and lying?"

"No."

"You weren't trying very hard, were you?"

"I guess not."

"You told your brother-in-law, Larry Provance, that everyone knew Sharon was suicidal, but you weren't able to give him any names, were you?"

"I don't remember that."

"You were fully aware of this alleged suicide note the day that your brother-in-law came to your house to talk, yet you didn't tell him anything about it, did you?"

"No."

"Mr. Guthrie, do you remember talking to Don Perry about what happened to Sharon?"

"Yes."

"Did you tell him that it happened at one o'clock in the morning?"

"Yes --- No."

"That's what he testified to. Are you saying that he is mistaken and lying?"

"No, I am saying that he might have been mistaken about the time."

"At the end of the conversation you told him *By the way everything is going great with us.*' Were you referring to your relationship with Sharon?"

"Yes."

"Did you tell him prior to your move to South Dakota that you were going to divorce Sharon?"

"Yes."

"When your brother-in-law asked you what you told Don Perry, what did you tell him?"

"I don't recall."

"Did you ever talk to Don Perry about the rumors of the affair between you and Myra Conner?"

"Yes."

"Did you tell him that it wasn't true because you were impotent, as a result of the assault in Lincoln, Nebraska?"

"Yes."

"So, all of these times when you were telling the church session and Don Perry this story about being impotent, you weren't having any trouble having sex with Myra Conner, were you?"

"No."

"Did you tell law enforcement that Sharon had been sleepwalking since 1975?"

"Yes."

"Are you the only one that ever saw Sharon sleepwalking?"

"That's right."

"Did you ever talk to anyone about it?"

"I thought the girls knew about it."

"On April 29th, did you go to Patricia Minor complaining of a sleeping problem?"

"Yes."

"Did she offer you the drugs Ambien and Xanax?

"Yes."

"Did you tell her that you didn't want those because they didn't work for you?"

"No --- Patricia wrote a prescription for Ambien and I took it to Sharon and she said Ambien didn't work. Sharon and I went to Patricia and she corrected the prescription."

"Mr. Guthrie, did you hear Patricia Minor testify that she offered you Ambien and Xanax, but you declined them because they didn't work for you?"

"Yes, I heard her testify. Sharon said those medications didn't work."

"So, then, it's all Sharon's fault?"

"I'm not saying that."

"Are you saying that Patricia Minor is either mistaken or lying?"

"Mistaken, yes --- lying, no."

"Didn't Patricia Minor write a prescription for Temazepam that day for you?"

"Yes."

"Did you have it filled at the K-Mart pharmacy?"

"Yes, I did."

"Isn't it true that later you filled the same prescription at Statz Drug?"

"No, I did not."

"Mr. Guthrie, did you sign for it?"

"Yes, I signed for it, but I didn't know what I was getting."

"Did you go back to Patricia Minor on June 9th, still complaining of having sleeping problems?"

"Yes."

"Did you take the Ambien that she offered you?"

"I did."

"Wasn't that the same drug she offered to you before, and you said that it didn't work for you?"

"I told her it didn't work for me. There is --- never mind."

"Did you tell law enforcement that Sharon was hooked on Benadryl?"

"She was."

"Did she take that for her allergies and her sleep?"

"Yes."

"Knowing that Sharon was hooked on Benadryl, didn't you twice go get a prescription for a more powerful sleeping drug?"

"No."

"During your affair with Myra Conner, weren't you afraid of getting caught?"

"Yes."

"Weren't you afraid of getting caught because you would lose your job?"

"No."

"You were sneaking around with Myra Conner, weren't you?"

"Yes."

"Were you meeting down by the river in Orleans?"

"Yes."

"Did you talk to Myra Conner about leaving Sharon and getting together with her?"

"Not directly."

"Myra Conner testified that you had those conversations. Is she also lying or mistaken?"

"No."

"She testified that the two of you had many conversations about the reason you wouldn't leave Sharon, and that was because you were afraid of losing your job. Is that correct?"

"About losing my job, yes."

"Were you happy with the relationship, just sneaking around and seeing her a couple times a week?"

"No."

"You loved Myra Conner, didn't you Mr. Guthrie?"

"No."

"You didn't love her?"

"No."

"Was it just for the sex?"

"Yes."

"Did it upset you when she broke off the relationship with you in January of '99?"

"To some degree --- yes."

"Did you continue to have contact with her?"

"She called me."

"Did you also call her?"

"Occasionally."

"Did you make a request to see her again after she broke it off?"

"Yes, I did."

"Did you see her again the end of February --- or early March?"

"Yes."

"Did you tell law enforcement that Myra Conner found out about Sharon's death through her church?"

"I called her."

"But, you told law enforcement that she found out through the church."

"I guess I did."

"Well, Mr. Guthrie, do you guess you did or is that what you told them?"

"I did --- yes."

"Isn't it a lie that you called her?"

"I called her and then she called me back."

"About a week after Sharon's death, did you have a conversation with Myra Conner about getting together?"

"She called me."

"Did you ask her if you could get together with her?"

"No, I did not."

"So, is she mistaken or lying about that?"

"Yes."

"When she told you no, didn't you hang up on her?"

"That's right."

"You were mad at her because you wanted to get together, weren't you?"

"No."

"Where did you go after Sharon's funeral?"

"To Casper, Wyoming, to see Karen and Eddy Neilson."

"What's your relationship with the Neilsons?"

"Friends."

"What's your relationship with Karen?"

"Just a friend."

"I have here an envelope addressed to you. Who is this from?"

"Karen."

"I have a card here. Who is this from?"

"Karen."

"Mr. Guthrie, do you remember seeing this envelope and card?"

"No."

"Don't you remember receiving this in the mail?"

"No."

"Mr. Guthrie, would you please read to the jury what is imprinted inside the card?"

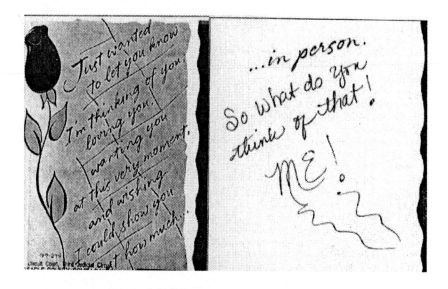

Just wanted to let you know I'm thinking of you
and loving you, wanting you at this very moment
and wishing I could show you just how much
...in person.

"Mr. Guthrie, Karen Neilson handwrote something on the inside of this card. Please read this to the jury."

So what do you think of that! Me!

"So, Mr. Guthrie, you get this type of card from Karen Neilson and you say that you are just friends?"
"That's right."
"Weren't you actually making plans to move out to Casper, Wyoming?"
"Yes."
"I have no further questions."

Redirect by the Defense

"Bill, did you kill your wife?"
"No, I did not."
"No further questions, Your Honor."

Witness for the Defense – Michael Waldner

"Mr. Waldner, Judd Robbins testified earlier for the State. Are you familiar with his name and have no doubt regarding his credentials?"

"Yes --- no doubt about that."

"Is it correct that I retained you as a computer consultant to consult with me regarding this case and also to review materials that were furnished to you through the cooperation of Mr. Robbins and Mr. Moore?"

"Yes. I received the data directly from the State's Attorney's Office in what is called a jazz drive format, which means the information was already acquired off the hard drives of the Guthrie computer. The data was in a special forensics format, so once taken from the hard drive it can't be tampered with or changed and requires special software to actually look at it and read the information."

"Did you have to obtain some special software before you were able to look at the information and read it?"

"Yes."

"Was that software expensive?"

"The cost was approximately five hundred dollars."

"Did you have to purchase any other hardware or software to be able to analyze this data?"

"Yes. I spent three hundred dollars, so I was able to read the jazz drive format."

"Mr. Waldner, what else did you need available to examine the data from a forensic point of view, so that your examination didn't alter information that was on the hard drives?"

"Once I had the information and the software, I only needed another computer system to actually view the information."

"Did you conduct various searches at my request?"

"Yes, I did."

"What was the first search you did?"

"Basically, I looked for a suicide note."

"Did you find anything?"

"No."

"Mr. Waldner, I have here a typewritten note that the defendant found in his office. Did you specifically conduct a search of the Guthrie computer trying to determine if this note was located in the hard drives?"

"Yes, I did."

"Were you able to locate it?"

"No, I was not."

"Is there anything in particular regarding what type of computer or printer would have generated this note?"

"The initial copy that I looked at was a photocopy. When I looked at the quality of the print with a magnifying glass, it appeared to be printed off an ink jet printer."

"Mr. Waldner, can you tell us anything else about the type of equipment that this note might have been printed on?"

"Not from just that document, no."

"Would it be possible that this note typed on the computer without being saved could still be found on the computer after it was printed?"

"The possibility of it being there immediately or very soon after they had printed it --- yes, it could still be there."

"In your opinion, how long would that note remain there?"

"Basically it would remain there until either somebody printed something else, or the particular area where the document was stored on the computer before it was printed was overwritten by either another file or another file that is being printed."

"I have here a document from the materials on the Guthrie computer that you reviewed. Was this found in the area storage indicating that it was an unsent e-mail?"

"That is correct."

"On the computer-generated lines, the fourth line from the top, the last word says *sent*. Would it be fair to say that the author of the note thought that the note was sent?"

"Quite possible --- yes."

"Mr. Waldner, has this happened to you whenever you have used e-mail?"

"Yes, sir."

"I have no further questions."

Cross-examine by the State
Questioned by Moore

"Mr. Waldner, is it correct that the jazz cartridge you received is the same information that Mr. Robbins had?"

"That's correct."

"You testified that you searched for the alleged suicide note and didn't find anything regarding that note, correct?"

"Yes, sir."

"Did you also go through and confirm everything that Mr. Robbins had found?"

"Yes, the majority of his information."

"Mr. Waldner, were all of the searches for drugs correct?"

"Yes."

"How about the searches for bathtub accidents? Were those also correct?"

"There's no reason not to believe that they weren't."

"I don't have any further questions."

Witness for the Defense – Cindy Orton

Ms. Orton is a fingerprint expert. Her training revolves around crime scene processing and latent print examination. A latent print, opposed to another type of print, is a chance impression and sometimes can be hidden. If a person touches something he will most likely leave an impression of the ridges of his fingers, which would commonly be referred to as his fingerprint. During a latent print examination one can't see the print. An examiner will use various chemicals to bring out a hidden print, which is called a latent. It would then be preserved and compared against a record print of an individual to identify that one or more of his fingers touched the object."

"Ms. Orton, is a fingerprint record made purposefully for identification purposes, such as law enforcement might use?"

"That is correct. A controlled recording is normally what you would see on a fingerprint card. Ink would be placed on the surface of the friction ridge skin on the finger that you want to record and rolled onto a white surface."

"Is it correct to say that one method of identifying a latent print is to compare it with a known or record print?"

"That is correct. If you have an unknown print on an object, I would study that print and use the three basic points of comparison in the characteristics of a print. When you look at your fingers you have ridges on them that flow in a pattern. Within that pattern there are points of identification. As you study the points of comparison with the record and the latent print you look for the same points of comparison to be in the same relative position, in the same direction, and the same type of point. If there aren't any unexplainable dissimilarities and the two match, then you have identification."

"Ms. Orton, what do you do if there isn't a record print available?"

"Without a record print you can't get a controlled rolling of a person's print. The next best thing is to take an item or items that the individual has touched on a regular basis and process them for latents. If we find latents that match on several of the items an individual has touched, then we can strongly assume the prints to be his prints. This is very difficult to do because a latent print is usually just a partial print. Very seldom is the whole print found like what would be rolled on a fingerprint card. If a record print is available, one wouldn't need much portion of the skin to make identification, but without a record print it becomes more difficult. For example, if I had a latent print from one side of the finger, it might not be much to work with, so in order to find that exact same latent on the individual's belongings is very difficult. One would have to have that exact same spot where they had left the same impression on something else."

"Ms. Orton, if you had the left half of a thumb print that you were trying to identify and you find the right half of another latent thumb print, is there any way to say they came from the same thumb?"

"There is absolutely no way to identify it unless there is some overlapping in the center that can be identified."

"Where have you had the opportunity to investigate suicide notes?"

"In the military."

"What did you do with this typewritten note that I gave you to examine?"

"I processed the document for latent prints by using a chemical called Ninhydrin. Perspiration contains alphamino acids and Ninhydrin, for whatever reason, reacts to alphamino acids and turns a bright red or purple color. Ninhydrin has been used extensively over the years for processing porous items for latent fingerprints that may have been left by perspiration."

"Were you able to find any fingerprints on this note?"

"Yes, there were quite a number of fingerprints on the document."

"Ms. Orton, why did you pick the four prints located around the edge of the page?"

"Mainly because they were good prints and because of the time constraints. I wanted to at least start with those to determine if we could eliminate them as being placed there either by William Guthrie or Gregory Wilson because they had touched this note. Since those four were good strong prints, I marked them and began to do the comparisons."

"Please explain the differences between prints on a fairly porous object as opposed to a relatively hard object?"

"A porous object like this typewritten note is often good to work with because if there is perspiration on the finger or other contaminants, such as oils that may have come from the back of the neck, paint or blood, those types of things will soak into a porous document. That makes it much more sturdy and stable to work with. On a nonporous item like a plastic bottle where fingers might be sweaty or oily, the print could easily be wiped away, which makes nonporous items very fragile."

"After you eliminated me as a possible source of the four prints, did you receive a set of Mr. Guthrie's record prints from the Beadle County Sheriff's Office and also eliminate him as the source of those same prints?"

"Yes, I did."

"Ms. Orton, you refer to two of the prints as B-1 and B-2. Why did you use the same letter?"

"I used the same letter because they were made by the same finger or thumb. Prints A and C were two totally different fingers or thumbs, so I concluded that were at least three different prints on the document."

"Are the prints labeled B-1 and B-2 on the left middle side of the page consistent with someone holding it and reading it?"

"Yes, because of the location on the paper it would likely be the left thumb, so I first search the left thumb and then I do all the other nine digits."

"Ms. Orton, since there were no record fingerprints for Sharon Guthrie, did you make some attempt to find latent prints for her?"

"Yes. I was provided with numerous items that either belonged to Mrs. Guthrie or ones that she had handled. I have been working on those items since January 10th using Ninhydrin. This process can sometimes take anywhere from twenty-four hours to several weeks before prints will show up. It can be accelerated a bit by the use of heat and humidity, but for whatever reasons the sensitivity of the prints that may be left don't always react right away. Each day I look at the same documents and sometimes new prints will start to develop."

"Regarding the typewritten note that we are dealing with, just because someone handles an object, how likely is it that prints will be left?"

"That would depend on what is on the individual's hands. If the person has just washed his hands and dried them prior to handling the object, most likely there wouldn't be any prints that we could develop. If the individual is anxious, ill or running a fever, he may have sweaty palms. Also, if the individual has been touching oily parts of his body, he would be more apt to leave a print. Perfume, make-up, or lipstick on the fingers would be more likely to leave a print."

"You stated that perspiration is one of the principal means by which fingerprints can be detected. In your opinion Ms. Orton, were the prints on this document from sweaty hands?"

"Yes, from very sweaty hands because they were all over the place. There was red and purple all over the front and back of the document."

"When you were looking at Sharon's personal items to find latent prints of hers, why did you select check blank copies?"

"Sometimes the flimsy part of the carbon copy will receive fingerprints very well, but I didn't have any luck with those."

"What other items of Sharon's were given to you?"

"There were several envelopes from anniversary cards. I specifically was looking for a print of a left-hand thumb because of the way you hold an envelope and pull the card out. I also had two of her Bibles, one of which she used extensively."

"Ms. Orton, you have investigated approximately forty plus suicide notes. Is it common or uncommon to find prints on suicide notes?"

"It's very common and that is why Ninhydrin is specifically used. It's believed that anybody contemplating suicide is going to be anxious and sweaty."

"No further questions."

Cross-examine by the State
Questioned by Moore

"Ms. Orton, were you able to identify if Sharon Guthrie had ever touched that note?"

"No, I was not."

"Is it true that older people have less amino acids in their hands than younger people have in their hands?"

"That could be possible, but I don't know that answer."

"Were you able to affirm that the same person made all of the same fingerprints on that document?"

"No, I could not."

"Is it correct that B-1 and B-2 were the only two that you know are the same prints?"

"That's correct."

"Did you find any of the defendant's prints on the note?"

"Of the four prints that I examined --- no."

"Did you find any of Mr. Wilson's prints?"

"Not any of those four. I had been advised that they had both touched the document, so I only worked with A, B-1, B-2 and C because of the time constraints."

"Did you compare the prints to the Guthries' daughters?"

"No."

"How about the Guthries' sons-in-law?"

"No."

"Did you examine any of the members of the church?"

"No."

"How about the defendant's secretary?"

"No."

"Ms. Orton, do you know where the defendant kept this document for seven months?"

"No, I do not."

"Did you check the document for prints of Myra Conner?"

"No."

"How about Karen Neilson?"

"No."

"Would you have been able to check for more prints if the defendant would have given you this document in June?"

"Yes, I could have."

"I have no further questions."

Redirect by the Defense

"Ms. Orton, just so there is no mistake. Is it correct that from the latent prints on the materials provided to you, that you could neither identify those four prints as Sharon Guthrie's or eliminate them as not being created by Sharon?"

"That is correct."

"Nothing further."

Recross by the State
Questioned by Moore

"Ms. Orton, did look at certain items of Sharon's to see if you could find a left thumb print?"

"Yes."

"Did you also look at numerous checks, two Bibles, and a photo album?"

"I didn't process the photo album."

"Why not?"

"Because it is a nonporous item, and I was hoping there would be enough on the other items that were porous. I also didn't want to deface the photo album and the likelihood of finding Sharon's prints would be better on the porous items, which I may add, are still developing."

"Did you find any usable prints on any of those?"

"Yes."

"Did any of them match the prints on the note?"

"Not as of yet that I can tell from the bits and pieces that I have."

"I have no further questions."

Witness for the Defense – Mitch Rivers

"Mr. Rivers, tell us about the drug searches that you did on the Guthrie computer during the time of Sharon's death?"

"I was preparing for a conference, so I took my laptop computer with me to Wolsey. When I got there, my laptop wouldn't function; so Bill allowed me to use his computer. I sent some e-mails, and then I also did research on several of the medications that we had found in the house that were given to law enforcement. I remember looking up Temazepam, which is also, Restoril, and I specifically remember looking up Ativan. I looked up some other medications, but those I can't remember. I looked at the anti-hypertensive medication that Sharon was taking. I used Excite and Lycos, but not AOL search because it's too slow. There is one other search engine I used, but the name evades me."

"Mr. Rivers, if the searches entered into evidence would bear the dates of May 15th and May 16th, would this possibly be the time frame that you did those searches on Bill's computer?"

"That would be correct."

"No further questions."

Cross-examine by the State
Questioned by Moore

"Mr. Rivers, did you do the search regarding Temazepam on May 4, 1999?"

"No, I would not have had the opportunity to do that."

"Did you do any of the searches for drugs in April?"

"No, I was not there in April."

"I have no further questions."

Witness for the Defense – Suzanne Hewitt

"Ms. Hewitt, did you assist me in finding your mother's items which Ms. Orton has been working on to identify latent prints?"

"Yes, I did."

"What can you tell me about this handwritten note on a napkin?"

"It's a note that my mom wrote to my dad four or five years ago."

"When did you first find this note?"

"My husband found it about a month ago and brought it to me."

"What did you do with this napkin note when you found it?"

"I talked with both of my sisters, and we didn't feel it was necessary to show it to anyone."

"When you were looking for documents of your mother's, was this note placed with the items to be transported to Cindy Orton?"

"Not at first, but it was later."

"Was this note subsequently removed from the materials that were taken to Madison?"

"No, it was just left on the table."

"Ms. Hewitt, as part of the psychological autopsy investigation of your mother, did you talk to Dr. Berman?"

"Yes, I did."

"Did Dr. Berman ask you about your family history and various aspects concerning your mother and father's relationship?"

"Yes."

"Did he ask you if there was any family history of mental health issues?"

"Yes. I told him that as far as I knew the family problems with mental illness were on my father's side."

"Ms. Hewitt, have you been treated for depression?"

"I was about nine years ago after my twin daughters were born, but I'm not now."

"Did you tell Dr. Berman that information?"

"I don't believe I did."

"I have no further questions, Your Honor."

Cross-examine by the State
Questioned by Moore

"Ms. Hewitt, when Mr. Wilson requested your mother's personal items, did you know at the time why he wanted them?"

"No."

"I have here a typewritten note that is addressed to you and dated May 13, 1999. When did you first see this note?"

"Yesterday before lunch."

"Was this note ever mailed to you?"

"No."

"Your father testified that he found this note on June 10th, 1999. Did he ever mention this note to you when he spoke to you numerous times on previous occasions?"

"No."

"When you had the tape recorder with you at your father's house, did you ask him about your mother committing suicide?"

"Yes, I did."

"Didn't you basically beg him for a reason why she would have done that?"

"Yes."

"On the day of the taping, did your father tell you about this note?"

"No."

"To your knowledge, did anyone other than your father and his lawyer know about this note before yesterday?"

"Not to my knowledge."

"Before your mother's death, did you talk with her about Lexi's wedding and help her plan it?"

"Yes."

"This note here implies that she was upset about your wedding. When was that?"

"Fifteen years ago on December 21, 1984."

"Was your mother still upset about your wedding?"

"No, we hadn't talked about it for probably ten years. "

"Did the topic of your wedding ever come up between you and your mother while getting ready for Lexi's wedding?"

"Yes, but it's been kind of a long time family joke and we had all gotten over it."

"Is it correct that your parents didn't like your husband at first, but had accepted him?"

"For the most part --- yes."

"Ms. Hewitt, has your husband gone fishing with your father?"

"Yes."

"Was he getting closer to your mother in the last couple of years?"

"Yes."

"Did your mother have a problem with Lexi's husband-to-be?"

"Not to my knowledge."

"In the years that you have known your mother, has she ever sent you a typewritten note?"

"Not that I can remember."

"Have you ever received handwritten notes from your mother?"

"Yes --- a lot."

"Ms. Hewitt, have you had the opportunity to read this typewritten note?"

"Yes."

"Does this note look like something your mother would write?"

"Not that I can think of --- no."

"Is it correct that the handwritten note on the napkin, from your mother to your father, was written when they lived in Orleans?"

"Yes."

"Please explain what the note on the napkin pertains to."

"Basically Mom was writing to Dad about a note she had found to '*your sweet darling*' and was saying that she knew about his affair."

"I have no further questions, Your Honor."

Gregory Wilson states that the defense rests.

Rebuttal witness for the State – Mamie Dubrook Questioned by Moore

"What was your position in the church when Bill Guthrie was hired in 1996?"

"I was the secretary for the PNC, which is a group of four people from our church in Wolsey and four people from the church in Bonilla. We get together to interview ministers. I would receive résumés from the different ministers and take them to the meetings; then at the meetings we would make phone calls and follow up on them."

"Would you please read the highlighted portion of the defendant's résumé regarding his work reference?"

"Village officer, Rawlins, Wyoming, 1982 - 1989."

"Did you ever check that reference?"

"No, that was a long time before we were hiring, so we didn't go back that far."

"Ms. Dubrook, there was testimony that the defendant was a police officer in Sinclair. Is that included on his résumé?"

"No, it isn't."

"Thank you, I have no further questions."

Judge Martin addresses the jury. "I believe that tomorrow the testimony should be wrapped up. Again, I admonish you that it is your duty neither to converse amongst yourselves or with anyone else on any subject connected with this trial, nor to form or express any opinion thereon, until the case is finally submitted to you. I would admonish that you not listen to the television or radio or read the newspaper regarding this matter. We will be in adjournment until 9:00 o'clock tomorrow morning. Thank you."

Judge Martin, the defendant, and counsel are in judge's chambers. "I realize that all of the witnesses have not testified, but I feel that we can go ahead with the instructions because any further witnesses will be covered under these instructions. In the event that it is not, I will visit with you when all of the witnesses have completed their testimony and ask if there are going to be any changes in the instructions or any new proposed instructions."

Judge Martin proceeds with settling the instructions:

Number 1- both sides have rested; it is now the
duty of the Court, and so forth.

Number 2 - in this action the defendant William
Boyd Guthrie is accused by the State, et cetera.

Number 3 - an indictment is the statutory method
of accusing a Defendant of a crime. It also includes
the presumption of innocence, the burden of proof,
and reasonable doubt.

Number 4 - homicide, the killing of one human being
by another, et cetera.

Number 5 - the elements of the crime of murder in
the first degree.

Number 6 - to find the defendant guilty of murder
in the first degree, et cetera.

Number 7 - premeditated design to effect the death
means, et cetera.

Number 8 - is the specific intent instruction.

Number 9 - the intent, which an act is done is shown
by the circumstances, et cetera.

Number 10 - motive is what prompts a person to act,

et cetera.

Number 11 - is the direct evidence instruction and circumstantial instruction.

Number 12 - is the video deposition instruction.

Number 13 - a statement made by a Defendant other than at the trial, et cetera.

Number 14 - the expert witness instruction.

Number 15 - the credibility of a witness may be attacked. Number 16 - refers to the typewritten transcript of the tape.

Number 17- regarding note taking.

Number 18 - you are the sole and exclusive judges of all questions of fact.

Number 19 - if you believe any witness has knowingly sworn falsely.

Number 20 - the weight of the evidence is not determined by the number of witnesses.

Number 21 - the function of the jury.

Number 22 - the function of the Court.

Number 23 - arriving at a verdict in this case.

Number 24 - if under the Court's instruction and the evidence.

Number 25 - consider this case carefully and honestly. Number 26 - in order to return a verdict all jurors must agree.

Number 27 - when you have retired to your jury room. Number 28 - and the two verdict forms.

Other than number 5, which will be revised, there are no objections to the proposals. Judge Martin asks if there are any other instructions that the Court should give at this time. Mr. Moore replies that the State has none. Mr. Wilson states that he only had the one that was addressed already and was opposed by Judge Martin.

Before adjourning the proceedings, Judge Martin states that he will have the clerk set up all the exhibits the next morning. He instructs Michael Moore and Gregory Wilson to be back at the courthouse at 8:30, so they can examine the exhibits to make sure they are all accounted for.

January 20, 2000

Trial Day Six

Judge Martin, the defendant, and counsel are in judge's chambers. "Mr. Wilson, you indicated that you wished to have a bad acts instruction. Please specify the bad acts that were admitted into evidence which you feel should be covered."

Mr. Wilson's list regards the extramarital affair by Bill Guthrie, the lies that he told to conceal the affair, the bathtub incident, the stairway incident, the overdose incident, and the incident in Lincoln, Nebraska, a fabrication to facilitate the continuance of the affair. He named the incidents where the youngest daughter stated that her father slapped her on the face and knocked her down. Also, her testimony about her father's alleged mistreatment of her mother, and her testimony regarding her father's threat to kill himself if she didn't go home with him from their camping trip.

"Mr. Wilson, I will hold on to my original determination on this matter. The affair is evidence of motive and part of this whole continuing course of action. All of these things, as far as I am concerned, are evidence that intend to connect the accused with a commission of crime and are not bad act's evidence. The only one that I can see that would be considered bad acts is the statement that Danielle made regarding the defendant slapping her, which wasn't even asked of her. It was just kind of said by her and I don't believe that it's such a significant item that it's going to make a difference."

Michael Moore requests a continuance. "Your Honor, after the State was informed on Tuesday of the alleged suicide note turned over by the defendant, Mr. Robbins reviewed the original computer seized at the church and informed us that the note was not on it. We were discussing this note with the Guthrie family and were informed that there is a second computer, which was hooked up to a printer in August and was located in the Guthrie home in Wolsey. The computer was taken from the house and put into storage and has remained there until I requested Les Hewitt to bring it to my office. We had the hard drive taken out of the computer and we mailed it overnight to Mr. Robbins. He received the hard drive yesterday afternoon. When I spoke with him last night he indicated that he had found the note. I don't believe that it was the whole note, but there is enough of it to identify that it was typed on August 7, 1999. Your Honor, I would ask to at least continue the case until tomorrow to allow Mr. Robbins to get here tonight, so I can present this evidence."

"Excuse me, Mr. Moore, are you referring to the typewritten note, which Ms. Orton testified did not have my client's fingerprints on it?"

"Yes, Your Honor."

"Your Honor."

"Mr. Wilson?"

"I have not yet had a chance to consult with my client this morning. I was contemplating a motion for continuance, so if this representation by the State bears out, obviously I will become a witness in this case."

Judge Martin allows a brief recess so Gregory Wilson can speak with his client, then everyone returns to judge's chambers.

"Your Honor, our computer expert found another note on the second computer that could be considered a suicide note. He will testify for the State that this note was typed on August 11, 1999, but it will take him overnight to arrive here."

"Mr. Wilson?"

"Your Honor, I will ask for a recess until Monday. I spoke with Ms. Orton this morning. Regarding the note written on the napkin that was introduced yesterday, she stated that it is a possibility this is what we are looking for --- something written with emotion in the deceased's handwriting. She said that good latent prints could be found on it. The paper isn't the best in terms of print, but she said that she is getting some reaction to the prints, but it's just too early to tell whether they are going to be identifiable."

"Anything else, Mr. Wilson?"

"Yes, Your Honor. I would also ask the Court's assistance in procuring the confidence in my file. I will write William Guthrie on it and label it client notes. If the State is going to introduce evidence, I will undoubtedly become a witness, of which, I would not be able to counsel, so substitute counsel would have to be obtained."

"Mr. Moore?"

"Your Honor, I would oppose any further continuance other than tomorrow. It's not my fault that this note was not provided to us in August or September. If the defense wanted to wait until January to produce it, they will have to live with the consequences. We have a jury waiting and now we wait for fingerprints? Judd Robbins will be here tonight and ready to testify tomorrow. I will make the hard drive available to the defense as soon as Mr. Robbins arrives here."

"Mr. Wilson, is there anything else you would like to put on record?"

"Your Honor, I have come to the inescapable conclusion that I cannot proceed as counsel for my client, given the fact, that I will be called to testify. The State apparently is going to be allowed to introduce evidence regarding the typewritten note that Bill Guthrie found in his office in June and gave to me in confidence."

Mr. Wilson hands Judge Martin an envelope. "I ask that the Court seal this envelope with all of my notes regarding this case and place it in safe keeping. If I am going to testify I will need these notes, but if I don't testify I will need them returned to me."

"The record may reflect that Mr. Wilson has given the Court a folder noted State versus William Guthrie, Gregory Wilson's file, confidential, do not open without a court order and dated January 20, 2000. I have sealed the folder and it will remain in the Clerk of Court's office."

"Thank you, Your Honor. I have spoken briefly with Keith Traverse, whom I am an associate with, and his comment was that he anticipates that he would be a witness as well as myself. I do not see how we can continue with the trial, so I move for a mistrial."

"Mr. Wilson, why do you feel Mr. Traverse would also be a witness?"

"Your Honor, my associate recalls seeing this note in question one time when we met with our client."

"Mr. Moore, does the State have anything to offer?"

"Yes, Your Honor. I would oppose the motion for mistrial. I feel they can offer the evidence through the defendant and obviously through Mr. Traverse, which would eliminate the need for Mr. Wilson to testify as a witness and he can continue to represent his client."

"Mr. Wilson, do you have a response?"

"Your Honor, I am basing this on my recollection of Mr. Traverse's involvement and on the knowledge of my involvement. He would have no notes to verify if that was the date that he met briefly with Bill Guthrie and myself when the note was given to me. I, on the other hand, would have my notes with my handwriting, complete with the date, and describing the document. Mr. Traverse's testimony would corroborate mine, but would not be anywhere close to the certainty or precision that I would be able to utilize because of my notes."

"Mr. Moore, does the State have anything to say?"

"Your Honor, I would just point out that obviously a mistrial would be extremely prejudiced to the State at this point. I feel that Mr. Traverse could corroborate the defendant."

"Mr. Wilson, I will take your motion for mistrial under advisement. I suggest that we listen to what Judd Robbins has to say and then I will re-address any motions that anyone wants to make. Tomorrow we will hear the testimony of the State's witnesses in which it will call for foundational purposes and when that is done, we will readdress this whole situation."

Judge Martin leaves chambers and enters the courtroom to inform the jury that it has become necessary to adjourn for the day, and court will continue the next morning at 9:00 o'clock.

January 21, 2000

Trial Day Seven

Judge Martin, the defendant, and counsel are in judge's chambers.

"Your Honor, before recessing yesterday, the State advised that it had seized a second computer of my client's. The State's computer expert Judd Robbins has analyzed it and the State intends to produce evidence from that second computer and offer testimony today. At this time, I would make motion to suppress any evidence regarding that computer on the grounds that it was done without the benefit of a search warrant, which is consequently in violation and against my client's rights to search and seizure."

"Mr. Wilson, do have any legal authority for the State not being able to go back in and search the house when they already had a search warrant?"

"It is apparent, Your Honor, that this second computer was stored in the Hewitt home for safe keeping. A search warrant was issued somewhere around the end of July, and I believe the period for exercising the search warrant is ten days. No warrant was exercised regarding the seizure of this computer, which is my client's property. The authority that I have at this point is a constitutional prohibition against search and seizure."

"Mr. Moore, any comments from the State?"

"Your Honor, I would oppose Mr. Wilson on the grounds that the search warrant, which in fact, isn't the evidence that I'm using in my case as chief. The computer was at the Hewitt house and brought to me by Les Hewitt."

"Mr. Wilson, I will have to agree with the State on this one. I am not sure if you would call this a search as long as it was turned over by Mr. Hewitt and nothing was done by law enforcement to seek out this evidence. The fact of the matter is, as I see it, the possibility of another computer being relevant in this case was generated by you when the defense revealed and turned over this note. Your motion to suppress this evidence is denied. Let's get back into the courtroom."

Rebuttal Witness for the State – Deputy Jim Sheridan Questioned by Moore

"Deputy Sheridan, during the search on July 27th, was a computer located in the southeast bedroom at the Guthrie house seized?"
"No, it was not."
"Did this computer look like it was being used?"
"No."
"When did you arrest the defendant?"
"I arrested him late in the afternoon on August 27th."
"I have no further questions."

Sally Gerhard, secretary at the Beadle County State's Attorney's office, testifies that on January 18th around five o'clock, a computer was brought to the office. She immediately called a technician; he came to the office, opened the computer, took out the hard drive, and placed it into an antistatic bag. She then placed the packaged hard drive into the box, sealed it, prepared the label, and overnighted it UPS to Judd Robbins.

Rebuttal Witness for the State – Judd Robbins Questioned by Moore

"Mr. Robbins, I have a typewritten note here that was recently turned over to me by the defense as a suicide note. Did I fax a copy of this to you on Tuesday, January 18th, requesting you to attempt to locate this alleged suicide note?"

"Yes. I went through the standard forensic procedure of connecting the hard drive up to my lab computer, and I made a complete copy. I then looked for the existence of a part, or all of, the alleged suicide note."

"What relevant information did you find on the hard drive regarding this note?"

"Microsoft Works is a program that has several capabilities, one of which is word processing. There was evidence of a temporary word processing file in this directory that contained contents of some of the words that appeared in the alleged suicide note. The temporary word processing work was done on August 5th, 1999. The next day, August 6th, I found a short temporary file with William Guthrie's name on it and the indication of the primary C drive and the Winword directory being accessed. Specifically it's a temporary word processing document that indicated that on August 6th something was being worked on. I'm not exactly sure what, but it was verification that activity was happening now, not in the Microsoft Works directly, but in the Microsoft Word directory."

"Mr. Robbins, are you saying that William Guthrie was using this second computer on August 6th?"

"That's what it looks like to me."

"What else did you find during this investigation?"

"I also found a three-page file named WBBULL.DOC, in the Winword directory that was also being worked on at approximately 5:13 p.m. on August 6th, twenty minutes after the other document. It contained what looked like a three-page church bulletin with parish notices for August of 1999. I also found information that looked like a copy of an earlier church bulletin from March of 1998. It looked like it was a first pass copy of an earlier file to begin an editing process to create an updated new file for perhaps upcoming bulletins."

"Mr. Robbins, what other file did you find?"

"I also found a file in the Winword directory called Sharon.doc. It was created on August 7, 1999, and it was last modified that same day."

"What does this file say?"

"It says, *May 13, 1999. I love you Mom.*"

"When you compared this to the alleged suicide note, are there any similarities between the two documents?"

"Yes --- a number of them. The font appears similar, the left margin is precisely the same at one and a quarter inch, and the top margin is precisely the same at one inch. The spacing and structure of the May 13, 1999, note is the same. Generally there is a space after a comma before the year, but I didn't find a space in either what was on the hard drive or in the alleged suicide note. The final line doesn't have a period at the end of that clause and also has an extra space before the word *Mom*. *Mom* is capitalized and there is a period after the word *Mom*."

```
0384 May 13,1999.
0398
0400 I love you  Mom.
0419 ...............................................      . . .
0489 ...............................................      . . .
0559 ...............................................      . . .
0629 ...............................................
0699 ...............................................
0769 ....█████....█████...█████...........................
0839 .....................................................
0909 .....................................................
0979 .....................................................
1049 .....................................................
1119 .....................................................
1189 .....................................................
1259 .....................................................
1329 .....................................................
1399 .....................................................
1469 ...............................................I......
1539 .......@..................#............#.............
1609 .............7....Times New Roman....Symbol..&.Arial..5.Courier New.
1679 ..........................."........h.......6F.<8..........
1749 ............1.......'.WILLIAM GUTHRIE.WILLIAM GUTHRIE...........@.@.
1819 @.@.....@.@...@.....@...@.....@.@.....@.@.@.@.....@.@...@.@.@.@.....@.
1889 ..@....@.@.B2C.@.@.@.@.@.@.@...@May 13,1999.
1934
     I love you  Mom.
```

"Mr. Robbins, is the *May 13, 1999* and *I love you all Mom* actually saved in Sharon.doc on the hard drive?"

"Yes."

"Did you ever find any other parts of the letter in the hard drive?"

"No."

"Could this file named Sharon.doc have been edited at any time where you wouldn't necessarily see it?"

"Yes. In a short note of this kind, what I see as a first pass of the document could have been saved, structurally prepared, and then filled in later in a minute or two. If the computer was turned off at the end of typing the note and printing it, there would be no record of those two sentences."

"Would that be because those two sentences were actually saved, Mr. Robbins?"

"Not likely. Certainly it's not obvious that they were saved in this form in this name. This file was not modified after this and nothing was saved on top of this, so there is no record of any middle sentences on the file on this computer."

"Mr. Robbins, am I correct in saying that you could add sentences to that, but if you print it and turn the computer off, that there wouldn't be any note in the modification date?"

"That's correct."

"Please tell us what I have here?"

"This is another file that I found in the Winword directory, called WBBULL.DOC, which was created August 8, 1999, at 1:03 a.m. It looks like a subsequent edit to the file that had been saved a day or two earlier as WBBULL. Again -- it is a first pass at an August church bulletin in 1999."

"I have State's Exhibit 69. What is this, Mr. Robbins?"

"This indicates that the document was created by Microsoft Word, that the font used was Times New Roman, and that William Guthrie's name is here as the probable owner or author of this document."

"Is it correct, Mr. Robbins, that these documents show that there was activity on this computer on August 8, 1999?"

"Yes, they do."

"As you continued your investigation, did you find any other files?"

"Yes, I found a file in the Winword directory called XYZ.doc which was modified on August 11, 1999, at 4:06 p.m."

"Mr. Robbins, will you please read this document that was created three months after Sharon's death?"

Dear Bill,
I am writing this letter as we agreed upon
Concerning our marriage.
I am upset with all the time you spend with
Everyone but your family.

I am upset will the time you spend away
Hunting and fishing from me.
I'm upset that Danielle hates me and you
Won't or don't do anything about it.
I'm upset that you don't do anything to
Separate Danielle and her boyfriend that
Relationship can only get worse.
I'm upset you haven't confronted them
On sleeping together.
I'm upset that you have had an affair and have
Not come clean with me,
I have thought of ending my life and you
Would have to face up to it.
Believe me I know how I can do it.
I'm upset that I have hurt Suzanne and
I don't know how to fix it and you won't help.
I'm upset that you have never spoken to Lexi
And Mitch about their living together without marriage.
I'm upset that I could leave this world and
No one would miss me.
Sharon

"Mr. Robbins, was this the document created on August 11, 1999?"

"Yes."

"According to the Winword directory, when was the last time before August of 1999 that this computer had been used?"

"The Winword directory had only been used once in the preceding half a year and that was in mid-March of 1999. The document was called FUNORDS.DOC."

"I have no further questions."

Cross-examine by the Defense

"Mr. Robbins, referring to the words William Guthrie located at the top of the document, would that have been something that the person operating the computer would have typed in or something that was already present on the software on the computer?"

"I would expect that it would have been present on the software."

"Would that be something that would automatically be generated by the computer whenever the software file was activated or utilized in some way?"

"It is probably an indication of the person who first installed the program."

"Mr. Robbins, from your reports, isn't it correct to say that this home computer had been in use way back to 1986?"

"Yes."

"In all likelihood, would that have been when the William Guthrie tag would have been generated?"

"In all likelihood --- yes."

"Would the William Guthrie tag be particularly significant to this case, Mr. Robbins?"

"Only that William Guthrie's name was there in a file and it indicated that the Winword directory was the focus of attention on August 6, 1999."

"Can you explain why in document 67, line 1749, the name *William Guthrie.William Guthrie* also appears?"

"Similarly this suggests that the owner, the installer, or licensee of the software, probably Microsoft Word, was purchased or licensed back in the mid '80's."

"Just for clarification, Mr. Robbins, is it correct that when the *William Guthrie.William Guthrie* was put on the computer, that this was not when the *I love you* was put on?"

"Yes."

"Mr. Robbins, you testified to the similarities of the note taken off the computer and the faxed copy that was sent to you. Would you please note for the jury the differences between those two documents?"

"In the final sentence, the words *I love you all,* the word *all* was added to the phrase *I love you.* I didn't see any other visible differences. The rest looks the same."

"Are the margins set document by document or can they be preset in some other fashion?"

"Generally there is a default and all new documents receive the default numbers, but they can be changed manually document by document."

"Mr. Robbins, have you had the opportunity to compare the note from May 13, 1999, to the letter written August 11, 1999?"

"Yes."

"I don't type a lick, but it did strike me as being odd that every first letter of each sentence in the August 11th letter is capitalized. I won't ask whether that is correct or not, but I would ask that you note that. When you compared both the note and the letter, do the sentences run from one line to the next?"

"Yes."

"When a sentence runs from one line to the next in both of these documents, is the first letter of each line capitalized in both documents?"

"Can you explain why the first letter of each line might be capitalized?"

"If the author of the document were to simply type each line and capitalize the beginning of the sentence as most of us are taught to do that would explain why the first letter is capitalized."

"Mr. Robbins, is it a possibility that there is some type of default in the software that would automatically capitalize the first letter of every line?"

"Yes, there is a possibility that some software may automatically capitalize the first word of what it perceives to be a sentence, and it can be set up to do this."

"If that were the case, how would that be changed so it wouldn't happen?"

"A person would have to go to the options choices in the software's control mechanism to tell it to do that or not to do that."

"Based on what we have heard, we have three options to explain the differences in the two documents. First, we could say that the author was the same author; second, that the authors are, in fact, two different authors; and third, that the software was automatically causing the first letter to be capitalized. The author either changed it in one document and not the other, or we again have two different authors, one who changed it and one who didn't. Correct, Mr. Robbins?"

"That's too complex to look at. The two places you pointed out in the letter where the line appears not to be capitalized at the beginning are, in fact, simply the last words of a long sentence on the preceding printed line. Generally, if someone types a long sentence ending with a period and then hits the return and goes to the next line, the new sentence would begin with a capital letter. In this case, the words simply end the sentence, and based on the margins, they would automatically wrap around to the next line and be printed as not capitalized."

"Another difference, Mr. Robbins, is that the sentences on the letter tend to run to the end of the margin, whereas they don't on the note. Could the note be a predecessor of the document found in Sharon. doc?"

"It not only could be, but I think it was."

"Could that also be an attempt to recreate the note?"

"I don't think so. Your point about the period is a difference, and the word *all* would suggest to me that it would not be an attempt. Anybody attempting to copy the note would have copied those couple of differences right away."

"How about if they were trying to do it from memory, Mr. Robbins?"

"Memory, huh? I really couldn't comment on some unknown approach to memory in this case."

"No further questions."

"The State rests, Your Honor."

Rebuttal Witness for the Defense – Rev. Larry Boutelle

Reverend Boutelle has known Bill Guthrie for three years. He did not know Sharon, but at Bill's request he officiated at her funeral. After her death, he and Bill went fishing on June 11th at Lake Thompson.

"Reverend Boutelle, while you and Bill were fishing, did he discuss Sharon's death with you?"

"He mentioned to me that a suicide note had been found in a book that he used for preparing worship."

"Do you know what kind of book that he was talking about?"

"I pictured a book of worship that often has prayers and pieces of liturgy that we might use in a worship service. I'm not certain that he told me that, but that's what I recall from memory."

"Were you discussing these matters in confidence?"

"As friends."

"Did Bill authorize you to testify here today as to the issue of confidence?"

"Yes."

"Did Bill tell you any of the specifics about the suicide note, such as, what he had done with it?"

"He told me that he had informed you about it. I'm not certain how he put it, but he clearly gave me the impression that the State's Attorney and the sheriff were not aware of it."

"Did you have any discussions with Bill regarding feelings that he was having due to Sharon's death, such as anger?"

"Yes, but I'm not certain that we put it in the context of anger. Given the depression and the grief that Bill was experiencing, I would say that anger was involved."

"No further questions, Your Honor."

Cross-examine by the State
Questioned by Moore

"I have just one question, Reverend Boutelle. Did you ever see the alleged suicide note?"

"No."

Judge Martin, the defendant, and counsel are in judge's chambers. Also present is Keith Traverse, Mr. Wilson's law partner, who has been called as a witness for the defense regarding the alleged suicide note.

"Your Honor, I don't know if this is necessary, but I understand from my associate, Mr. Wilson, that there has been some discussion between the Court and counsel regarding my potential testimony. I thought that I should make record, so I am assured that I am not violating some ethical ruling by testifying."

"Mr. Traverse, the Court has no problem with you testifying and allowing Mr. Wilson to continue to represent the defendant. Mr. Guthrie, do you have any problem with Mr. Traverse testifying?"

"Absolutely not, Your Honor."

Keith Traverse is excused from chambers. Gregory Wilson states that his fingerprint expert, Cindy Orton, doesn't have any additional evidence at this time. Judge Martin denies her further testimony, since she doesn't have anything more to offer the jury that would be probative.

Rebuttal Witness for the Defense – Keith Traverse

"Mr. Traverse, when did you meet Bill Guthrie?"

"I met Mr. Guthrie in our office on July 27, 1999, when you asked me to be in on a meeting with him."

"Did I discuss this case with you prior to that date?"

"Yes."

"Also, prior to that date, did you have the opportunity to see a note given to me by Bill Guthrie?'

"Yes, I did. I don't believe I saw the original, but I saw a photocopy of it."

"Did we discuss the location of the original document?"

"Yes, it was in your file."

"Mr. Traverse, is there any particular reason why you recall seeing that document prior to the 27th of July?"

"Yes. Quite some time earlier when I was in Huron, I had a brief conversation with Agent Lindberg and Deputy Sheriff Sheridan. They had asked me if I was representing Mr. Guthrie, which brought the case to mind; and I recalled that I had seen the note."

"Did you assume at that time law enforcement had not seen the note?"

"Yes."

"I have no further questions."

Rebuttal Witness for the Defense – William Guthrie

"Bill, I'm showing you a letter that Mr. Robbins found on the computer that came from your home in Wolsey. Did you create this document on that computer on August 11th of 1999?"

"Yes."

"Did you draft this document as a letter to you from Sharon?"

"Yes, I did."

"Will you please explain this document?"

"In about March, Sharon and I were talking about the differences that we were having in our marriage. We agreed to separately write down the differences and see what we could do about them."

"Bill, do I understand that you were writing down your grievances regarding Sharon and that she was to do the same concerning her grievances with you?"

"Yes. When we came together and started talking about them, I had written mine down, but she hadn't written hers down. We still went ahead and talked about the differences that we had with each other."

"So, Bill, what is this letter?"

"It is a recollection as to what her letter would have been. In June, when I was talking with Rev. Larry Boutelle, he said that there would come a time when I would probably feel some anger and some loss. He said that I would probably even need to put together a sermon on anger, which I didn't do. When I started thinking about this, I felt that those differences we had with each other might have contributed to what happened to her. I wanted to bring out those things and just try to remember the things that were creating the pain."

"Mr. Robbins testified that this suicide note I have here was created on August 7, 1999. Bill, did you create this document?"

"I probably did, but I --- I don't remember it."

"Bill, you testified earlier that you gave this suicide note to me on or about June 15, 1999. Did you keep a copy of that document for yourself?"

"No."

"I have no further questions."

Cross-examine by the State
Questioned by Moore

"Mr. Guthrie, did you type this letter regarding the differences with your wife?"

"I did."

"Why did you type the words, *I thought of ending my life and you would have to face up to it?*"

"That was a statement that she had made. And I would have to face up to that, yes."

"You typed that in there, Mr. Guthrie?"

"Yes, I did."

"What about the typed words, *Believe me, I know how I could do it.*"

"Sharon said that."

"Mr. Guthrie, did you type this to make yourself feel better?"

"I typed that to try to --- yes, make myself --- not make myself feel better --- no, but to try to bring some reason into what had happened."

"Was this so you could justify to yourself that she had committed suicide?"

"At that point."

"Mr. Guthrie, didn't it made you feel better because you knew that you had killed her?"

"No."

"I have no other questions."

"Ladies and gentlemen, the evidence is done. The defense has rested and the State has no other witnesses. We will take a short recess; whereas, I will be settling the instructions in chambers, and then I will be back out here to read the instructions to you. Counsel will make its closing arguments and the case will be submitted to you. Again, I admonish you that it is your duty to not converse among yourselves or with anyone else on any subject connected with this trial, nor to form or express any opinion, thereon, until the case is finally submitted to you."

In chambers, Judge Martin asks the attorneys if there are any other motions that need to be made.

Michael Moore states that he has none. Gregory Wilson, on behalf of his client, moves to enter its order for a judgment or acquittal, or in the alternative, a directed verdict of not guilty.

"Mr. Moore, does the State resist this?"

"Yes, Your Honor."

"The motion is denied. Mr. Wilson, do you have any other motions?"

"No, Your Honor."

"Mr. Wilson, is it correct that your motion for mistrial has been withdrawn?"

"Yes, Your Honor."

"Counsel, after the closing arguments are completed and before the jury starts deliberations, I will inform the jury who the two alternates are and excuse them. I will also tell them that they are still under the admonition not to discuss the case with anyone because they may be called upon."

Michael Moore begins closing arguments for the State.

"Ladies and gentlemen, I told you at the beginning of this trial that there are four ways a person dies. Natural death, accident, suicide, or homicide. Now that you have heard the evidence in this case, you know that Sharon Guthrie's death was not a natural death and that she didn't die of an accident. You have also heard a lot of evidence regarding suicide, so you know that it wasn't suicide. That leaves homicide.

"Throughout this trial many witnesses have testified and you have consumed a lot of evidence. Sharon Guthrie, fifty-four years old, is dead and died in her bathtub because of a large amount of Temazepam in her system. Testimony has shown that the Temazepam was prescribed for the defendant, Bill Guthrie, not her.

"Sharon loved doing children's sermons on Sundays, loved her three children and her grandchildren, and looked forward to seeing them grow up. She was excited about the upcoming wedding of her daughter and that Lexi was going to wear her wedding dress. Bill Guthrie took all of that away from her. He wants you to believe that Sharon committed suicide. As a last ditch effort to make you believe she committed suicide, Tuesday of this week the defendant produces a suicide note and claims to have found this note last June after his wife's death. It's not really a suicide note. Sharon doesn't say that she's going to kill herself and she doesn't say good-bye to everybody. If the defense thought it was authentic or genuine, you would have seen it long before last Tuesday.

"I told you in my opening statements what the evidence would be, and now that you have heard it you know that Sharon did not commit suicide, but that Bill Guthrie committed pre-meditated murder.

"In June of 1992, the defendant was a minister at a church in Orleans, Nebraska. Approximately a year and a half later, Bill Guthrie begins an affair with Myra Conner, which continues until 1996. They sneak around and see each other as many times as possible. The rumors start flying around Orleans causing him to move to Wolsey, but the affair continues with Myra Conner until she breaks it off in January of 1999.

"Soon after the breakup, incidents begin to happen to Sharon. Late March, early April, she trips on a string across the basement stairs in their home and almost falls down the basement steps. April 3rd, a lamp falls into the bathtub. The defendant has been doing searches for bathtub accidents on the computer. Coincidence, I don't know. April 15th, Sharon is groggy and can't go to work. The doctors can't find anything wrong with her. April 21st and 22nd, again Bill Guthrie spends two hours on his computer, searching the Internet for bathtub accidents and household accidents.

"Late April, more searches are done on the computer, this time for drugs. Benadryl didn't work, so Bill Guthrie has to find something a little better. April 29th, he makes an appointment with Patricia Minor complaining of a sleeping problem. He has no history of a sleeping problem and has never before told anyone that he was having a sleeping problem. Patricia Minor prescribes Temazepam for him. This is the drug that killed Sharon. We specifically know that Bill Guthrie looked up Temazepam on the Internet on May 4, 1999. On May 12th, Sharon refilled one of the defendant's prescriptions at Statz Drug. On May 13th, the day before Sharon died, Bill Guthrie filled the second prescription at K-Mart Pharmacy.

"On June 9th, almost a month after Sharon's death, Bill Guthrie goes back to Patricia Minor again complaining of a sleep problem. This time when she prescribes Ambien, a medication of which he refused before, he now accepts it. That same day he is interviewed by law enforcement. The next day Bill Guthrie finds the answer to all of his problems --- the suicide note.

"July 27th, a search is done at the Wolsey residence and at the church office. We thought that the computer that was seized from the office contained the most damaging evidence until this week. We now know that the second computer's evidence is even more damaging since on August 7th and 11th, Bill Guthrie was sitting at his computer at home typing up suicide notes. He says he was feeling sorry, so he typed this one up. What else is he going to say now that we have caught him?

"Judge Martin instructed you on motive. Why did Bill Guthrie kill his wife? Well, first of all, it was a terrible marriage with a lot of marital discord and he wanted out. He knew that if he divorced Sharon, all of the things that he had done before would ruin him and he wouldn't be able to be a minister anymore. No one would hire him as a minister. He couldn't divorce Sharon, so he struggled and stayed with her, which was fine. He could live with the marriage because for five or six years he was having sex with Myra Conner at every opportunity. All that was fine until she broke up with him.

"Bill Guthrie told his youngest daughter that he hated her mother, he thought that she was fat and ugly, and he was disgusted by her. He didn't want to hug Sharon, he didn't want to hold her, and he didn't want to touch her. For years he talked about divorcing Sharon. The youngest daughter testified that the tension and the stress in the marriage were so bad that she left home after she turned eighteen and graduated from high school.

"Suzanne and her husband, Les, testified that Bill Guthrie told them that he was going to divorce Sharon after Lexi's wedding. He shared this news with them a short time after the breakup with Myra Conner. The defendant hated his marriage to Sharon and he wanted out, but he couldn't chance a divorce.

"Another motive? Let's talk about the affair, which is an age-old motive of lust for another woman. Bill Guthrie sure wasn't having any lust for his wife Sharon. He hadn't had sex with her for years, claiming that he was impotent. He wasn't experiencing any trouble having sex with Myra Conner the many times that they were together down by the river or in motel rooms. I'm not saying that everybody that has an affair kills his or her spouse to get out of a marriage, but Bill Guthrie did! I asked him if he loved Myra Conner and he said that he didn't. He answered yes when I asked him if it was just for sex.

"In the small town of Orleans, when the rumors were flying around about the affair, what does Bill Guthrie do? He doesn't stop the affair, but talks with Myra Conner about his fear of getting caught and losing his job. What does he do to avoid getting caught? He lies! He tells his executive presbyter that the rumors aren't true because he is impotent and can't have sex. Then he goes to the session and the congregation of the church and tells them the same lies --- that the rumors are not true. As their minister and a man of God, he lies to them, and all that time he is having sex with Myra Conner. Bill Guthrie's reason for being impotent? An alleged rape that supposedly happened in Lincoln, Nebraska. More lies. We know that the defendant wasn't impotent. Myra Conner testified that he didn't have any problems having sex with her.

"The rumors of the affair didn't stop, so Bill Guthrie is asked to leave the church in Orleans. When he gets to the Wolsey and Bonilla churches, he tells the session that he has some problems and needs to go back to Nebraska for counseling. He tells them that it won't interfere with his Sunday services since he would go during the week. More lies! He isn't going there for counseling, but to see Myra Conner and continue with the affair.

"Then, in January of 1999, Myra Conner tells the defendant that it is all over --- she's tired of sneaking around. Bill Guthrie is upset by this news, but the contact doesn't stop. They still talk and then they see each other again the end of February, early March. They are again intimate. Again, Myra Conner tells him that she is ending the affair, but leaves the window open saying that she is a single woman. Very conveniently Sharon dies!

"Bill Guthrie tells law enforcement officers that the church notified Myra Conner of Sharon's death, but he admits under oath that he called her right after Sharon's death and told her that Sharon had died.

"Sharon's funeral was Monday, May 17th, and the following Tuesday or Wednesday, Bill Guthrie converses on the phone with Myra Conner asking her if they can get together. He couldn't have been grieving as much as he wanted people to think when here he is trying to get back with his lover. She refuses to see him, and he accuses her of betraying him and hangs up on her.

"That doesn't discourage him very much. Needing a shoulder to cry on, Bill Guthrie goes to Wyoming to see some old friends, Karen and Eddy Neilson. In June, Karen Neilson, who according to the defendant is just a friend, sends a card that says, *Just wanted you to know, I'm thinking of you, loving you at this very moment, and wishing that I could show you just how much.* He says that this card is from just a --- friend?

"Let's talk a little bit about how Bill Guthrie researched and planned his wife's death. When you look at the evidence, he tells you how it's going to happen. Remember the unusual incidents start happening soon after Myra Conner dumps him. These unusual incidents are not just coincidences. Remember the string accident when he asked Sharon to go to the basement to look at something that he had done down there earlier that day. She starts down the steps, feels the string, and sits down with Bill right behind her. The next day Sharon tells her daughter Suzanne what had happened. When Suzanne speaks with her father about it, he says that Sharon wasn't supposed to be talking about it, that he was taking care of it and had called the police. Later he says that Sharon just tripped on her shoelace. If she had just tripped on her shoelace, why was he telling Suzanne that he didn't want anyone to talk about it? Les Hewitt testified that he went over to the house and found wood shavings, like what a drill would make on one side of the steps and chipped plaster on the other side. Then we have the sleepwalking incident, which you can also refer to as a practice run. Sharon didn't go to work because she was very groggy and out of it. Bill Guthrie originally told Sharon's co-workers at Reed Clinic that Sharon had a headache. He took Sharon to the doctor at 2:00 o'clock that afternoon and claimed that he carried her up there from the car. His story was that Sharon was sleepwalking the night before, getting up and taking Benadryl and drinking chocolate milk. He said there were bottles of Benadryl on her nightstand. Pretty similar to what he told us happened on May 14th, but now he says there were red cups being used. The nurse in the office testified that Bill Guthrie proclaimed he didn't do anything to Sharon. Was he feeling guilty? We also know that Benadryl comes in capsules, which are easy to take apart and put into someone's drink.

"Friday, April 16th, Bill Guthrie drafts an e-mail to his daughter Lexi, but never sends it. One of the things he writes is in regard to Sharon falling asleep in the bathtub with water running all over the floor. She was asleep in the same tub that she drowns in on May 14th. Either he was psychic or he was planning how to kill her. A month before her death he puts her in that tub asleep with water running all over the floor.

"The electrocution incident? First, it's important to remember what was on the computer. April 21st about 10:00 p.m., Bill Guthrie begins searches for bathtub and household accidents in different search engines. For two hours he sits there doing that and obtains thousands of results. On April 23rd, Sharon is washing her hair in the bathtub and he brings a lamp into the bathroom since the lights allegedly are not working. The lamp falls into the bathtub. The story is that the dog came in and knocked it over, but Sharon couldn't have seen that since she had her head under the faucet. Sharon said that they were having a romantic evening, but we know that's not true. Bill Guthrie didn't care about his wife; he wasn't having sex with her, and there wasn't a romantic evening. Maybe, just maybe, he told her that to get her into the bathtub. What really happened I don't know, but we know that Les Hewitt testified that when he went over the next day to check the lights for Sharon that one light was working and one was not.

"April 27th, Bill Guthrie does a search on the Internet for Ativan and Lorazepam. April 29th, he fills the same prescription twice. He has been to see Patricia Minor at the clinic complaining of a sleep problem. She offers him Ambien and Xanax, but he says that they didn't work for him, that he had tried them before. Now, when he testifies, he said that Patricia Minor was mistaken or lying; that he is telling the truth. He said that about several of the State's witnesses, that they were mistaken or lying. Patricia Minor testified that when Bill Guthrie refused the Ambien and Xanax, it was decided to give him Temazepam; so she gave him a handwritten prescription. He takes it to K-Mart, has it filled and signs for it at about noon that day. Then he calls Sharon at work, tells her he lost his prescription, asks her to have Patricia Minor call one into Statz Drug, and later picks it up. Bill Guthrie claims that he didn't know what he was picking up, but he went there, picked up the prescription, and signed for it. More lies!

"On May 12th, Sharon refills the prescription at Statz Drug at about 5:30 p.m. and signs for it. Bill Guthrie refills one at K-Mart the next day on May 13th. The next day Sharon dies in the bathtub with the Temazepam in her system.

"What's really unusual is that on June 9th, when Bill Guthrie goes back to Patricia Minor still complaining of a sleep problem, this time when she prescribes Ambien, he takes it. Why did he take the Ambien this time when a month and a half before he claimed that it didn't work for him? Ambien and Xanax only come in tablets. He wanted the Temazepam, which only comes in capsules, so he could take them apart and put them in Sharon's chocolate milk. On June 9th, he didn't really care if the medication was a tablet or a capsule. Sharon is dead --- he has already killed her. It doesn't matter anymore, so he takes the Ambien.

"May 14th, the morning of the drowning, Bill Guthrie tells numerous changing stories of the events that happened that day. Basically, what did stay the same was that he went to the church to pray and do devotions. When I asked him if he got in the tub to try to get Sharon out, he said that he did. Nancy Holst testified that she got soaked when she and Carter Mansgrove removed Sharon from the tub. Peggy Stevens testified that the defendant was not wet. Bill Guthrie says that Peggy Stevens was lying. Why would Peggy lie? If he did all the things that he said he did; if he got in that tub, if he tried to help her, he would be wet, but he wasn't. Bill Guthrie is a blatant liar! He did not help Sharon! If he had helped her, he would have been wet.

"Bill Guthrie says that he is telling you the truth and all these others are lying. This is the same guy that stood in front of his church and lied --- the same guy that lied to his bosses. Doesn't this offend you?

"What did Bill Guthrie tell Don Perry? When Mr. Perry phoned the Sunday after Sharon's death, the defendant told him that the accident happened at 1:00 o'clock in the morning. At the end of the statement, he suddenly throws in the comment that he and Sharon were getting along great. Well, we know that statement isn't true since he had been telling others that he was going to divorce Sharon. Mr. Perry has no reason to lie, but Bill Guthrie would like you to believe that Mr. Perry is lying.

"Sharon's brother, Larry Provance, testified that he overheard the defendant's changing stories regarding the accident. He has never observed his brother-in-law getting up early in the morning to go to the church to do prayers and devotions. Larry Provance goes to his brother-in-law to ask him what happened. Bill Guthrie won't tell him anything, he is evasive, and won't look at him. When Larry asks him about telling Don Perry that the accident happened at 1:00 o'clock in the morning, Bill Guthrie answers that he doesn't know what he told him. If you are telling people the truth, you remember what you told them. The truth never changes.

"Bill Guthrie had the opportunity, and he had the pills available to him. We know that he specifically acquired capsule pills that were easy to take apart and dump into chocolate milk, which was Sharon's drink of choice. He found an easy way to dump the pills in and shake them up in a carton of chocolate milk, which you can't see through. There isn't any bad taste, so Sharon didn't notice anything when she drank it.

"Lexi, the middle daughter, testified that she drank some chocolate milk in a large carton at the house in Wolsey and it was fine, but a smaller carton had been thrown away when the cleaning was done in the house.

"One of the ladies that helped clean the house found some white powder on the kitchen counter. Assuming that it was flour, she wiped it up. We know that when a capsule of Temazepam is opened and spilled on a counter, it looks like flour. Sharon was allergic to flour and her daughters testified that she wouldn't have left flour lying around.

"What did Bill Guthrie tell law enforcement when they interviewed him on June 9, 1999? He said that Sharon had been sleepwalking since 1975 or '76 and goes on to explain some of the incidents when she was sleepwalking. At that time there wasn't any reason to dispute that, but when talking to close family members, they said they had never seen Sharon sleepwalk. They hadn't heard anyone talk about her sleepwalking until April 15th. Was this April 15th sleepwalking incident a practice run?

The defendant told law enforcement that Sharon was hooked on Benadryl and that he would try to hide it from her. Yet, knowing that, he goes out and acquires a more powerful sleeping drug, and leaves it lying around the house, so he can kill her.

"Bill Guthrie tells us that on the night of April 15th that Sharon was having an anxiety attack. Did he say this to cover his bases, just in case something shows up that she had a heart attack? He says that she was shaking, had pain in her chest, and left arm, which are classic symptoms of a heart attack. He says that he slept really hard that night, but also remembers Sharon getting up and there were five bottles of Benadryl on the nightstand. Sounds a lot like the story of May 14th, except that he decides to go with the red cup story --- four or five of them. A photo taken that morning by Jim Sheridan shows one red cup on the headboard, not the nightstand.

"Bill Guthrie tells us that when he found Sharon, she was face forward lying down in the water, that he tried to get her out of the water, that he attempted to get the water out of her, and tried to get her out of the bathtub, but couldn't. He tells Suzanne that he actually did get her out of the bathtub, but we know that's not true. Nancy Holst and Carter Mansgrove removed Sharon from the tub. The defendant says that he tried to get her out. That's a lie! He was not wet! He certainly would have been wet if he had tried to get her out of the bathtub!

"Law enforcement asked Bill Guthrie if he knew what drugs his wife was taking. He says that he didn't know. We asked him what drugs he was taking. He names them for us, but doesn't tell us about the Temazepam that Patricia Minor prescribed for him for his sleeping problem. After further questioning, he then admits that he has a prescription for sleep, but doesn't remember what it is.

"When Bill Guthrie is asked about the affair, he says that there were some rumors in Nebraska, but denies having an affair. We tell him that we know about the affair, and he finally admits that it was three years ago. He says that he was working out things with Sharon. More lies. We know that he had seen Myra Conner in January of

1999. Finally, at the end of the interview he admits seeing her the end of January.

"When he is asked about suicide, he says that four years ago Sharon was suicidal, and then says nothing more about it. Bill Guthrie was asked if Sharon made any suicide threats when he told her about the affair. He said that she had made some suicide threats. When asked if he thought that this recent information regarding the affair would have triggered a suicide, he said it would not have because Sharon knew about the affair in January and that they were working things out. So, now Bill Guthrie is trying a suicide angle, something that we brought up to him. Now he is thinking about suicide.

"There are more lies. The defendant says that he worked for the sheriff's office in Carbon County, Wyoming, and also Sinclair. His résumé says that he worked for Rawlins. We know that he never worked for Carbon County. I don't know why he would lie about that, but he is lying.

"Bill Guthrie continually lied to his family, specifically Suzanne. She was asking him what happened from May 14th up to the time that she went to talk to him with the hidden tape recorder. He denied the affair and didn't seem to know anything about the pills Sharon took. Suzanne begged her father to tell her something; she didn't want to believe that her mother committed suicide. He just sat there and didn't say anything. Then, four days later on July 30th after the taping, Bill Guthrie decides to save the world. He meets Suzanne at her work place, admits to the affair, and tells her that he told her mother about the affair the night before she died. He says that is why Sharon must have committed suicide. More lies. Bill Guthrie told law enforcement that he told Sharon in January about the affair. He told Larry Provance, his brother-in-law, that he told Sharon in March about the affair. He wanted his daughter to believe that her mother committed suicide, so he tells her that.

"All this time Bill Guthrie doesn't tell Suzanne, Larry Provance or law enforcement that he has what he reports as a suicide note. The reason that he didn't tell anyone about the alleged suicide note is because it's not authentic --- it's not genuine. This note was brought in at the last minute to try to convince you that Sharon committed suicide. Well, that didn't work. Les Hewitt brought in the second computer that was located at the house, which showed that the note was written on it three months after Sharon died.

"You heard from the State's expert witness, Brad Randall, and the defendant's expert witness, Dr. Burns. They both basically said that the cause of death was drowning, but that Sharon would not have died in that bathtub if it hadn't been for the Temazepam in her system. They both told you that the manner of death couldn't be determined, and they didn't have all the evidence that you have. You can determine the manner of death. The two experts did have a little dispute over the amount of pills in her system, but both agreed that this drug killed her.

"You heard from a suicidologist who testified that he has never seen a suicide where the person was face down, face forward in a bathtub. He researched, talked to various people, and looked at all of Sharon's medical records for the last ten years. Out of twenty-seven risk factors, the ones found were regarding Sharon having complained of insomnia and that she was a middle-aged female. Out of those twenty-seven risk factors there were only two that he felt were questionable.

"There are four ways people die. There is only one way that Sharon died. It was homicide. I know that this case is circumstantial, but the circumstantial evidence is overwhelming. It leads anybody to the same conclusion that the defendant did this, that he researched it, that he planned it! Heck, he even tried it before. I would ask that you look at the evidence and find Bill Guthrie guilty of murdering his wife, Sharon Guthrie. Thank you."

Gregory Wilson begins his closing arguments for the defense. "It's a fundamental principle of our law that a defendant in a criminal case is presumed to be innocent. The prosecution has the burden of proving every element of the offense. In case of a reasonable doubt, you must return a verdict of not guilty. A reasonable doubt is based upon reason and common sense, the kind of doubt that would make a reasonable person hesitant to act. Proof beyond a reasonable doubt, therefore, must be proof of such a convincing character that a reasonable person would not hesitate to rely upon it. Motive is not an element of the crime charged.

"Where the case of the prosecution rests substantially, or entirely on circumstantial evidence, you are not permitted to find a defendant guilty of the crime charged unless the proved circumstances are not only consistent with the guilt of a defendant, but cannot be reconciled with any other rational conclusion. Each fact that is essential to complete a set of circumstances is necessary to establish that a defendant's guilt has been proven beyond a reasonable doubt. If the facts and circumstances are consistent with the innocence of a defendant, you must acquit. The guilt of a defendant may not be established alone by any admission made outside this trial.

"To assist you in deciding questions, you may consider the opinion with the reasons given for it by an expert. If any member of the jury has any reasonable doubt that the defendant committed the offense charged, then it is that juror's duty to give the defendant the benefit of such doubt and vote for a verdict of not guilty. No juror should surrender a conviction as to the weight or effect of the evidence solely because the opinion of the other jurors or for the mere purpose of returning a verdict.

"You will be given copies of the instructions that were read to you; that is the law of the case. In these past two weeks you have heard evidence, and it's now time for you to determine the facts of the case.

"Deputy Jim Sheridan was called first to testify. What was done to preserve evidence at the Guthrie house on May 14th, 15th, or 16th? Nothing! Also, Agent Jerry Lindberg didn't do anything to preserve evidence, and he acknowledged that the computer was mishandled when it was seized.

"The floor was wet when Deputy Sheridan arrived at the Guthrie house early the morning that Sharon drowned. Regarding the interview, Bill told Sheridan and Lindberg that Sharon was under a lot of stress at work. They caught him in a truth. Sharon was under stress at work.

"Bill told them that Sharon took her medications with chocolate milk. They caught him in a truth again; Sharon did take her medications with chocolate milk. Bill said that Sharon complained of sleep and anxiety problems. They caught him in a truth again. She did have sleep and anxiety problems.

"You heard from a computer expert from Pierre who had the computer in his possession for quite some time before it was finally delivered to

Judd Robbins. Mr. Hutchins acknowledged that the software he used to inspect the computer didn't preserve it as evidence.

"You heard Judd Robbins testify. Look at the exhibits that he introduced. The document *Worst Pills Best Pills* was self-stored on the computer. Remember, Mr. Robbins explained that sometimes when you access a website on the Internet, the website automatically starts downloading information onto your computer without you knowing it or doing anything to cause it to do so. It was uncertain when *Worst Pills Best Pills* was accessed; there isn't any date on it. Probably Mitch Rivers trying to do some research after Sharon's death?

"The Lycos search? Again --- there was no date on it. Remember Mitch Rivers testified to using Lycos to search again for Lorazepam or Ativan, which he knew were Sharon's exhibits --- no date. Ambien, Exhibit 13 --- no date. Exhibit 13a, connected to 13 --- no date. Exhibit 14 --- no date.

"Then we get to the bathtub accidents. Those do have dates on them, there's no doubt about it. I will get to those later. As you are looking at these documents, remember the instruction on circumstantial evidence. Remember the drugs that Sharon was taking. Remember that she didn't like to complain. Again, remember the instruction on circumstantial evidence.

"During Mr. Moore's closing statements, he said Bill Guthrie is accusing people of lying. *'Was that person mistaken or lying'* were Mr. Moore's words when he would ask Bill a question. Those words were not my client's words --- I want you to remember that. I'm not accusing anybody of lying, but people do make mistakes. We are all human.

"Nancy Holst recalled that she and Sharon did have a conversation about taking a prescription weight control medication called Phen-fen. Also, she remembered that Sharon was taking a sedative called Ativan. When I asked her if she remembered that Bill did daily meditation at the church in the mornings --- she didn't remember. She told Jerry Lindberg that Bill did do daily meditations at the church in the mornings. Was she lying? No, she was mistaken; that's all it is. I wouldn't for a second suggest that she was lying. She also testified when she first started CPR on Sharon that Sharon's body was warm, as in body temperature.

"Peggy Stevens arrives --- Bill is not wet. That's pretty significant. She is wrong. I'm not suggesting that she is lying, but she is wrong. How do we know that she's wrong? Suzanne tells us that she is wrong because she remembers that her father's knee was wet. We know at the very minimum that Peggy is wrong to that extent. Bill was wet! How much, we don't know. Heaven knows, at that point, no one is worried about Bill's clothes being wet. That was the last thing on their minds. Bill's clothes were wet, and we know that fact by at least two witnesses.

Peggy Stevens stated that Sharon's body was cold to the touch, which is again contradicted by Nancy Holst who said that Sharon was still very hot from the bath water. Which of them is right, which is wrong; we don't know exactly.

"Susan Fenski, the ER nurse, put the lavine tube into evidence. Why did she testify? This is a big deal because this tube didn't draw out a clump of pills the size of a golf ball.

"My notes say that Dr. Rogers stabilized Sharon's pulse. That takes us back to Dr. Randall's testimony that Sharon could only have been under the water a few minutes at the most because they couldn't have resuscitated her as much if she would have been under any longer.

"Dr. Randall, the medical examiner from Sioux Falls, testified that there wasn't much to dispute. Sharon did have an overdose of Temazepam. Dr. Burns agreed with him that in theory, as few as five pills, but in all likelihood, more. Dr. Randall did go the extra step and offer his opinion that it was likely in the neighborhood of twenty pills. I asked him if, in his opinion in estimating that number of pills, was that based on his experience with suicide overdoses, and he said yes. I asked him if it was true that the multiple kind of drugs that Sharon had in her system was consistent with suicide overdose, and he said yes. He agreed with Dr. Burns that the effects of those drugs would be felt in as little as fifteen minutes. The amount of Temazepam in Sharon's system was probably not fatal. He pointed out that the other two drugs found in Sharon's stomach contents and in her blood were Sharon's prescriptions, which takes us back to the comment that multiple kinds of drugs are consistent with a suicide overdose. Dr. Randall talked about how capsules glob together and would have expected to see some of the capsules drawn out with Sharon's stomach contents, but you saw the NG tube. It's a small diameter tube, not a stomach pump. Dr. Randall seemed a little perplexed that there were no remnants of the Temazepam capsules. He said it would be common to find remnants of gel caps like this if her stomach had been pumped within minutes. Sharon's stomach was never pumped. I am not suggesting that anyone did anything wrong, but the fact is, there were no gel caps or pill fragments found in Sharon's stomach contents.

"Kate Sands. Her first reaction was that it was flour on the kitchen counter, but we know that also along with flour there were baking soda, baking powder, powdered sugar, and pancake mix in the house.

"Peggy Stevens testified that Bill's clothes weren't wet and that he didn't have shoes on. I was scratching my head about that. He had just been over to the church, so he must have had his shoes on. Hey --- it's mid May, it's nice out, and the church is right next door. He was dressed casually in a T-shirt and baggy sweat pants, so he went over there barefoot. That's all there is to that.

"Janice Polo confirmed that the hall carpeting was wet. The prosecution caught Bill in a bunch of lies. We caught Bill in another truth --- she confirmed that. She didn't see the red cup on the nightstand or the headboard, and Sharon's clothes were on the right side of the bed, same side as the cup.

"Ilene Best, who helped do the vacuuming, saw Sharon's clothes in the entry way to the master bathroom where Sharon was found. She said it looked as if Sharon had stepped right out of them and left them lie there.

"Myra Conner said Bill lied to her a number of times, said that he was going to divorce Sharon and move in with her. It's pretty clear that Bill strung her along --- he just wanted the sex. You shouldn't feel sorry for Myra Conner; she's a big girl and knew what she was doing. She had her eyes open and knew exactly what was going on; and just like Bill, she let it go on for years.

"Lisa Scott said Sharon was pretty private about her personal life. She also said Sharon made it clear to her that Bill caught her and saved her from falling down the stairs. She also pointed out that Bill was rude with Sharon on occasion, but at the same time, she generally observed their relationship to be good. She was there the morning when Bill brought Sharon into the clinic suffering from an apparent overdose.

She said that Bill was upset saying that he had carried Sharon into the clinic. Bill was caught in a lie there. I don't think any of us believe that Bill carried her in. Sharon also talked to Lisa Scott about the shock incident, which wasn't an electrocution, since Bill got the shock. Sharon told her that the dog knocked the lamp over into the tub. Lisa Scott also commented that Sharon was not necessarily withdrawn, but again, very private.

"Shawna Brady thought Bill and Sharon were well suited for each other and also confirmed that Sharon didn't confide in anyone very much. Regarding the stairs incident, she testified that Sharon told her that if Bill hadn't caught her she would have fallen down the stairs. When Sharon came into the clinic on April 15th, Shawna Brady's suspicion was that Sharon overdosed on Benadryl. Then when Sharon came to work the next day, she heard Sharon say that she basically had no memory of the day before, which brings us to the drug information on the side effects of benzodiazepines regarding loss of memory. The day of the funeral, Shawna Brady heard Bill tell Patricia Minor that Sharon must have had a second prescription filled.

"This brings us to Patricia Minor, regarding Bill's sleeping pill prescription. She did not say that Bill asked for the Temazepam --- she never said that. Go back to the instruction on circumstantial evidence. I'm not asking you to believe right now what my client told you, but to go with what Patricia Minor told you. Under the circumstantial evidence instruction, isn't it reasonable to conclude that she suggested the Temazepam? Absolutely! Patricia Minor acknowledged that by eliminating the first two drugs that it would logically take her to the Temazepam. Remember that circumstantial evidence instruction.

"Sharon reported to Patricia Minor that she had a family history of sleep problems. Patricia Minor confirmed that she prescribed the drug Ativan for Sharon for anxiety. Remember that Sharon started complaining of her sleep problems back in March. Patricia Minor told you that Sharon wasn't the type to complain; and when she finally brought the problem up, it's a pretty good bet that Sharon had been suffering with difficulties of getting to sleep for some time. Sharon was saying that she was having trouble sleeping, not that Bill was telling her that she was having trouble sleeping. This was what Sharon was feeling, not what Bill was telling Sharon.

"Patricia Minor also confirmed that Sharon was a very private person. She sometimes gave Sharon samples of pills, wrote them down on Sharon's prescription list, but Sharon wouldn't speak to what anyone might have done prior. Sharon talked about her financial concerns with Patricia Minor. Patricia Minor commented that the change in Sharon's demeanor seemed to start about the time she started complaining about these sleep problems.

"On April 15th, the day that Sharon was brought into the clinic, Patricia Minor's conclusion was that Sharon overdosed on Tylenol P.M.

Patricia Minor was the one who wrote the Temazepam prescription for Bill --- the pills that Sharon overdosed on. One prescription for fifteen pills, plus three refills equaling a total of sixty pills. Later that same day, Sharon tells Patricia Minor that Bill lost his prescription and asks her if she would call one in for him at Statz Drug. Patricia Minor knows Sharon, doesn't ask any questions and calls it in. Bill picks up that prescription later on that same day. Jon Hilton, the pharmacist at K-Mart, filled Bill's prescription twice. One was filled on April 29th, and then again on May 13th, an appropriate number of days later. Remember it was a prescription for fifteen pills, so on May 13th, he is down to two pills, so he gets it filled before he runs out. That makes sense. That is certainly under that instruction regarding circumstantial evidence and consistent with the theory that Bill is not guilty with regard to misusing that prescription.

"Remember when I asked the pharmacist from Statz Drug what is meant on the third column of the sign sheet where it says *yes* or *no* counseled. Ann Cruse said that is where they note whether they *do* or *do not* counsel a customer when picking up a prescription. If the pharmacist circles *yes* that means that the patient was counseled as to the side effects, when to take it, et cetera. If they just sign for it, the prescription is given to the customer; they pay for it and leave. On April 29th --- check the record sheet. You will see where when Bill picked up the prescription, that the column says, n*ot counseled.* Is that consistent with Sharon calling Bill on the afternoon of the 29th saying, hey Bill, I need a prescription picked up at Statz Drug. Would you do that for me? Is that consistent with Bill going to Statz and saying, I'm supposed to pick up a prescription for Sharon Guthrie, and Statz

Drug saying, here it is, sign here. Bill picks up the prescription, takes it home, and gives it to Sharon. Remember that circumstantial evidence instruction.

"Look at the side effects of benzodiazepines. Remember that Sharon did pick up that second prescription at Statz Drug on May 12th --- two days before she overdosed.

"Lexi Rivers testified that her mother took her medications with chocolate milk, that she liked chocolate milk and drank a lot of it. Bill did work for law enforcement in Sinclair, Wyoming. If you remember, Lexi testified that Sinclair is right next door to Rawlins and both are in Carbon County. Whether Bill worked for Sinclair Police Department, the Rawlins Police Department, or the Carbon County Police Department --- who cares? There is no reason to question her ---she is right. Her father did work for one of those law enforcement agencies.

"Lexi Rivers testified that her mother talked to her about the April 15th overdose incident. Sharon said that she had taken too many diet pills with Benadryl, and the combination of the two pills was causing her problems. Interestingly enough, Sharon told Lexi that after the April 15th incident, Bill told her to quit taking diet pills and to quit worrying about her weight. Sharon also told Lexi about tripping on the stairs and again Sharon made it clear that Bill caught her and kept her from falling.

"Dr. Reed treated Bill for the bathtub shock incident and described it as an anxiety attack. That is pretty interesting, not because it happened to Bill, but it was interesting considering the symptoms that Sharon was having. Pretty good medical description of an anxiety attack.

"Les Hewitt talked about going over to look at the stairs after Sharon tripped. Said that he saw some little wood filings on the floor, but no hole, no string, no wire. Just a few little wood shavings. Have you ever had a banister come loose and every time you pull on it, it kind of pulls out a little bit from the wall? It is screwed into plaster and when it comes out, some plaster comes out of where it's been screwed into the wood. How the screw peels that stuff out of there kind of reminds you of wood coming out of a drill. He also checked the light fixture in the bathroom shortly after the lamp almost fell into the tub.

He found a bad starter in the light, which is a little device that is on older fluorescent light fixtures and is necessary for the light to turn on.

"Don Perry said Bill told him Sharon died at 1:00 o'clock in the morning. That's obviously not right. It's not right under any circumstances --- it's just not right. I don't think Mr. Perry was lying, but he was wrong. Either that or we caught Bill in an upset moment and Bill misspoke. Either way, we all know that Sharon didn't die at 1:00 o'clock in the morning. Dr. Randall established the fact that Sharon was only in the water a few minutes. I think that Don Perry recalled the conversation with Bill incorrectly.

"Don Perry also testified that there might be some concern with the Presbytery if Bill were to get divorced. I'm sure it would; most churches would have some concern.

"Remember when I asked Don Perry about talking to a Chief Cassidy in Lincoln, Nebraska? In the interview with Jerry Lindberg, he referred to a Chief Crosby. When I asked him about that, he said he was confident he had said Chief Cassidy. I spoke to Jerry Lindberg later and he said that Mr. Perry was using the name Crosby. That's a point I want to make. It's a little thing, but it's a good example of how people can be wrong. Not intentionally with any devious intent, but they can be wrong.

"Suzanne Hewitt testified that her mother expressed some concerns regarding the Reed Clinic where she worked. She said there were lots of white powdery substances in the house. She talked about the dog being blind in one eye, hyperactive, and running into things. She confirmed that her mother knew how to use a computer because she used one at work. She testified that her father's knee was wet on the morning of May 14th when her mother drowned.

"Suzanne Hewitt said her father told her that he was going to divorce her mother after the wedding. She talked about the hormone pills that her mother was taking and how Sharon called them *happy pills*.

"Suzanne also said that her father started talking about Sharon's sleepwalking in March. That would have been around the same time Patricia Minor stated that Sharon began to complain about sleeping problems.

"Interestingly enough, when Sharon talked to Suzanne about tripping on the stairs, she told Suzanne that she didn't know what tripped her. Not a string --- not a wire --- not her sandal. She didn't know what it was.

"Suzanne made it very clear that the few bottles of pills we have here are a small fraction of what was really in the house.

"Suzanne also talked about the incident when Bill was shocked. Sharon told her that she heard Bill yell at the dog, she saw the lamp fall, and Bill grabbed it. I would ask you to search your memory now. See if you recall anyone testifying that Sharon claimed to have had her head under the water when the lamp fell.

"Suzanne doesn't remember her father going over to church in the morning to pray and do devotions. How long has it been since Suzanne lived at home?

"Suzanne said that her father had told Sharon of the affair before she died and that he was going to divorce her. We know now, because of the note on the napkin, that Sharon actually knew about the affair years ago.

"You heard the tape of the conversation between Suzanne and Bill. Suzanne was pleading with her father to tell her the truth. Dad, you've got to tell the truth. Dad, I have already lost my mother. I don't want to lose my father. I don't want my kids to lose their grandpa. If you listen to that tape again, I want you to look at the sequence in which that statement was said. Suzanne says to her father. I know you cheated on Mom. You told them that you cheated on Mom. You admitted to it. That's a motive, Dad. They talked to Myra Conner. Then Suzanne says, Dad, you have got to tell them the truth. Now, what's this truth? It's not about the affair because Suzanne knew that law enforcement was aware of it because her father admitted it to them and they have talked to Myra Conner. What is this truth that Suzanne was pleading with her father to tell law enforcement that would keep her from losing her father and her kids from losing their grandfather?

"Danielle Guthrie had been out of the house for about a year and a half. She told of the incident five years ago when they were living in Orleans. She said that her parents had a big fight and her mother blamed her. Sharon blamed her fifteen-year old daughter for her and Bill's problems with their relationship. She testified that her mother made the statement that sometimes when she was driving home from work she thought about turning her car into oncoming traffic. She also added that her father kind of manipulated her with some similar threat about suicide. If you don't come home with me, I will throw a rope around a tree and I will be dead by morning. That's Dad being manipulative, but that's not what Mom was talking about.

"Later, when Danielle and Sharon's relationship got a little better, she moved away to go to college. Sharon told her daughter that she was very stressed about the financial circumstances at the clinic. We heard Danielle talk about the relationship between her parents. She said that her mother did not sleepwalk. Again --- she hadn't lived at home for about a year and a half. She did remember that when she was still at home her parents had a morning routine. It included her father getting up fairly early --- at least early enough to go to coffee with Sharon and then for her mother to leave Wolsey by about 8:10 to be to work at 8:30. So, there was a little corroboration there when Danielle said that her dad never went over to the church to pray in the morning. Remember that Danielle had been gone from home for a year and a half.

"Danielle described how her mother would bathe. She said that Sharon would kneel down on her knees with the water running in the tub, lean forward to get her hair wet, and then wash her hair. Seems odd to me for someone to wash their hair that way when there was a bathroom with a shower just off the master bedroom, but that's the way Sharon liked to wash her hair --- there doesn't seem to be any dispute about that.

"Danielle testified that she taught, or attempted to teach, her mother how to do searches on the Internet and also noted that Sharon did know how to e-mail.

"Larry Provance talked about sleepwalking as a child and he stated that when you are sleepwalking, you don't know that you are sleepwalking, otherwise, it wouldn't be sleepwalking.

"Jerry Lindberg caught Bill in another truth when he checked on how long it would take to fill a bathtub. Jerry said seven minutes, thirty seconds to fill an empty bathtub and a lot less time if someone was in the tub. It took eleven minutes for the tub to overflow. That is even the more important number because Bill's version was that he

found Sharon facedown in the bathtub with the tub ov
he returned to the house.

"Regarding Dr. Berman's risk factors. I had him ide
exhibit without the risk factors. The reason I did that
doing a psychological autopsy, as he calls it, he has one s
that is probably pretty neutral --- the medical records. People in the
medical profession write down what they observe as accurately as they
can. The other part of this psychological autopsy that he relied on
was the interviews with people. Dr. Berman didn't seem to want to
talk about it too much, but it's pretty obvious that he can't have a solid
opinion unless he has some good information.

"Everybody said that Sharon was a happy-go-lucky person. Is this
the same person who has known that her husband has been cheating
on her for years, had to move out of Orleans because he was cheating
on her, and then continued this affair when they moved to Wolsey? Is
this the same happy-go-lucky person who lived in the same home with
this relationship that Danielle described? I want you to think about
that.

"Dr. Berman probably surprised us all when he said that the most
used method of suicide when a firearm is present is a gun. Forty some
percent. Everyone knows that women don't commit suicide with guns,
right? They wouldn't want to destroy their looks that way, but it's the
most common method of suicide. The second most common method
is drug overdose. The old saying goes that statistics don't lie, but you
can make them mean anything you want. Logic? Common sense
as Dr. McGrath called it, and says Dr. Berman has got a forty-two
percent chance of being right. Dr. McGrath also pointed out that the
last available year for which we had information that there were almost
six times as many suicides in South Dakota as homicides.

"Joan Colby, a member of the session at the church in Wolsey, said
she worked with Bill on a regular basis delivering home communion
and was frequently at the church to open it up for funerals. When she
needed to plan some activity with Bill, she always knew that she could
contact him and had done so dozens of times at the church early in the
morning. What does early in the morning mean, Joan? 6:30 - 7:00
o'clock? The State can argue what it wants to argue. Put a hand on the
Bible and swear to tell the truth. That was Joan Colby's testimony.

Joan Colby said Sharon had talked to her a little bit about the troubles that she was having sleeping. Not long before her death, Sharon confided to her that she was thinking about cashing in her retirement account at the clinic.

"Remember Dr. Berman testified that one suicide could trigger another. Joan Colby told you of a recent suicide that affected the Wolsey area prior to Sharon's death.

"Think about how many times that Bill had already moved. If it was really time to divorce Sharon, was having to move one more time going to bother him? He had moved several times already, picked up, and started over. Ending the marriage with Sharon and having to move one more time, would that have made a difference to him? He wasn't getting rich over there in Wolsey.

"Dr. Burns talked about the quantity of five pills --- probably more than that, but to say how many more is just an absolute guess. The high concentration of drugs found in Sharon's stomach contents means nothing. Both Dr. Burns and Dr. Randall explained the difference between concentration and amount. A teaspoon of sugar in a little water makes the water sweet, but a teaspoon of sugar in a gallon of water can't be noticed. We know there was a large concentration in Sharon's stomach, at least five pills --- probably more. Dr. Randall guessed twenty pills, based on his experience with drug overdoses regarding suicides.

"We know the Lorazepam was in capsules. Sharon's prescription, Ativan, was in tablet form. Sharon had two of her prescriptions plus the Lorazepam in her system. Those were sleeping pills. Sharon liked to take pills --- lots of pills.

"Dr. Burns said the pills had to have been taken within the last four hours which makes the possible conclusion that Sharon took them that morning of May 14th. Tablets--- not capsules. They would have floated around in the chocolate milk and would have been noticed somehow, unless Sharon took them intentionally herself.

"Dr. Burns confirmed that gel capsules dissolve in about an hour. Assuming that Sharon took those five or twenty capsules of Temazepam at 7:00 o'clock in the morning when Bill went over to the church, you wouldn't have expected to find any gel capsules in Sharon's stomach over an hour later when they started drawing the contents out of her stomach.

"Remember that Mitch Rivers testified he saw samples of the medication Prozac in the house.

"Reverend Larry Boutelle testified when he went fishing with Bill on June 11th that Bill told him, in confidence as a friend, that he had found a suicide note in a liturgy book in the church office. Bill told him that he had talked to his attorney about the note. You heard Bill testify that he gave the note to me on June 15th. You heard Keith Traverse testify that he saw the note sometime before July 26th.

"The State's theory is that Bill is a liar. They've proved it fifty times over --- they've mentioned it a hundred times over. He is an adulterer; we got that point after the first ten witnesses. Bill cheated on Sharon and they had a horrible relationship. He had a motive --- he was cheating on his wife. Myra Conner broke off that affair five years later than she should have. Five years later than he should have, but she broke it off. It's over, she said she's dating another man. Remember her testimony. Don't count on my recollection of it; don't count on Mr. Moore's recollection. Myra Conner broke it off.

"The trip on the stairs? Take Sharon's word for it; Bill kept her from falling down the stairs. If he was trying to kill her, why didn't he push her instead of grabbing her to keep her from falling? Did Sharon trip on a shoelace? Take Sharon's word for it. Nobody saw any string on that stairway. Sharon made it clear several times that Bill kept her from falling.

"The bathtub incident when Bill was shocked. Again, please take Sharon's word for it. The dog hit the lamp cord causing the lamp to dive towards the tub. Whether Bill got shocked or Bill got burned or just got scared like some of us do --- take Sharon's word for it. Again, if he were trying to kill her, wouldn't he have let the lamp fall?

"Sharon told somebody that she leapt out of the tub. I don't intend to be rude, but picture this. She is on her knees, bending over washing her hair; the lamp gets knocked over. The lamp is falling towards the tub, and she leaps from the tub before it hits the water. Take Sharon's word for it.

"Les Hewitt said the starter was out in the light. How do you fake a burned out starter in a fluorescent light fixture? Do you think Bill is capable of that? The light was malfunctioning with the burned out starter, Sharon put the lamp in the bathroom, and the dog came in and hit the cord.

"Yes, these sound like a pretty unusual string of circumstances, but remember the overdose on April 15th. Remember that Bill called in sick for Sharon and then later he took her into the clinic. Sharon told her daughter Lexi that she herself did the overdose. Nobody put Benadryl in her chocolate milk or Tylenol P.M., or whatever it was. They tested for narcotics. There were no nasty drugs in her system. Take Sharon's word for it.

"Sharon was trying to lose weight and she was taking diet pills. The diet pills probably aggravated her sleep problems, and she took Benadryl, which has a depressant effect.

"That brings us to the unsent e-mail. The little word that says *mail sent* means the author thought it was sent --- Bill thought it was sent. Mike Waldner testified to that. The e-mail talked about the overdose that Sharon admitted that she did on April 15th. This isn't some grand plot. This is exactly what happened on April 15th; and the date of the e-mail is April 16th. This isn't history, it's an e-mail that Bill thought he sent to Lexi about something that she had talked to Sharon about the next day. Like I said --- take Sharon's word for it. Sharon said that she herself was at fault for the overdose. Somebody should have seen this as a suicide gesture and advised Sharon to talk to someone about getting some help. They should have referred her to a counselor, but they didn't --- it wasn't done.

"Why would Bill run the risk of being caught with duplicate prescriptions? Bill had one prescription for sixty pills, fifteen at a time, with three refills. All he had to do was wait six weeks, fill the first one, two weeks later fill it again, which would be four weeks down the road; then fill it again. Why would he do something to get a prescription that is sure to be picked up on? Why would he sign for it when he already had access to sixty pills?

"Why would Sharon cause a duplicate prescription to be issued? Sharon told Patricia Minor that Bill had lost his prescription and asked her if she would phone another one in. Nobody talked to Bill that day. Patricia Minor testified that Sharon asked her to duplicate the prescription for the pills --- to reissue the prescription by phone.

Patricia Minor asked Sharon if she wanted it filled at Statz because that's where they usually get their prescriptions. Sharon said yes. Bill didn't need that second prescription. Sharon had been having trouble sleeping for months. She had the mild dose of Ativan that Patricia Minor had given her. Maybe Sharon's low dose wasn't working, but Bill's pills were.

"Just maybe Sharon really did figure out how to do those Internet searches that Danielle showed her and there was another reason why Sharon wanted that Lorazepam prescription. Bill certainly didn't need it. He already had sixty pills, and all he had to do was wait six weeks from the original prescription date, taking them on a day-to-day basis just like he was supposed to do. That's not what happened. He didn't need that second prescription, but apparently Sharon did. Go back to the circumstantial evidence instruction.

"The State's theory is that Bill, for some unknown reason, caused this duplicate prescription to be issued, then emptied the pills into a quart jar and carefully calculated a non-fatal dose because he wanted it to appear to be a drowning accident. There is no evidence that Sharon actually drank chocolate milk that morning. The State's theory is that Bill carefully timed giving her this chocolate milk so that the full effect would take place just after she got into the bathtub. Not before because he couldn't carry her into the bathroom. Additionally, besides timing the Temazepam dose just right to hit her just as she got into the bathtub, remember there isn't any evidence of foul play here. In terms of the bruising on her body, there are no indications that she was dragged into the tub, only indications than she got into that tub by herself. I'm being cynical and forgive me, but that's got to be the State's theory. How else would it work? He is going to drown Sharon; he does all the bathtub searches, and he can't get her into the bathtub from the bedroom because she is too heavy. Think about the facts. He timed the dose carefully and then somehow he got Sharon to take the tablets. He says, here Sharon, here's your glass of milk, never mind the tablets floating around in it. Or, here Sharon, it is 7:00 o'clock in the morning; take your sleeping pills. Remember she had tablets in her stomach that morning. How did that happen?

"Did she get up in the middle of the night and take them? No, that's what Bill says --- that can't be true. He has been caught in so many lies. Is there no way that we can catch him in the truth? Did Sharon take the pills herself after she woke up that morning? We don't know, but we know with absolute one hundred percent certainty that she took tablets not capsules. Sharon's name is on the prescription bottle for the tablets. She took those tablets that morning --- they were in her stomach. Four hours was Dr. Burn's testimony. That could only happen if she took them herself. By accident --- intentionally --- as a suicide gesture --- an attempt?

"Could it be that this happy-go-lucky person committed suicide? Was she the same person that knew about the affair for years? Was she the same person that wrote that note on the napkin years ago? Is this the same happy-go-lucky person who Dr. Berman described, the one that blamed Danielle to her face for the marital problems that she and Bill were having? Is this happy-go-lucky, no-risk-of-suicide person that Dr. Berman described the same person that talked about taking her hormone pills --- *happy pills* as she called them? Is this the same person that had Prozac in her house?

"I don't mean to be unkind to Sharon, but Bill Guthrie is charged with murder. You can't let being kind to Sharon's memory cause you not to look at what is a real possibility that Sharon overdosed herself to commit suicide.

"Is this the same Sharon who admitted to her daughter Lexi that she took too many drugs and said that Bill was going to take her on a cruise when she lost weight? You have heard the relationship between Bill and Sharon described. Is this the same Sharon that was lied to about an affair that her cheating husband was having and yet Bill moved her with him around the country several times?

"Is this the same happy-go-lucky Sharon whose husband told his three daughters that he was going to divorce their mother after Lexi's wedding? Bill told Sharon that also. Yes --- he has been caught in so many lies that it's hard to believe him, but you can believe the three daughters. None of them would tell their mother that their dad was going to divorce her after Lexi's wedding.

"Is that reasonable --- is that rational? Sharon was looking at losing her husband, a philanderer, a liar, and a cheater. She had a job, and the possibility of losing that job was facing her. Now, is this the same person that Dr. Berman described? She has Lexi's wedding coming up.

Lexi, a petite 5'2" little thing, is going to wear her dress; and Sharon is wondering how she got to be two hundred pounds at 5'1. How did I end up to fifty-four years old with a husband that has been cheating on me? How am I going to go to Hinton for the wedding and face these people that knew me when I was thin, and now Bill is going to divorce me? That morning on May 14th, did Sharon take five pills as a suicide gesture to get some love, to get some attention, to get some control back in her life? Is that what she did? We don't know. Did Sharon take twenty pills to try to kill herself? We don't know. We will never know, but ask yourself this question. Is there a reasonable doubt?"

Michael Moore begins the State's rebuttal. "Ladies and gentlemen, this case is about over and almost in your hands. When the defense talked about the Temazepam on April 29th and that Sharon had Lorazepam, remember the evidence stated that Sharon didn't have the Lorazepam until May 6th.

"When Mr. Wilson said that this isn't a draft of this purported suicide note, ask this question. Why did the defendant on August 7th type the date of May 13, 1999? Why did he do that? In this case, look at all the facts; don't look at one thing.

"Mr. Wilson told you several times to take Sharon's word for it. I don't know how many times he told you that. Then when he said that Sharon told Patricia Minor that Bill Guthrie called her and wanted those pills now, Sharon is not telling the truth. Don't take her word for that, but only when it's convenient for the defense.

"I want you to look at all the evidence. I want to point out that we never presented evidence that Bill Guthrie would lose his job because he was going to get a divorce. What I said was that if Sharon and Bill were going through a divorce, the lies would have to come out. He lied to his church in Orleans, he lied to the session there, and he lied to his boss. Then when he came to Wolsey, he lied; plus he was having an affair with a parish member. He would lose his job for those lies and for his conduct, not a divorce. That's what the defendant was afraid of, and that's why he got rid of Sharon. He dug a hole too deep to get out, and this was the only way out.

"We talk about beyond a reasonable doubt. I believe that's the first thing that the defense told you. The best way I can explain this is to have you think of the picture of Mount Rushmore. Take Lincoln's head out of that picture. You still know what the picture is beyond a reasonable doubt. You don't have to concentrate on the holes. Look at the whole picture, and you know what it is. You know what the whole picture shows you that Bill Guthrie is guilty.

"Ladies and gentlemen, if any of you have the least thought that Bill Guthrie didn't do this, I want you to remember how Sharon died. Remember that on April 3rd he was on his computer looking up bathtub accidents. On April 21st and 22nd, for two hours he was on the computer looking up bathtub and household accidents. Remember how Sharon died.

"Remember the draft of the e-mail which says Sharon was in the bathtub on April 16th. This is the only thing in evidence that states that. Everybody else who heard about this incident never heard that. Remember that one month later she died in that bathtub.

"Remember that Bill Guthrie acquired the drug Temazepam and signed for it twice. Remember that Temazepam only comes in capsule form, and that this was the drug that killed Sharon.

"Remember how Bill Guthrie continually changed his story regarding what happened to Sharon.

"Remember the alleged suicide note that Bill Guthrie brought into evidence on Tuesday of this week. What did we find then? An attempt to make other suicide notes in August three months after Sharon died.

"I ask you to remember all of these things. There isn't any other rational explanation of what happened to Sharon. The defendant, Bill Guthrie, killed her and I ask you to find him guilty. Thank you."

At 1:57 p.m., Judge Martin excuses the two alternates, and the bailiff escorts the remaining twelve jurors to the jury room. Martin instructs Michael Moore and Gregory Wilson to make sure that every one of the exhibits is present and available for the jury members.

During deliberations, the jury makes a request to again listen to the tape recording of Suzanne Hewitt and her father. At 4:49 p.m., the jury is called back into the courtroom to listen to the tape and then escorted back to the jury room to continue deliberations.

At 6:49 p.m. the jury is back in the courtroom. A roll call of jury members is taken, and each member is asked to answer with an affirmative response that he or she is present.

"Ladies and gentlemen of the jury, have you reached a verdict?" Judge Martin asks.

"Yes, we have."

"I will have the clerk read the verdict. Will the defendant please rise?"

"The State of South Dakota, Plaintiff, versus William Boyd Guthrie, defendant. We, the jury duly impaneled to hear the above entitled matter, find the defendant guilty of homicide, murder in the first degree, dated this 21st day of January, 2000."

Bill Guthrie, upon hearing the guilty verdict, loses the strength in his legs and sits down in his chair. His attorney helps him to his feet.

Judge Martin thanks the jury, the attorney, and the whole court system. He announces to the jury that they are now at liberty to visit with people about the case if they wish to do so and excuses them.

Bill Guthrie is escorted out the courtroom and taken back to the jail to await his sentencing.

Epilogue

William (Bill/Dr. Bill) **Boyd Guthrie** was sentenced to life without parole on January 24, 2000, and is serving his sentence at the South Dakota State Penitentiary in Sioux Falls, South Dakota. At his sentencing, he was informed by Judge Eugene Martin that he had the right to ask the governor of South Dakota to commute his sentence. He also had the right to appeal the decision of the jury to the Supreme Court and if he could not afford the costs of an appeal, he would have the right to apply for assignment of counsel.

Bill Guthrie made an appeal on October 23, 2000, to the Supreme Court on the following issues:
(1) whether expert testimony was properly allowed on the question of suicide
(2) whether the motion for judgment of acquittal was properly denied
(3) whether the circuit court properly denied a defense motion to suppress evidence obtained during trial
(4) whether he was entitled to offer surrebuttal testimony of his fingerprint expert
(5) whether certain communications by Guthrie to his superior fell under the "clergy privilege" in SDCL 19-13-17 and whether this privilege was waived under SDLC 19-13-26
(6) whether the Circuit Court properly allowed the State to play the tape-recorded conversation, to have the jury read a transcript of this recording, and to permit live testimony regarding the same conversation.
Issue (4) lacked sufficient merit for discussion.

An opinion was filed on May 16, 2001. The first-degree murder conviction was upheld 3-2 by the Supreme Court of South Dakota. The justices ruled that although Judge Eugene Martin should not have allowed a prosecution suicide expert to tell jurors that he did not believe Sharon Guthrie killed herself by overdosing with drugs, the high court determined that the testimony did not unfairly taint the trial.

Bill Guthrie asked for his name to be removed from the Presbytery membership and is no longer considered an ordained Presbyterian minister. It has been noted that he has been doing some teaching in the GED program and also conducting Bible studies at the prison. He declined an interview with PS Chilson, stating that his lawyers advised him that as long as they are working on a court solution, he would not be able to give an interview to anyone.

Judge Eugene L. Martin, at the age of 59, retired from the bench on February 1, 2001, after serving twenty-three years as a circuit judge. The Guthrie case, during his long career, was only the second murder case that he presided over in the eleven counties that make up the Third Judicial Circuit in the State of South Dakota. He and his wife now reside in Rapid City, South Dakota, where he established a mediation and arbitration business. He works with attorneys and their clients to attempt the settlement of civil lawsuits out of court to reduce the court load in a quicker and less expensive manner.

A mild-mannered soft-spoken man, Martin is the father of two grown children, enjoys tennis and taking walks. One family pet, a cat, shares their home. He is very active in the Catholic religion and enjoys singing in the choir along with his wife.

Michael Moore, 35, is still serving as State's Attorney in Beadle County. The Guthrie trial was the first murder case that he prosecuted, and it was this case that prompted South Dakota to create its own computer forensics unit. To date, he has also prosecuted a homicide regarding the death of a young man that was injected with Oxycontin, a narcotic pain medication.

In October of 1999, two months prior to the Guthrie trial, Michael Moore married his current wife, Candice, and is now a father to a little girl, Mikena, born on January 31, 2003.

During an interview with Michael Moore, PS Chilson asked if there were any other avenues left for Bill Guthrie to pursue. He said that habeas corpus would be one, but Guthrie would have to show a violation of his constitutional rights and/or ineffective assistance of counsel.

PS Chilson asked how sentencing is determined regarding life in prison or the death penalty. Michael Moore said that in South Dakota the prosecutor makes this decision before going to trial and has to file notice to seek the death penalty. The notice is typed and just has to be signed. There are fifteen to twenty different aggravated circumstances that a prosecutor has to look at. If it meets one, the prosecutor can seek the death penalty. Moore stated that when he looked at the aggravated circumstances in the code, that a couple of them could have fit the Guthrie case, but it was marginal. After reviewing other death penalty cases, he didn't think that this was one of them and did not sign the notice seeking the death penalty.

Tracy Kelly, Deputy State's Attorney, has since moved away from Huron due to her husband's job transfer. Michael Moore stated that she was a tremendous help to him throughout the Guthrie trial.

Jim Sheridan still works at the Beadle County Sheriff's Department as a deputy.

Bill Guthrie's attorney declined an interview with PS Chilson and also the use of his real name. He appealed to the South Dakota Supreme Court the trial court's monetary sanction of $8866.00 for violating a reciprocal discovery motion. The Supreme Court turned it back to Judge Eugene Martin in Beadle County. On November 5, 2001, Guthrie's attorney appeared before Judge Martin. After two hours and no decision, this was again turned over to the Supreme Court. November 20, 2002, the Supreme Court ruled that Guthrie's attorney must pay a monetary penalty for waiting too long to disclose an alleged suicide note that he introduced during the murder trial. However, the high court trimmed the amount that he must pay for violating a court order that set a timetable for disclosing evidence. The Supreme Court said that the penalty should be cut to $5500.00 to take into account his ability to pay. The Supreme Court said that the smaller penalty would still send a message to attorneys and prevent future abuses in disclosing evidence.

The Presbyterian churches at Wolsey and Bonilla hired a new minister. The churches underwent a loss of several members due to the actions of Bill Guthrie. The children of the church trusted Dr. Bill and suffered many disappointments throughout this ordeal.

The relatives, though they miss Sharon terribly, continue to rebuild their lives by their faith. The three daughters differed in their opinions during the trial, and this situation remains the same. The youngest daughter, **Danielle**, is now married and has one child. Last noted, **Lexi**, the middle daughter, keeps in contact with her father in prison and firmly believes that he is innocent. She remains split from her two sisters. After the death of her mother, **Suzanne Hewitt**, the oldest daughter, stepped up to the plate and took over the care of her grandmother. Nanette Guthrie died on October 30, 2001, at the age of 84. Of course, Bill Guthrie was not at his mother's funeral.

Two years after the death of her mother, **Suzanne Hewitt** felt that the people of the community still avoided her and her family because of her father's crime. Some could not understand why and how she could testify against her father. On May 20, 2001, Suzanne granted an interview with a local radio station. She invited people to call in and ask her any questions that they wished to ask.

"We have Suzanne Hewitt in the studio with us this morning for our edition of Talk of the Town. Suzanne, of course, is the daughter of Sharon Guthrie, and we are going to be talking a little bit about the Guthrie murder trial. Good morning, Suzanne, thank you for being here with us."

"Good morning and thank you for having me."

"Your father, William Guthrie, is serving a life sentence for murdering your mother. I bet you are glad the whole thing is over with."

"I am very glad it's all over with. In my mind, justice has been served."

"Where do you draw your strength from?"

"First and foremost --- God, my faith, my background, and church. God has been there for me. Anytime I needed strength --- prayer big time. The second and foremost is my husband and family. My husband has been very supportive --- he has been my backbone. Then I would have to give some credit to the people I work with."

"Can you tell us what kind of a person your mother was?"

"My mom wasn't a perfect person by any means, but she was a great mom --- she was my friend. Most people you talk to say she was a wonderful person. She was great with kids --- she was great with my kids. In the beginning she didn't like my husband, so that was kind of a drawback; but they became friends as our marriage progressed. She was a wonderful person."

"Your mother worked at Reed Clinic?"

"Yes, she did. The patients there liked her --- the people she worked with liked her. She was fast friends with all the ladies who worked there."

"We should mention to our listeners this morning that if anyone has questions to ask of Suzanne, to give us a call. We'll put you on the air. Now, don't be chicken. I know some people tend to get a little chicken in these instances."

"People don't know what to ask. I'm an open book. If you have a question, no matter how little or how big, I'm here to answer it."

"So often times, Suzanne, we hear about jury trials on the news; however we just get little tidbits of it; and it's different when you come face to face with a person who's been through it."

"Right. My big thing is that I don't want people to be afraid to ask me questions. I don't want people to be afraid to talk to my family or me. As with any crime, you need to be able to say, 'I don't know how you feel, but what can I do for you --- what can I do for your family?' I think the biggest thing in a crime is the family is embarrassed, and they shouldn't have to be embarrassed. I didn't commit the crime --- I didn't do the things that my father did. I'm not embarrassed to stand up and say I'm a strong person. I have strong beliefs and this shouldn't have happened."

"Suzanne, don't you think that people just don't know what to say to you when they meet you face to face?"

"Exactly, and that shouldn't be. People should feel it's okay to say what they think. If you think I'm wrong, tell me I'm wrong. If you don't agree with how I feel about this whole thing, that's fine. You can say that, but I'm going to tell you how I think, and I'm going to tell you how I feel, too."

"Describe what's happened to your children throughout all of this."

"I have one child that has been teased and tormented at school. I don't know if it's things the kids have heard at home or opinions they have heard in the media. I don't know, but that's not fair. My kids didn't do what their grandfather did, and they shouldn't be teased for it."

"Suzanne, you mentioned before that it's sad that the family has to be the ones who have to suffer."

"Yes, it is. With my father now in prison and my mom gone, I don't have a lot of people to turn to if I need something. I don't have my mom to be able to call. People shouldn't have to suffer --- I shouldn't have to suffer for what my father did."

"What has life been like after the trial?"

"To be quite honest --- it's been quite lonely. I feel everyone has distanced themselves. People don't know how to react to me. They don't know what to think of me. That's sad! I think my mom had a lot more friends --- I think my family had a lot more friends than what I've seen. But, there again, I don't think people know how to react."

"Suzanne, do you feel you have been wronged by the press?"

"I think so. I feel like they put it into writing that I was against my father's rights. I felt that everything I did, I was protecting my mother's rights. My mother was no longer here, and I felt like someone needed to protect those rights that she had and that's why I did what I did. That's why I went in and taped my father --- I felt like I wasn't getting the truth. That's why I went to the state's attorney's office. That's why I went to the sheriff's department. I wanted to get to the truth, and I wanted justice served for my mom."

"It's really put you in a predicament, hasn't it?"

"Yes, it has. I've been the bad guy in everything, and I've lost a lot of family because of that."

"Not that you would have cause to visit the prison, Suzanne, but have you heard how your father is dealing with life in prison?"

"No, I have not. I don't have anything to do with him anymore. I consider myself Sharon Guthries' daughter. That's probably very cold-hearted, but that's just how I feel at this point."

"Suzanne, your parents lived in Wolsey. Explain what the reception has been over there since the trial?"

"I think that, there again, people don't know what to say or how to react because they knew my parents a year longer than they knew me. They saw my father as a minister or as a fishing buddy. They didn't see his anger; they didn't see how he treated his family. They never saw that. They saw what was in the church and what was in the public, but they never saw what was behind the scenes. They never knew the things I went through growing up, and I think that's the big thing. I think the people of Wolsey just don't know how to react to me. I go there; and if I go to church, they are always kind and they always ask how I'm doing, but I never felt like I was welcome there anymore. It's very uncomfortable."

"How have your husband and your kids dealt with the aftermath of the trial?"

"I think that we've all done very well --- I really honestly do. I think we have God first in our life as a family, and I think with that we've been given the strength to move on. I think now that the appeal process is done, now that I can voice my opinion, I think we'll be able to move on and be able to get on with life."

"By the way listeners. If you have any questions or comments for Suzanne, please give us a call."

Caller #1: One of the jurors called in and expressed how serving on the jury was one of the hardest things she has ever done in her life and doesn't want to do that again. To know everyday that someone is in prison because of the part she played being a jury member is very upsetting to her.

"Suzanne, have you talked with any of the jurors?"

"I would like to hear from the jurors because I wasn't on that side of it. I would like to hear how they felt and how they reacted and what they thought. What was the big thing that brought them to believe that my father was guilty --- what in the trial made them think that?"

Caller #2: This individual told Suzanne that she appreciated her honesty and said that we need more people to come out and be honest about issues. She told Suzanne that there are other families that have skeletons in their closets. Family members with drug abuse, alcoholism, domestic violence, theft, criminal records, etc. She said, "Sin is sin in the eyes of God. There's no degree of sin."

Caller #3: "I think you did a good job helping bring someone to justice like that. Suzanne, you should be rewarded."

"Thank you."

"Suzanne, isn't it good to hear from the public and know what they are thinking? That's what we wanted this morning."

"Yes, it is."

Caller #4: "First, Suzanne, I want to commend you for your strength. This has not been an easy situation for you. You actually lost both parents through this. You mentioned that you have not spoken to your father."

"Not since he has gone to prison in Sioux Falls. I've sent him a couple letters and not gotten a whole lot of response back."

"Would you like to ask him again if he would admit to murdering your mother?"

"I would love to --- I would love to ask him."

"I'm sure growing up as a child, as any child, you were taught honesty?"

"Especially being a preacher's daughter I was taught that from early on."

"Again, I commend you for your strength and am happy to hear you on the radio this morning."

"Thank you. We need to voice feelings and opinions and not be embarrassed about them and be able to move on through the pain and heal through the pain."

"It has to be difficult, Suzanne, when you have people talking behind your back."

"After my mom died, it amazed me that when I was walking through a store, I would see people talking; and I would feel they were talking about me, and the minute I walked up they would get quiet. I would ask myself --- were they talking about me? You get a feeling of paranoia when you've been through something like this. You just feel like everyone is talking about you and downing you. I don't want that for my mom --- I don't want that for my family. I've picked myself up by the bootstraps. It's time for healing, and it's time to be able to move on."

"Suzanne, why are you here today?"

"I want people to know that my mom was a good person, and that I'm not a bad person. I made the choices that I did because that was what I needed to do. I prayed about it, and I felt like I was led in the direction to be on the opposite side of my father --- that was my conviction. I needed to protect my mom; and if in doing that, they found my father guilty, then that's what needed to happen."

Caller #5: "Suzanne, I went to school with your parents in Nebraska. I was there when you were born. Your mother was a wonderful and kind lady, always happy, smiling and upbeat. She was a good leader of children. Looking back, your father was always troubled; but we didn't know how troubled he was. The entire thing is such a tragedy because it has hurt so many people. I can attest to the fact that instead of knocking you and your family down, it has made you stronger. I hated it that you had to go through this, but you and your family are going to be winners. You are going to come out on top and be fine. You're doing a good job, Suzanne."

"Thank you."

"That was a very emotional phone call, Suzanne."

"Yes, it was, and I know exactly who that was; and she is a wonderful lady."

"Something like this must be so difficult to go through emotionally."

"It has been. It's like a movie that you see on television. It's somebody else's life; and now here I'm in the midst of it and it's my life. It's my life --- it's a movie. It's been an uphill battle for the last two years."

Caller #6: "I think your mother was such a great person and always happy. I have probably been one of the ones who have avoided you, but it was because I felt you didn't want to talk. I just congratulate you for coming forward, being honest enough to do this. We did see problems with your father. We felt that he wasn't treating your mother right. I'm sorry that I've avoided you, but we just think the world of you."

"Thank you very much, and you don't need to avoid me."

"Suzanne, people come to you and they don't know what to say. What would you like them to say?"

"I'd like them to just tell me how they feel. I'd like them to tell me how their kids are, how their grandkids are, how their parents or grandparents are doing. You don't necessarily have to talk about what happened. If you would like to talk about what happened --- I'm an open book. I've always been willing and able to talk about what went on and what happened, but I've always felt like people have shied away and there's no need for that. People don't know what to say. You never know what to say to a family member, but just the fact that you're there for that person makes a big difference than by not saying anything. A hug ... a pat on the shoulder saying, *'You'll make it.'* That kind of stuff is what people need."

"Suzanne, did you know any of the jurors?"

"No, I did not. I recognized a few faces from around town, but I've not seen any of them since the trial. If any of them want to talk to me or give me their opinions, I'm open to that."

Caller #7: How do you get along with your sisters since the trial?"

"One of them I have contact with, and one of them I do not."

"You don't have contact with the one who thought your father was innocent?"

"Yes."

"I want to thank our callers for calling in this morning and especially thank Suzanne Hewitt for visiting with us regarding the murder case of her mother."

Author's Words

Small town murders are a rarity and particularly unusual when a man of the cloth is involved. I ask you to remember that only a small percentage of clergy commit crimes and a much smaller percentage commit murder. We must continue with our faith and believe in the many good clergy that stand in our pulpits and preach the Word of the Lord.

Serving God as a minister seemed to be Bill Guthrie's life's work. Why murder? Why not get a divorce and continue to serve churches and preach the gospel. We most likely will never know why he murdered his wife. What began thirty plus years ago as a union between two young people in the eyes of God ended in tragedy, in the eyes of God. Only Bill, Sharon, and God know the actual details of that fateful day on May 14, 1999.

Bill Guthrie was never clinically diagnosed as such, so one can only speculate, but it appears that he clearly has what is described as narcissistic personality disorder. The more common name is self-centeredness. People with this disorder react to criticism with feelings of rage, shame, or humiliation. They take advantage of others to achieve their own goals. They are self-important and exaggerate achievements and talents. They are preoccupied with fantasies of success, power, beauty, intelligence, or ideal love. They have unreasonable expectations of favorable treatment and require constant attention and admiration. They lack the ability to understand the effects of their behavior on others. They often feel entitled to special treatment by others and can become demanding, angry, and easily offended.

Prior to hiring Bill Guthrie, the churches in Wolsey and Bonilla were not informed of his affair in Nebraska. They seemed happy with his easily understood sermons and his friendliness. It has been revealed that he could not remember the names of the church members very well. The session overlooked what he lacked because they were so happy to have a full-time minister.

Bill Guthrie asked that he be referred to as Dr. Bill since he had his doctorate degree. Since the investigation and the trial there has been some question whether he really had a doctorate degree.

Bill Guthrie assured the church board that he would do lots of things, but somehow they never got done. He consistently balked when it came to doing home or hospital visits. Could it be that to him making a call meant picking up the phone and dialing? He would exaggerate his pastoral reports and actually did not put in the time regarding church business that he documented on his reports. He would become angry and pout when he didn't get his way with the church session. His résumé seemed to be much exaggerated and false. He was good at making up stories. He constantly complained of headaches and backaches --- anything to get attention. You be the judge. Doesn't this sound like narcissistic behavior?

The churches knew that Bill Guthrie had some problems, but they never would have thought that this man who stood in front of their church preaching the Word of the Lord would be capable of having an affair with another woman or murdering his wife. Who would have thought?

It has been noted that Bill Guthrie especially like redheaded women --- that they were his passion. The woman that he was having an affair with ... red hair. The friend in Wyoming ... red hair. Another known friend ... red hair.

Bill Guthrie was known to be very controlling and very catty. All of the decisions in the family had to be his and his only. As it was witnessed by many in public, when Sharon would say something that he disagreed with, he would cut her down right then and there. People strongly felt that he didn't treat Sharon with the respect she so deserved.

Bill Guthrie couldn't wait to have his deceased wife's possessions removed from the house. How heartless of him to tell his daughters at the cemetery that he might remarry someday and he wanted their mother's belongings removed from the house immediately. Wasn't this gesture of his a suspicious sign? Thinking back, of course there were lots of signs, but no child wants to believe his or her parent is capable of murdering the other parent.

Numerous sympathy cards were sent to Bill Guthrie, and some ended up in a wastebasket. The others --- who knows? Hopefully, the family got to see them first. Rumor has it that he took the memorial money with him to Wyoming after the funeral, so we can only assume that he didn't share the cards with his family.

After Sharon's funeral, someone came to the manse to check on Bill Guthrie and found him in the basement. He told them that he had fallen down the basement steps and lay on the floor all night. Funny thing is --- when that person walked through the living room, there was a movie playing in the VCR.

Bill Guthrie was known to visit pornographic websites. A few months prior to Sharon's death, he attempted to blame his thirteen-year-old grandson, saying that Derrick stole his credit card to get on the porn sites. During Judd Robbin's search of the hard drives on the computer at the church, a large number of pornographic sites were found that Bill had visited. Since this information was not relevant it was not used as evidence during the trial. It has been said that Bill Guthrie had asked the church board for more hard drive space.

Bill Guthrie taught his children the Ten Commandments, then proceeded to make a mockery of them by breaking most of them. It is known that he could be very cruel when it came to disciplining his children. According to family members, it was felt that some of the punishments that he inflicted on them could today be considered child abuse. He stated in front of the congregation on Mother's Day in 1999 that his father's actions would be considered child abuse today, and yet he inflicted the same punishments on his children.

Bill Guthrie didn't stop with his children. There was a time when he was angry with his grandson, Derrick, and began to beat on him with his hand. Derrick's mother and her friend witnessed this and removed Derrick from the scene. There was another time that Derrick was told to lie for his grandfather or deal with his wrath.

Bill Guthrie received the following letter prior to his arrest. The postmark reveals that it was mailed from Wolsey. This letter was found during the search at the church office and was not relevant evidence. The following is the actual letter with typographical errors:

Bill

this will be an anonomous letter because I was very close to your wife and for all peoples benefit you dont need to know who wrote this. I know a lot about you and your past. I think it would be in the best intinerst of everybody if you would resign you job and leave town. I dont want to bring this stuff out to the public to get you fired but we both know that it would. Nebraska, wyoming, doctorate degree. Just a few off the things you dont want brought out to the public ! ! ! ! ! ! ! !

If you resign by 7–15–99 and leave town by 8-1-99 I promise I will never speak of this. Its up to you. dont be stupid, you've already done enough stupid things GOOD_BYEX ! ! ! ! ! ! ! ! ! ! !

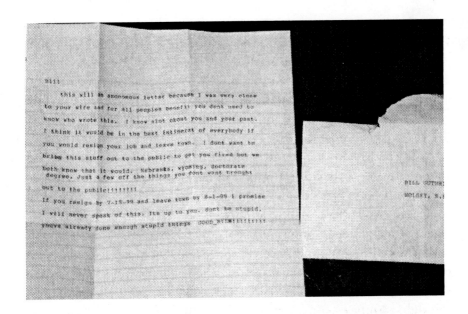

It appears that Bill Guthrie's actions got him nowhere, but free room and board in a prison cell for the rest of his life. How ironic that he went from one house of sinners to another house of sinners, only on different terms. It has been said that he had a dream to have a prison ministry. Well, it seems that he has fulfilled that dream. To date, he still maintains his innocence.

During an interview with Suzanne, I asked her if she had ever had the feeling that her mom might have committed suicide prior to the alleged suicide note being presented at the trial? She stated, "I knew she wouldn't have killed herself. I was like on the fence because she would never have been caught dead naked. That was the biggest point she would have made. Mom always said she would have to face God if she killed herself and she wouldn't want to have to explain to Him why. On the other hand, I knew my dad was a minister and I knew he wouldn't kill anybody. But, I have resolved myself to know that Dad gave her the drugs in the red cup in her chocolate milk, but the drowning is what killed Mom. So, in his mind, he did not kill her. She swallowed them; she drank the chocolate milk, so in his mind she did it herself. He's not thinking that he put the drugs in the milk."

After the trial was over, by request of the family, Sharon's body was moved from the Wolsey cemetery to a cemetery in Nebraska. Prior to the move, the defense requested that the casket be opened, so fingerprints could be taken to determine if Sharon's prints were on the alleged suicide note. Since it had been close to a year since Sharon was buried, Suzanne was told that the whole hand might be needed in order to get a good print. Permission was given, but Suzanne did not allow them to remove her mother's hand. Cindy Orton did succeed in getting a good print without the use of Sharon's whole hand, and it was determined that Sharon's prints were not on the alleged suicide note.

The good news is that Bill Guthrie is now **Serving Time** for his actions. Prison bars control him, and he will never have power over the many beautiful memories of Sharon. The bad news is that this controlling man took Sharon away from her children, grandchildren, great grandchildren, siblings, relatives, and friends. The scary thought is that if Bill hadn't produced the alleged suicide note, it could be a possibility that he would be a free man today and would have gotten away with murder. Thanks to computer forensics and Judd Robbins this didn't happen.

Why didn't Sharon leave Bill? This question has been asked many times since her death. One reason and most likely the most important one--- she loved him. When she married, her dream to be the wife of a minister was fulfilled. Her marriage vows were an oath that she took for life.

Sharon's last living day in church was on Mother's Day. Bill Guthrie escorted his wife to her pew, said many nice things about her, and kissed her in church --- something that he had never done before. Was this all a front? Was he preparing himself in front of the people of the church, so they would think that he was a terrific husband and would definitely never surmise that he was capable of murdering his wife?

Suzanne, during an interview, stated that for over a year after her mother's death she was angry with her mother for not standing up to her father. She felt that if her mother would have been a stronger person that she would be here today. She has since forgiven her mom.

Regarding the anger towards her father, Suzanne said she didn't know if there would be any point in time that she could forgive him, especially since she knows where he is for the rest of his life for what he did. She said that when her father dies, he will have to face God, not her.

Even though Sharon had an allergy to flour, she enjoyed baking while listening to Country Western music. She was a fan of Elvis Presley, car races, tractor pulls, and the Nebraska Cornhuskers football team. She was very talented at playing the violin and ministering to the children of the church, loved crafts, and sewing. Her favorite holiday was Christmas. She loved decorating the whole house and the giving of gifts. Sharon was described by many as being bubbly, always upbeat, always smiling, and having a good word for everybody. She never cut her husband down to anyone. She was always proud of him and was his enthusiastic cheerleader. Sharon was a caring person and very loving person, and sometimes referred to as the hug giver. Speaking of giving, Sharon's eyes were donated to the Lyon's Eye Bank

Remember that Bill Guthrie has been convicted of murder; his family has not. This terrible crime is his and his alone, and in no way the fault of his family. Suzanne, Lexi, and Danielle have suffered enough through the loss of their mother and even though their father is still living, in all reality they lost both parents through this tragedy.

Though this a true story, I have brought into existence my experiences and feelings in describing what the Guthrie family, in all likelihood, went through at the hospital, dealing with Sharon's death, at her funeral, and finally with dispensing of her possessions. The sudden loss of my father due to drowning in a stock dam and my mother's untimely death by suicide allowed me to depict my feelings as I wrote portions of this book.

Even though it has been sixteen years since my mother's death, I clearly remember the day that my two sisters and I went through her house to decide what to keep and what to put on the auction. My mother loved doing crafts and could make something creative out of anything. As I pulled out pieces of ribbon, a button, a pinecone, it didn't matter what --- I would cry. To this day I still have some of her craft supplies and items that she created. I even wept when I sorted through her tools, nails, screws, et cetera, when emptying the cupboards in her basement. Granted, the death of a loved one crushes you and the funeral is the last physical connection, but when you remove all of the belongings from a loved one's home, it is most stressful. It is your final good-by and an end of an era. When my sisters went through our mother's clothing, I wasn't ready to tackle that emotional event at the time, but later I felt that I should have done that with them.

My brother, two sisters, and I suffered through bad feelings towards one another after the death of our mother. We were hurting so much that we struck out at one another. We eventually forgave each other through our faith and our love. With both parents gone, we did not want to be split as siblings. I pray that Suzanne, Lexi, and Danielle will again become as close as they once were. As we all know, life is too short to hold grudges, especially with family members.

I was very intrigued with Dr. Alan Berman's testimony. I learned so much regarding the risk factors for suicide. After my mother's suicide, I did some research; but I was unaware of the many risk factors. Maybe --- just maybe, if I had known that these numerous risk factors existed, I could have stopped her from completing suicide. Of course, I'll never know that for sure, but I do pray that those who read this book may learn from Dr. Berman's facts, hopefully never having to use them.

A murder-suicide in our family happened prior to my mother's suicide. Mom's uncle killed his wife, then turned the gun on himself. Mom talked about this quite often and kept the newspaper clipping lying on her dining room table. Did we see this as a sign that she would complete suicide? No. Who would? The fact that our mother couldn't get over realizing that her uncle did this didn't give our family any warning signs. She didn't seem depressed or any different to us than usual.

Dr. Berman's testimony regarding the ways people complete suicide, whether they are male or female, was quite interesting to me, especially since my mother did own a gun. She used a single-shot rifle with one shot to her heart. Actually, I have misquoted that fact. That one shot hit more than one heart.

Bill Guthrie's attorney spoke in his closing arguments stating that women don't commit suicide with guns. They wouldn't want to destroy their looks that way, he said. Of course, I realize that he was defending his client, but some women do use guns to take their lives. My mother is proof of that. In my opinion, he didn't do much research. I agree with him that women worry about their looks, but that doesn't stop them from using a gun. It is known that when men complete suicide using a gun that most place the gun in their mouth, then pull the trigger. The male species don't care if they destroy their looks; they just want to get the job done.

There are people who fear that if suicide is talked about that it will give someone the idea. That is false. There are many completed suicides that possibly could have been prevented if it had been discussed. Being aware of the risk factors could save a life. Our schools don't have a problem with teaching our children about the dangers of drugs and smoking, but some will shy away from the subject regarding suicide. Several years ago, I approached a school official on conducting a suicide informational program and I was refused. He said that if the school would do this program and a child would complete suicide after this program, then the parents would come down on the school. I was very disappointed at his reaction. I strongly feel that if the students are taught risk factors that they might possibly save a friend's life, since it is a fact that kids talk to kids. When someone feels that their friend might be considering suicide, they can go to the school counselor, another adult, or the parents.

Remember that talking about drugs doesn't make someone take drugs, talking about smoking doesn't make someone smoke, et cetera. Though we can't save everyone, knowledge is the key that can help prevent some suicides from happening. We are teaching our children to report weapons to school officials, why not the probability of a friend thinking about suicide? I feel that this is very important.

Some schools are incorporating information about suicide and I hope that more do.

Why did I want to write this book? The idea was planted when a friend of mine who attended almost every day of the trial stated that someone should write a book about this murder. A writer is always looking for an interesting story, and this looked to be the one. As an aspiring writer, I decided to take on this challenge; so I took the first steps needed to begin writing this book. I didn't attend the trial at all. Actually, the day that Bill Guthrie was found guilty of murder, I was celebrating my fifty-first birthday. As my research and writing continued I began to live the whole experience as if I had been there. As I wrote and re-wrote and re-wrote and re-wrote, I found that I could relate with the pain that Suzanne, Lexi, and Danielle were going through.

Six years have gone by since Sharon's murder and even though this story centers on Bill Guthrie's murder trial; I wanted to write this book for Sharon, so people will remember her. I didn't personally know Sharon; but as you read, she was described by the many who knew and loved her as an upbeat, fun-loving person.

I want to sincerely thank Suzanne Hewitt for interviewing with me. It took a tremendous amount of soul searching and courage for her to be there for her mother and go against her father.

Thank you Michael Moore and Judge Eugene Martin for your interviews and your assistance.

Ann Cruse, was a tremendous help when I needed information regarding drugs or the correct spelling of drug names.

A special thanks to my good friend, Jan, who has been a wonderful support to me through, not only the writing of this book, but through other times.

There are others that deserve my thanks, but they have asked to remain anonymous. An immeasurable amount of gratitude to the wonderful person that spent numerous hours proofing and editing this book.

About the Author

Pamela S Chilson has lived her entire life in South Dakota and currently resides in Huron. Her rural upbringing and small town way of life contribute to her style of writing, which has been a passion most of her life. Her topics vary, but the desire to tell a story is always there. With infinite support and encouragement from her husband Doug, other diversified books are simmering on her back burner.

Writing consumes a large part of Chilson's daily routine. Two fiction books, one for adult readers, and one for juvenile age are now in progress. When not writing, Chilson manages the family rental business. Hobbies include bowling, reading, horseback riding, and crafts. Spending time with her grandchildren is high on her list of activities.

PS Chilson's first book, a child's learning book, features actual photographs of her and her husband's small dog that was adopted from the local humane society. This book also includes learning lessons along with two question-and-answer pages.

Contact <u>dougdc@basec.net</u> to order PEPE'S FIRST *SCRAPBOOK* *"Learning With Pepe."*

Printed in the United States
35377LVS00004B/46-210

About the Author

William A. Miller is the director of Woodland Pastoral Associates and former director of the Department of Religion and Health, Fairview Hospital, Minneapolis, Minnesota. He is the author of several books on a variety of subjects dealing with personal and interpersonal dynamics. His master's and doctor's degrees are in psychology, counseling, and clinical studies. He has undertaken graduate work in industrial relations.

For nearly twenty years, Dr. Miller has given seminars, workshops, and lectures throughout the United States and in Canada and Europe. He is widely known for his presentations on Shadow, self-image, grief, stress, and motivation. He and his son, Mark codirect Miller Associates—a professional consulting firm specializing in Just In Time theories and practices, incorporating interpersonal dynamics.

Communications to Dr. Miller or requests for information about seminars, lectures, and consultations should be addressed to 2005 Xanthus Lane, Minneapolis, MN 55447.